Culture,
Ideology,
Hegemony

T0346626

Also by K N Panikkar:
British Diplomacy in North India (1968)
Against Lord and State: Religion and Peasant Uprisings in Malabar (1989)
Culture and Consciousness in Modern India (1990)
Communalism in India: History, Politics and Culture (1991)
The Concerned Indian's Guide to Communalism (1999)
Peasant Protest and Revolts in Malabar (1990)
Towards Freedom, 1940 (1998)

Culture, Ideology, Hegemony

Intellectuals

and Social Consciousness

in Colonial India

K N Panikkar

Anthem Press
London

Anthem Press is an imprint of
Wimbledon Publishing Company
PO Box 9779
London SW19 7QA

This edition first published by Wimbledon Publishing Company 2002

First published by Tulika, India (hardback) 1995
First reprint (paperback) 1998
Second reprint 2001

British Library Cataloguing in Publication Data
Data available

ISBN
1 84331 052 X (hbk)
1 84331 039 2 (pbk)

1 3 5 7 9 10 8 6 4 2

Printed by Newton Printing Ltd, London, UK.   www.newtonprinting.com

Contents

Preface   vii

Acknowledgements   xi

1 An Overview   1

2 Cultural Trends in Pre-Colonial India   34

3 Historiographical and Conceptual Questions   54

4 Culture and Ideology   86

5 Search for Alternatives: Meaning of the Past
  in Colonial India   108

6 Creating a New Cultural Taste: Reading a
  Nineteenth-Century Malayalam Novel   123

7 Indigenous Medicine and Cultural Hegemony   145

8 Marriage Reform: Ideology and Social Base   176

Glossary   200

Index   201

Preface

This book is part of an enquiry to understand and explain how Indians, under colonial subjection, came to terms with their past and present, and thus to envision a future for their society. These tasks—investigating the nature of the past, perceiving the reality of the present, and conceiving the shape of the future—were complex and difficult, for they were mediated by ideologies, both inherited and imposed. The past had to be invoked if the present was to be changed, and the present could not be ignored in conceiving the future. Colonialism, by selectively appropriating and expropriating the past, tended to privilege the present and to fetishize the future. Overcoming the debilities of tradition and the impediments of subjection, therefore, was a necessary pre-requisite for ushering in a new order which, among other things, included the formation of a nation-state. The cultural and ideological struggles in colonial India, expressed through a variety of socio-cultural movements and individual initiatives, were directed towards its realization. This process, however, was not a unilinear and undifferentiated progression; it was riven with contradictions, contentions and ruptures. The cultural–intellectual 'renaissance' did not necessarily merge with nationalism, nor was the latter a logical outcome of the former. Yet, the social consciousness generated by intellectual–cultural endeavours was integral to the process of the nation in the making.

During this phase of history, to borrow D.D. Kosambi's evocative phrase, Indians were engaged in a 'creative introspection', which meant not only exploring the vitality of the indigenous epistemological tradition, but also assessing it in the context of the advances made by the west. Regional and thematic differentiation was not an expression of the disparate and heterogeneous character of this quest, but a sign of its strength and vitality. It embraced a wide range of issues; its stirrings were felt by almost all religious and caste groups; and it extended to almost all parts of the country. It was neither homogenous in content nor uniform in intensity; yet, cumulatively, it created the intellectual and cultural climate for the emergence of a new India.

Most investigations of this theme have for long remained within the parameters of ideas and movements for socio-religious reform and regeneration. What brought about this awakening and how its essence was disseminated, were the major concerns of the early historiography on the subject. Colonial and nationalist historians were both trapped in this paradigm, the former focusing on the instrumentality of colonial rule and the latter on the influence of indigenous tradition. To both, the past was a focal point; the contention was only about how and why the past was invoked. The departure from these concerns in recent times, particularly by Marxist historians, has considerably enlarged the scope of enquiry. Marxist historians have focused on the limitations of the 'renaissance', the societal context of ideas, and the contradictions in the formation of consciousness. The intellectual history of colonial India is thus illumined by a sensitivity to the nature of class formation and class values as well as to the material conditions of human existence.

The essays which form the chapters of this volume draw upon the methodology which informed this departure. They locate intellectual history at the intersection of social and cultural history and thus seek to narrate, explain and contextualize the formation of social consciousness and the role of intellectuals in shaping it. This inter-relationship, viewed in the light of ideas and movements impinging upon a variety of issues, forms the core concern of these essays. Some conceptual and thematic problems are set out in general terms in the first chapter, and later chapters, each focusing on a particular area, are devoted to their elaboration and empirical elucidation. Thus there is a continuity and inter-relatedness which knit these essays, even when they deal with apparently disparate themes like medicine, family and literary fiction. They are a series of micro-analyses converging on a central concern, namely, the formation of social consciousness. The multiple thematic focus is not accidental but intentional, adopted in order to illumine the multi-dimensional and complex character of the cultural–intellectual endeavours. A counter-hegemonic project, both through 'hidden' and 'public transcripts', directed against the 'earthworks' and 'fortresses' that colonialism was raising around the state in India, was posited in these endeavours. A reconstitution of the past was also germane to this project, as reforming the present was inevitably linked with the perception of the nature of the past. Both collectively contributed, among others, to the early impulses which laid the cultural–intellectual foundations of a modern nation-state in India.

Given the thematic and spatial canvas of these essays, a variety of sources in the holdings of several archival offices, libraries and private collections had to be consulted. Apart from the major archival repositories in India—the National Archives of India, the Maharashtra State Archives, and the Tamilnadu State Archives—this study draws upon the material available in a large number of libraries all over India, particularly pamphlets, tracts, journals and newspapers, from which a substantial part of the information is culled. They are far too many to be listed here. Outside India, the India Office Library, the British Museum Library, and the library of the School of Oriental and African Studies in London; the Bodelian Library and the library of the Institute of Oriental Studies in Oxford; the Public Library and the library of the Centre for Christian Studies at Edinburgh; and the Bibliotheque Nationale in Paris, have been extremely useful. I would like to express my gratitude to the officials of all these institutions.

These essays have been presented at seminars and as lectures in several universities in India and abroad. The universities of Bombay, Kurukshetra, Jaipur, Bhubaneswar, Sambhalpur, Goa, Mangalore, Calicut, North Bengal and Darbhanga; Madras Institute of Development Studies; Centre for Development Studies, Thiruvananthapuram; School of Oriental and African Studies and London School of Economics, London; College de France, Paris; University of Rome; the national universities of Cuba, Costa Rica and Panama; and College de Mexico are some of them. I am grateful to these institutions for providing me the opportunity to benefit from the comments of their faculty.

Financial support for undertaking research in India and

abroad came from different organizations. Grants from the Indian Council for Social Science Research, University Grants Commission and Jawaharlal Nehru University, New Delhi, enabled the collection of materials from different repositories in India. Indian Council for Cultural Relations, New Delhi, sponsored my visit to London. For working in London and Edinburgh, financial support was also provided by the British Council and the Charles Wallace Trust. A senior research fellowship of the Nehru Memorial Museum and Library, New Delhi, and an invitation from the Maison de Sciences l'Homme, Paris, enabled me to write parts of this work. My gratitude to all these institutions for their support.

To my postgraduate and research students I owe a special word of thanks. Most of my ideas were initially presented to them and their response and comments have substantially contributed to their elaboration and refinement. The interaction with my colleagues at the Centre for Historical Studies, Jawaharlal Nehru University, has been equally fruitful. Among them, S. Gopal, Romila Thapar, Bipan Chandra and R. Champakalakshmi have read earlier versions of some of the chapters and offered comments. Chandramohan, Rusheed Wadia, Venkatachalapathy, Padmavathy and Arundhati Mukho-padhyaya helped me in collecting material from different libraries in India.

Finally, but for the silent support of my wife, Usha, this book would not have been possible. By shouldering the responsibilities of running the home, particularly during my long stints away from Delhi, she helped me to pursue my research. So did my daughters, Ragini and Shalini, and their husbands, Pithamber and Raman, by their understanding and affection.

New Delhi   K.N. PANIKKAR

Acknowledgements

An Overview
Revised text of the Presidential Address at the Modern Indian History section, Indian History Congress, thirty-sixth session, Aligarh, December 1975.

Cultural Trends in Pre-Colonial India
First published in *Studies in History*, Vol. II, No. 2, July–December 1980.

Historiographical and Conceptual Questions
First published in S. Bhattacharya and Romila Thapar (eds.), *Situating Indian History*, New Delhi, 1986.

Culture and Ideology
First published in *Economic and Political Weekly*, Vol. XXII, No. 49, 5 December 1987.

Search for Alternatives: Meaning of the Past in Colonial India
Paper read at the seminar 'The East and the Meaning of History', University of Rome, November 1992.

Indigenous Medicine and Cultural Hegemony
First published in *Studies in History*, Vol. VIII, No. 2, July–December 1992.

Marriage Reform: Ideology and Social Base
First published in *The Indian Historical Review*, Vol. IV, No. 1, July 1977.

1 An Overview

Pandit Jawaharlal Nehru, referring to the crisis of his self-identity, expressed the cultural dilemma of Indians under colonial subjection in the following words:

> I have become a queer mixture of the East and the West, out of place everywhere, at home nowhere. Perhaps my thoughts and approach to life are more akin to what is called Western than Eastern, but India clings to me as she does to all her children, in innumerable ways. . . . I cannot get rid of that past inheritance or my recent acquisitions. . . . I am a stranger and an alien in the West. I cannot be of it. But in my own country also, sometimes, I have an exile's feeling.[1]

A century or so before Nehru wrote this, the beginning of this dilemma, a crisis of identity, was experienced in the rapidly growing colonial cities of Calcutta, Bombay and Madras. The intellectual ambivalence of Rammohun Roy in Bengal, Bal Shastri Jambekar in Bombay and Gazula Lakshmi Narasu Chetti in Madras gave expression to this crisis.[2] The period between Rammohun and Nehru witnessed the subjection of the Indian middle class to the hegemonic influence of British colonial values and ideology leading to the

---

[1] Jawaharlal Nehru, *An Autobiography,* London, 1947, p. 596.
[2] Rammohun Roy maintained two houses in Calcutta, one for entertaining his European friends and the other for his family to live in. It is said that in the first house everything was European except Rammohun, and in the second, everything except Rammohun was Indian.

development of an intellectual and cultural provinciality.[3] Simultaneously, there was a struggle by the intellectual leaders[4] of the nineteenth century against this provinciality, on the one hand, and against the ideological basis of the traditional order, on the other. Rammohun's crisis of identity was an early expression, and Nehru's despondency the culmination, marked by partial success and partial failure, of this struggle. Even though the intellectual basis and ideological premises of this effort considerably differed from individual to individual, there was a unity of purpose—an urge to create a new life and society—which informed the intellectual struggle as a whole. Scholars who have examined the course and nature of cultural and intellectual developments during the colonial rule have tended to overlook the importance of this struggle in the making of our intellectual attitudes and cultural norms. The perspective of some of them has been confined to an elaboration, either conscious or unconscious, of the colonial ideologues' scheme of the western impact and the Indian response to it, leading to the clubbing of intellectuals into mutually exclusive categories such as 'conservatives', 'reformers' and 'radicals'.[5] Alternatively, the concepts of 'acculturation', 'westernization' and 'modernization', divorced from the realities of the specific historical context in India, have found favour with others. A few

---

[3] The reference is to the attitude of the English-educated middle class towards the colonial metropolis and to their intellectual dependence on and adop-tion of colonial cultural values. See Edward Shills, *The Intellectual between Tradition and Modernity: The Indian Situation*, The Hague, 1961, pp. 27–28.

[4] I use this term to denote all those who were involved in the generation, adoption and propagation of ideas. Though it subsumes those who are generally called reformers, I include a large number of less-known individuals who had no reforming role in the strict sense of the term. The word 'leader' does not imply any hegemonic influence in society.

[5] This categorization found acceptance among a wide range of historians, from L.S.S. O'Malley and J.N. Farquhar to Salahuddin Ahmed and R.C. Majumdar. None of them takes into consideration the conflicting tendencies within each group and the significance of the ideas which do not fall within these categories. See L.S.S. O'Malley, *Modern India and the West*, London, 1968, p. 54; J.N. Farquhar, *Modern Religious Movements in India*, London, 1914; Salahuddin Ahmad, *Social Ideas and Social Change in Bengal*, Leiden, 1965, p. 27; and R.C. Majumdar (ed.), *British Paramountcy and Indian Renaissance*, Vol. X, Pt. II, Bombay, 1965, pp. 256–84.

others have adopted more sophisticated phrases—or are they frameworks?—like tradition–modernity continuum, tradition of modernity and modernity of tradition.

A change in perspective would, as a preliminary step, call for a detailed analysis of a variety of questions which still need to be addressed by social and intellectual historians. For instance, what was the nature of the changes that occurred in the immediate pre-colonial society and what was the intellectual tradition of that period? How did the intellectuals of the nineteenth century perceive the social, political and economic realities of their times? Did they have a vision of the future, and if they did, was it aimed simply at a rectification of tradition sanctified by the concept of a golden past, or maintenance of the status quo, or a total transformation? What were their programmes and methods? What were the intellectual and ideological bases which helped them to perceive reality and construct a vision of the future? Finally, and perhaps most importantly, how did the specific political and economic situation—that of colonial domination—in which they functioned affect their ideas, programmes and methods?[6] These are some of the questions which the following overview of the intellectual developments in the nineteenth century seeks to analyse.

The Pre-Colonial Context

The emergence of modern ideas and the development of social protest and religious dissent in the nineteenth century have been generally viewed as a consequence of the introduction of European ideas and institutions in India. To the British colonial and administrator–historians, this impact–response framework was useful in projecting the civilizing role of British rule and the manifold blessings bestowed upon the people of India by the dissemination of western knowledge.[7] The formula was very simple: familiarity with European history, institutions and languages and the concomitant influence of the European ideas of liberty, rationalism and humanism

---

[6] The importance of contextualizing all developments during the colonial period have been underlined by several scholars. See Bipan Chandra, *Nationalism and Colonialism in Modern India*, New Delhi, 1979, pp. 1–37.

[7] The characterization of the eighteenth century as a dark age was a part of this framework.

acted as the 'open sesame' which made Indians critical of their own institutions and consequently led them to embark upon a career of reform.[8] Many assumptions of this approach, notwithstanding its inherent ideological justification of British rule, can be found in the writings of Indian historians. Some have viewed the emergence of socio-religious movements as a contribution of the missionaries to Indian cultural life,[9] while others have ascribed the development of modern ideas exclusively to the influence of western education.[10] Without belittling the importance of western influence, it should be pointed out that such analyses not only ignore the complexities of the social and intellectual developments during the nineteenth century, but also overlook the elements of protest and dissent in the Indian intellectual tradition and the potentialities of social development in the eighteenth century before British intervention. Above all, they totally ignore the material conditions within which these develop-ments occurred.

Without going into details, the importance of the changes that occurred in the pre-colonial period may be underlined by referring to religious conditions in the eighteenth century and changes in the structure and organization of caste. Undoubtedly, Hinduism was beset with idolatry, polytheism and superstition. But these

[8] All developments during colonial rule, ranging from humanitarianism to nationalism, are accounted for within this framework. See O'Malley, *Modern India and the West*, pp. 54–66; B.T. McCully, *English Education and the Origins of Indian Nationalism*, New Delhi, 1966 (reprint), pp. 176–237; and Percival Spear, *A History of India*, Harmondsworth, 1968, p. 160. Charles Heimsath's *Hindu Social Reform and Indian Nationalism* (Princeton, 1964), in spite of his professions to the contrary, falls within the same framework. A comparatively recent and indeed more sophisticated appli-cation of this formula is a study of the emergence of Indian nationalism by Anil Seal. He writes: 'It is not possible to attack the general problem of this work, how modern politics and their genesis is clearly linked with those Indians who had been schooled by western methods.' Anil Seal, *The Emer-gence of the Indian Nationalism*, Cambridge, 1968, p. 16.

[9] B.C. Bhattacharya, 'Development of Social and Political Ideas in Bengal, 1858–1885', unpublished Ph.D. thesis, University of London, 1934, p. 13.

[10] 'A new ideology suddenly burst forth upon the static life, moulded for centuries by a fixed set of religious ideas and social convention. It gave birth to a critical attitude towards religion and a spirit of enquiry into the origin of state and society with a view to determining their proper scope and function.' R.C. Majumdar (ed.), *British Paramountcy*, p. 89.

religious beliefs and practices were being challenged by a large number of heterodox sects which emerged in almost all parts of India—the Satnami, Appapanthi and Shivanarayan sects in Uttar Pradesh, the Karthabajas and Balramis in Bengal, the Charandasis in Rajasthan and the Virabhramas in Andhra Pradesh, all of whom denounced polytheism, idolatry and caste distinctions.[11] The Karthabajas met in congregations twice a year in which caste distinctions were renounced: they ate together as equals and addressed one another as brother and sister.[12] Like the later nineteenth-century reformers, Charan Das invoked Vedic authority for anti-idolatry and anti-casteism. He claimed that his attempt was to propagate Vedic truth in simple Hindi for the benefit of the common man.[13] He was opposed to all rituals including the use of *tulsi* leaves for worship. These sects, again like the nineteenth-century reformers, placed a high premium on personal morality.[14] Numerically, they were certainly not insignificant; most of them had a following of twenty to thirty thousand. They were indeed different in methods of organization and functioning from the religious movements of the nineteenth century, but to dismiss them on that account as personal revolts without much social significance is to miss their real import. They have to be assessed and understood primarily as an expression of a developing trend of protest and dissent in the religious life of the people, characterized at the time by superstition and the tyranny of priests. Their failure or success apart—and this depended upon

[11] V.P.S. Raghuvanshi, *Indian Society in the Eighteenth Century*, New Delhi, 1969, pp. 143–46; P.N. Bose, *Hindu Civilization*, Vol. I, London, 1896, pp. 115–16; K. Veeraraghavcharyulu, *Mana Gurudevudu* (Telugu), 1963, pp. 120–36; and Jakkula Swaminathaiah, *Sri Pothuluri Veerabhrahmamgari: Jeevitha Charitha* (Telugu), 1954, pp. 162–70. (I am thankful to V. Ramakrishna, Department of History, Central University, Hyderabad, for providing me with references from Telugu sources on the socio-religious movements in Andhra Pradesh.)

[12] K.K. Datta, *Survey of India's Social Life and Economic Conditions in the Eighteenth Century, 1707–1813*, Delhi, 1961, p. 4.

[13] Beni Gupta, 'Charan Dasi Sect', *Journal of the Rajasthan Institute of Historical Research,* April–June 1974, pp. 16–30.

[14] Charan Das laid down that a man should not (1) Tell a lie, (2) Revile, (3) Speak harshly, (4) Discourse idly, (5) Steal, (6) Commit adultery, (7) Act violently to any creature, (8) Imagine evil, (9) Entertain hatred, and (10) Possess conceit or pride. Ibid. The Karthabajas also laid down ten rules of conduct.

various factors including the subsequent socio-economic developments—they 'testify to the reform movements manifesting in society
even independently of foreign influence'.[15]

This line of enquiry is also relevant to other aspects of
eighteenth-century society. A closer look at the changes in the
structure and organization of caste and the major trends in literary
and artistic expression would be particularly rewarding. The present
state of our knowledge of the eighteenth century, a no-man's-land
ignored both by medieval and modern historians, does not permit
detailed analysis of these issues. But there is enough evidence to
indicate the broad trends. For instance, it is possible to show that
substantial changes were occurring within the institution of caste:
fragmentation,[16] occupational mobility[17] and sanskritization,[18] for
instance. In the realm of intellectual activity, the eighteenth century,
like all other periods of Indian history, was not devoid of individual

[15] Raghuvanshi, *Indian Society in the Eighteenth Century*, p. 146. Montgo-
mery Martin, though with the pious hope of a Christian, wrote: 'Sectarian-
ism has spread itself in India, particularly among the once orthodox Hindus,
not a few of whom are passing from the grossest idolatry into the abstract
non-entities of deism.' Quoted by Raghuvanshi, ibid., p. 146. Also see H.H.
Wilson, *Essays and Lectures Chiefly on the Religion of the Hindus*, II,
London, 1862, pp. 76–77.

[16] Many examples can be cited of this process: the Kayasthas in Uttar Pradesh,
Kaibrathas in Bengal, Pancham Banjigarus and Panchalas in Mysore, and
Agradanis and Gangaputras in Bihar were forming new sub-castes during
this period. Raghuvanshi, *Indian Society in the Eighteenth Century*, pp. 79–
80. The reasons for fragmentation were many, including changes in
occupation, material position and secular sanction.

[17] The examples of changes in caste occupations are many. A large number of
brahmins worked as coolies in factories at Surat. In Mithila, 68 per cent of
the brahmins actually participated in cultivation, whereas only 12 per cent
lived on priestly work. Raghuvanshi, ibid., pp. 61–63. In Maharashtra,
tailors gave up their traditional occupation and took to dyeing. H.F.
Fukuzava, 'State and Caste System (Jati) in the Eighteenth Century Maratha
Kingdom', *Hitotsubashi Journal of Economics*, IX (1), pp. 39–44.

[18] Examples of higher caste claims and adoption of superior caste customs and
rituals in the eighteenth century are numerous. For instance, the Lingayats
in Mysore claimed superiority over sudras and the Jotephandas in Bengal
claimed vaishya status. Goldsmiths and potters started wearing the sacred
thread and abandoned the custom of widow remarriage. Francis Buchanan,
*A Journey from Madras through the Countries of Mysore, Canara, and
Malabar*, Vol. I, London, 1807, pp. 252–58, 214–15, 395; Ferminger (ed.),
Fifth Report on India Affairs, Vol. III, pp. 9–10.

brilliance.[19] Artistic and literary activities displayed a very high level of creativity, especially in literature and painting.[20] The move towards popular literature, both in form and content, rejecting 'the painted, the powdered and the obsequious'—a trend which had started in Malayalam and Bengali literatures as early as the sixteenth century[21]—gained emphasis during this period.[22] What happened to these tendencies after the British conquest of India is another story. It may not be rewarding to speculate upon the course of their possible development if colonial intervention had not taken place. Yet, a proper appreciation of these tendencies would enrich our understanding of the intellectual scenario of the nineteenth century. It would also help us to look for alternative explanations to the rather simplistic impact–response formula.

Enlightenment as Panacea

That the social practices and religious beliefs prevalent in the nineteenth century acted as impediments to progress was a conviction common to most nineteenth-century intellectuals.[23] Polytheism and

[19] Jai Singh of Amber in astronomy, Shah Walliullah of Delhi in Islamic religion and philosophy, and in literature, Mir, Sauda and Nazir in Urdu, Brajanatha Bodajena in Oriya and Bharathachandra Roy in Bengali are a few important names in this context.

[20] Hermann Goetz, *The Crisis of Indian Civilization in the Eighteenth and Nineteenth Centuries,* London, 1938. See also George Bearce, 'Intellectual and Cultural Characteristics of India in a Changing Era, 1740–1800', *Journal of Asian Studies,* November 1965. He writes: 'From 1740 to 1800 the culture of India was still the lively expression of a society that appears to be master of its destiny. . . . The society at its various levels, aristocratic and popular, produced in both variety and quality an impressive amount of art, music, literature and learning.'

[21] Kunchan Nambiar's *Ottan Thullalukal* in Malayalam and the *Mangal Kavyas* in Bengali are initial efforts in this direction. See K.M. George, *A Survey of Malayalam Literature,* New Delhi, 1968, pp. 108–26 and Sukumar Sen, *History of Bengali Literature,* New Delhi, 1960, pp. 112–21.

[22] Urdu and Telugu literatures are particularly important in this respect. See Bearce, 'Intellectual and Cultural Characteristics of India'; Muhammed Sadiq, *A History of Urdu Literature,* New Delhi, 1964, pp. 66–116; W.H. Campbell, 'The One Great Poet of the People', in V.R. Narla (ed.), *Vemana through Western Eyes,* New Delhi, 1969, pp. 50–67; and G.V. Sitapati, *History of Telugu Literature,* New Delhi, 1968, p. 36.

[23] Rammohun wrote: 'I regret to say that the present system of religion adhered to by the Hindus is not well calculated to promote their political interest. The distinction of castes and innumerable divisions and sub-

idolatry, they believed, negated the development of individuality, and supernaturalism and the authority of religious leaders led to conformity born out of fear.[24] Casteism was abhorrent not only on moral and ethical grounds but also because it fostered social division and 'deprived people of patriotic feeling'.[25] At the same time, it was realized that 'no country on earth ever made sufficient progress in civilization whose females were sunk in ignorance'.[26] The social practices and religious beliefs of nineteenth-century India were thus seen as features of a decadent society characterized by constraint, credulity, status, authority, bigotry and blind fatalism.[27] They were sought to be replaced by freedom, faith, contract, reason, tolerance and a sense of human dignity.[28] In short, while opposing the hegemonic values of a feudal society the intellectuals advocated the introduction and acceptance of values characteristic of a bourgeois order.

The means and methods by which this transformation could be effected was one of the major concerns of the nineteenth-century intellectuals. An analysis of their political perspective and their ideas on education would help elucidate this.

The nineteenth-century intellectuals were firm believers in the efficacy of enlightenment as a panacea. They traced the source of

---

divisions among them, has deprived them of patriotic feeling, and the multitude of religious rites and ceremonies and the laws of purification have totally disqualified them from undertaking any difficult enterprise.' Sophia Dobson Collet, *Life and Letters of Rammohun Roy,* Calcutta, 1913, p. 124. See also 'Project of a New Social Organization' and 'Practical Suggestions Relating to the Abolition of the Institution of Caste' in *The Weekly Chronicle,* 6 June 1853; 'Additional Hints Regarding the New Social Organization', *The Weekly Chronicle,* 11 July 1853; U.N. Tagore, *Bengalis as They Are and as They Ought to Be,* Calcutta, 1865; 'Thoughts on Indian Reformers', *The Enquirer,* January 1835; Keshub Chandra Sen, 'The Reconstruction of Native Society', in Prem Sunder Basu (compiled), *Life and Works of Brahmananda Keshav,* Calcutta, 1940, pp. 286–89; Mahadev Govind Ranade, *The Miscellaneous Writings,* Bombay, 1915, pp. 190–94; and V. Ramakrishna, 'Veeresalingam and His Times', unpublished M. Phil. dissertation, Jawaharlal Nehru University, 1974, pp. 50–57.

[24] Rammohun Roy, *Tuhfat-ul Muwahhiddin,* in J.C. Ghose (ed.), *The English Works of Raja Rammohun Roy,* 1906, pp. 945–46.

[25] Ibid., p. 929. See also Ranade, *The Miscellaneous Writings,* pp. 236–37.

[26] Keshub Chandra Sen, 'Promotion of Education in India', in Basu (compiled), *Life and Works of Brahmananda Keshav,* p. 48.

[27] Ranade, *The Miscellaneous Writings,* p. 166.

[28] Ibid.

all ills in Indian society, including religious superstition and social obscurantism, to the general ignorance of the people. The dissemination of knowledge, therefore, occupied a central place in their programme of reform.[29] Their ideas on education were different both in purpose and detail from the educational policy of the colonial rulers. While dissemination of the colonial ideology and utility for administrative needs were the main objectives of the educational policy of the British government, the educational programme of the Indian intellectuals was oriented to the regeneration of the country. The debates on education within the official circles were never concerned with how best Indians could be educated, but on the contrary, first, with how best the educational policy could serve the administrative needs[30] and second, and perhaps more important, with how best it could inculcate the colonial ideology in the minds of Indians. The alien rule was maintained not simply with the help of the police and the army but also by an illusion created by ideological influences. In creating this illusion, education, which could help project British institutions and values as the ideal, was conceived as an effective medium.[31] Therefore, the educational enterprise of the

---

[29] The emphasis on education was common to all, from Rammohun to Vivekananda. Rammohun believed that if they received proper education Indians would be worthy of respect by all men. Rammohun Roy, 'Modern Encroachments on the Ancient Rights of Females', in Nag and Burman, *English Works of Rammohun Roy*, I, Calcutta, 1945, p. 9. Given proper education, Keshub expected the poor, 'the men of consequence', to improve their conditions, and 'to forcibly stop outrage, cruelty and oppression'. Keshub Chandra Sen, 'Men of Consequence', in Basu (compiled), *Life and Works of Brahmananda Keshav,* p. 217. Veeresalingam looked upon the educated men as the protagonists of change. J.G. Leonard, 'Kandukuri Veeresalingam', unpublished Ph.D. thesis, University of Wisconsin, 1970, p. 165. Vivekananda was more positive about this: 'we must have a hold on the spiritual and secular education of the nation, you must dream it, you must talk it, you must think and you must work it out. Till then there is no salvation for the race'. Swami Vivekananda, *Complete Works,* Calcutta, 1970, Vol. III, p. 301 and Vol. IV, p. 362.

[30] The early policy of the East India Company of encouraging the study and translation of Indian classics was not a part of a cultural policy, as David Kopf argues, but an extension of the administrative policy. David Kopf, *British Orientalism and Indian Renaissance*, Berkeley, 1969, pp. 13–21.

[31] Macaulay's oft-quoted flourish, 'Indian in blood and colour but European in taste and manners', was not an accidental slip but an expression of this general urge.

government—covering vernacular, primary and university education—remained within the confines of colonial needs and did not
transgress the limits of colonial interests.

In their struggle against the ideological influences of the
colonial system of education, the Indian intellectuals strove to
formulate and implement an alternative based on science and mass
education through the medium of the 'vernacular' languages. One of
their basic assumptions was the inadequacy of the traditional and
literary education to meet the needs of the time. Rammohun's
objection to loading 'the mind of youth with grammatical niceties
and metaphysical distinctions of little or no practical use to the
possessors or to society'[32] was widely shared. Akshay Kumar Dutt,
the first Indian to propose a national scheme of education, totally
rejected the traditional system.[33] Vidyasagar ridiculed those who
believed that the *shastras* contained all scientific truth.[34] To Sayyid
Ahmad Khan, the traditional system of Muslim education was a great
stumbling block in the way of progress.[35]

The alternative proposed by them was 'a liberal and enlightened system of instruction, embracing Mathematics, Natural Philosophy, Chemistry, and Anatomy with other useful Sciences'.[36] In Akshay

[32] Rammohun Roy, 'A Letter on Education', in Ghose (ed.), *The English
Works of Raja Rammohun Roy*, p. 447.

[33] Akshay Kumar Dutt, *Dharamniti*, Calcutta, 1851, pp. 148–50.

[34] Vidyasagar compared them to the Khalifa who ordered the destruction of
the Alexandrian library. The Khalifa is reported to have said, 'The contents
of the books in the library are either in conformity with the Qoran or they
are not. If they are, the Qoran is sufficient without them; if they are not, they
are pernicious. Let them, therefore, be destroyed.' Quoted in Indra Mitra,
Karuna Sagar, Vidya Sagar, Calcutta, 1969, p. 732.

[35] 'The old Mohammedan books and the tone of their writers do not teach the
followers of Islam independence of thought, perspicuity and simplicity; nor
do they enable them to arrive at the truth of matters in general; on the
contrary, they receive and teach men to veil their meaning, to embellish their
speech with fine words, to describe things wrongly and in irrelevant terms.'
*Report of the Committee for the Better Diffusion and Advancement of
Learning among Mohammedans of India,* quoted in G.F.I. Graham, *The
Life and Work of Sayyid Ahmed Khan,* New Delhi, 1974 reprint, pp. 248–
49. Also see K.A. Nizami, *Sayyid Ahmad Khan,* New Delhi, 1974, p.15.

[36] Rammohun Roy, 'A Letter on Education', in Ghose (ed.), *The English Works
of Raja Rammohun Roy*, p. 474. The universality of science was taken for
granted by the Indian intellectuals. They did not face the question whether
science was 'western' or 'new' as in the case of China. About 1640, there was

Kumar's scheme of education the students were to be introduced to the rudiments of scientific knowledge at a very early age.[37] He considered science education to be the most urgent need of the times and, therefore, advocated the establishment of schools of technology, agriculture and ship-building.[38] The importance of a scientific out look and the acquisition of scientific knowledge was equally emphasized by Vidyasagar, Mahadev Govind Ranade, Sayyid Ahmad Khan and Veeresalingam.[39] Keshub Chandra Sen considered the absence of the scientific pursuit as the major drawback of the education imparted by the British government.[40] Even Dayanand and the Arya Samajists, in spite of their obsession with Vedic knowledge, recognized the importance of science education;[41] scientific subjects found a place in the curriculum not only of the Dayanand Anglo-Vedic institutions but also of the Gurukula at Kangri.[42]

This emphasis on science education was the result of a growing realization that scientific knowledge was crucial to the

a discussion in Peking as to whether the new sciences were primarily western or primarily new. The Chinese objected to the word 'western' used by the Jesuits in the titles of the scientific books which they wrote and translated. They insisted that it should be dropped in favour of 'new'. Joseph Needham, *Within the Four Seas: The Dialogue of East and West,* London, 1969, pp. 12–13.

[37] Akshay Kumar Dutt, *Dharamniti*, p. 161. (I am thankful to Arundhati Niyogi for translating Akshay Kumar's Bengali writings.)

[38] Ibid.

[39] Mitra, *Karuna Sagar, Vidya Sagar*, pp. 731–32; D.G. Karve, *Ranade, The Prophet of Liberated India*, Pune, 1942, p. 187; Nizami, *Sayyid Ahmad Khan*, pp. 70–71; and Veeresalingam, *Complete Works* (Telugu), Vol. VII, 1951, pp. 188–89.

[40] Keshub Chandra Sen, 'The Promotion of Education in India', in Basu (compiled), *Life and Works of Brahmananda Keshav*, p. 47.

[41] Lala Lajpat Rai, *A History of Arya Samaj*, edited by Sri Ram Sharma, Bombay, 1967, pp. 136–37.

[42] One of the three objects of the Dayanand Anglo-Vedic College was to encourage and enforce the study of English literature and sciences, both theoretical and applied. Although the Gurukula at Kangri was founded 'with the avowed aim of reviving the ancient institution of Brahmacharya, of rejuvenating and resuscitating ancient Indian philosophy and literature, conducting researches into the antiquities of India, of building up of a Hindu literature incorporating into itself all that is best and assimilable in occidental thought', its curricula contained courses on physics, chemistry and other science subjects. Lajpat Rai, ibid., pp. 138, 144. See also the prospectus of the Gurukula Mahavidyalaya, 1911.

progress of the country and to the development of modern thought and culture.[43] The intellectuals recognized the importance of disseminating the existing scientific knowledge for a rational approach to social problems; equally, they were aware of the need for higher intellectual pursuit of scientific studies which would create scientists who would 'grapple with the facts of nature, discover their laws and bend them to our material and moral uses and the general progress of the humanity at large'.[44] The intention was to create 'men of Science and not men whom accident has placed in the era of Science'.[45]

Working within the framework of its colonial needs, the British government was neither interested in general dissemination of scientific knowledge nor in encouraging higher pursuit of scientific studies by Indians. The Indian intellectuals were sharply critical of this governmental indifference. To Keshub Chandra Sen the most glaring inadequacy of the existing system of education was the lack of opportunity to pursue scientific studies.[46] 'I must say', wrote Mahendra Lal Sarkar, 'that our Government has hitherto afforded no opportunity, nor offered any encouragement to the pursuit of Science by the natives of this country.'[47] It was 'the want of opportunity, want of means and want of encouragement'[48] which prevented Indian students from pursuing scientific studies.

Several attempts were made by Indians to arouse an interest in science, disseminate scientific knowledge and promote scientific studies. In 1825 a Society for Translating European Sciences was established in Calcutta which published fifteen volumes of *Vigyan*

---

[43] Mahenderlal Sarkar wrote in the *Calcutta Journal of Medicine*, August 1869, as follows: '. . . the best method, and under the circumstances, the only method, by which the people of India could be essentially improved, was by the cultivation of the Physical Sciences; that the great defects, inherent and acquired, which were pointed out as the characteristics of the Hindu mind of the present day, could only be remedied by the training which results from the investigation of natural phenomena.'

[44] Mahenderlal Sarkar, *The Projected Science Association for the Natives of India*, Calcutta, 1872, p. xiv.

[45] Ibid., p. viii.

[46] Keshub Chandra Sen, 'The Promotion of Education in India', in Basu (compiled), *Life and Works of Brahmananda Keshav*, p. 47.

[47] Sarkar, *The Projected Science Association for the Natives of India*, p. xii.

[48] Ibid., p. xi.

Sebadi, a periodical devoted to the propagation of scientific knowledge.[49] This was followed by the establishment of a Mechanical
Institute with Tarachand Chakrabarty, an important member of
Young Bengal, as its president.[50] In 1833 the members of Young
Bengal published a bilingual monthly, *Bigyan Sar Sangraha,* which
dealt exclusively with scientific matters.[51] A sociologist who scanned
through the periodicals in Bengal during the first half of the nineteenth century noticed that:

> the whole intellectual climate in contemporary Calcutta was really
> and truly surcharged with Science and things scientific. In indi-
> vidual lectures and writings in journals and newspapers there was
> a constant demand for the study, teaching and dissemination of
> scientific knowledge. In the pages of the *Tattwabodhini Patrika,* in
> the columns of the *Sambad Prabhakar,* logic for technical schools,
> agricultural institutes researching on improved methods of cultiva-
> tion, was repeated again and again.[52]

The establishment of the National Institution for the Cultivation of Sciences by the Natives of India marked the culmination of
this awareness.[53] Similar efforts were made in other parts of the
country as well. In 1863 Sayyid Ahmad Khan established the Scien-

---

[49] Bela Dutt Gupta, *Sociology in India,* Calcutta, 1972, p. xv.
[50] Ibid., p. xvi.
[51] G. Chattopadhyay (ed.), *Awakening in Bengal,* Calcutta, 1965, p. xxv.
[52] Bela Dutt Gupta, *Sociology in India,* p. xvii.
[53] The aim of the institution was described as follows: We want an institution
which will combine the character, scope and objects of Royal Institution in
London and of the British Association for the Advancement of Sciences. We
want an institution which shall be for the instruction of the masses, where
lectures on Scientific subjects will be systematically delivered, and not only
illustrative experiments performed by the lecturers, but the audience would
be invited and taught to perform them themselves. And we wish that the
institution be entirely under native management and control. Mahenderlal
Sarkar, *On the Desirability of a National Institution for the Cultivation of
the Sciences by the Natives of India,* Calcutta, 1872, p. 8. The idea of
establishing this institution aroused considerable interest and enthusiasm.
Hindu Patriot (10 and 17 January 1870), *Indian Daily News* (12 January
1870), *The Bengali* (15 January 1870), and *The Indian Mirror* (7 January
1870) praised and supported this effort. Babu Gangadhar Chatterji wrote
an exhortative song for the Association. Babu Kalimohan Das considered
it the first step towards the regeneration of India from both the physical and
moral points of view. See *The Indian Mirror,* 15 March 1872.

tific Society at Ghazipur. Its primary object was the introduction of improved methods of agriculture in India by which the condition of the people could be improved.[54]

The initial policy of the British government to redirect education to a small section of society did not find favour with most of the intellectuals; they realized the importance of mass education for national regeneration.[55] Akshay Kumar advocated free and compulsory education and that educational facilities be made available to peasants and workers.[56] Dayanand went to the extent of suggesting that there should be a government order and national custom that nobody should keep their children at home once they attained the age of eight and those violating it should be severely punished.[57] To Vidyasagar 'the extension of education to the mass of the people' was the immediate need of the country.[58] The importance of mass education was equally stressed by Keshub Chandra Sen, Mahadev Govind Ranade, Veeresalingam and Sayyid Ahmad Khan.[59] Keshub Chandra Sen's popular magazine, *Sulabh Samachar,* was intended to enlighten and awaken the masses against oppression and exploitation.[60] In a series of open letters to Lord Northbrook, under the

[54] Nizami, *Sayyid Ahmad Khan,* p. 74.
[55] In one of his lectures in England Keshub Chandra Sen said: 'Up to the present moment the blessings of education are restricted to the upper ten thousand; but the mass of the people are really ignorant—most painfully ignorant.' *Keshub Chandra Sen in England,* Calcutta, 1938, p. 415; Akshay Kumar Dutt, *Dharamniti,* p. 153.
[56] *Tattwabodhini Patrika,* Shravan, Saka 1770, Vol. 2, No. 61, pp. 68–77 and Akshay Kumar Dutt, *Dharamniti,* pp. 153, 161.
[57] Dayanand Saraswati, *Satyarth Prakash,* 1972, p. 40.
[58] Mitra, *Karuna Sagar, Vidya Sagar,* p. 732. In another context, however, Vidyasagar maintained that 'by educating one boy in a proper style the Government does more towards the real education of the people, than by teaching a hundred children mere reading, writing and little of Arithmetic'. This was not because he considered 'education of the whole people' as undesirable, on the contrary, he considered it 'certainly very desirable', but because of the limited resources available for education. Ibid., p. 762.
[59] Veeresalingam, *Complete Works,* Vol. VII, pp. 202–04, 365, 372–75; Shan Mohammad (ed.), *Writings and Speeches of Sir Sayyid Ahmad Khan,* 1972, p. 231; Graham, *The Life and Work of Sayyid Ahmad Khan,* p. 152; and Ranade, *The Miscellaneous Writings,* p. 270.
[60] Keshub Chandra Sen, 'Men of Consequence' and 'England's Duty to India', in Basu (compiled), *Life and Works of Brahmananda Keshav,* pp. 277, 215. Also see *Keshub Chandra Sen in England,* p. 339.

pseudonym Indo-Philus, he made a passionate appeal for promoting mass education:

> How sad and pitiable is the condition of the dumb millions in India! Illiterate, poor, credulous, weak and helpless— often at the mercy of griping priests, rapacious zamindars, cruel planters and a vicious police—their lives are truly miserable. The education of the lower classes has hitherto been sadly neglected. We are apt to rejoice that more than half a million of men are under instruction in India. But how small and insignificant is this figure when contrasted with an estimated population of 151 millions? A hundred and fifty millions of souls have yet to be educated . . . time has shown that this 'rapid transfusion' [through filtration] was a mere dream. An efficient system of cheap vernacular schools must be organized by the state itself to benefit the masses directly. It is indeed painful to reflect that while the total education grant in Bengal is 18 lacs, only three lacs is devoted to the education of the middle and lower classes, and so much as 15 lacs spent on English schools and colleges.[61]

That the vernacular was the only medium through which knowledge could be disseminated to the masses was a conviction common to most intellectuals of the nineteenth century.[62] Conscious

---

[61] Basu (compiled), *Life and Works of Brahmananda Keshav*, p. 290. Similar ideas were expressed by Ranade, Veeresalingam and Vivekananda. Vivekananda wrote: 'The only service to be done for our lower classes is to give them education, to develop their lost individuality. That is the great task between our people and princes. Upto now nothing has been done in that direction. Priest-power and foreign conquest have trodden them down for centuries, and at last the poor of India have forgotten that they are human beings. They are to be given ideas; their eyes are to be opened to what is going on in the world around them; and then they will work out their own salvation.' Vivekananda, *Complete Works*, Vol. IV, p. 362; Karve, *Ranade, The Liberated Prophet of India*, p. 195; and Veeresalingam, *Complete Works*, Vol. VII, pp. 202–04, 273–75, 365.

[62] Sayyid Ahmad Khan gave emphatic expression to this idea: 'The cause of England's civilization is that all the arts and sciences are in the language of the country. Those who are bent on improving and bettering India must remember that the only way of compassing this is by having the whole of the arts and sciences translated into their own language. I should like to have this written in gigantic letters on the Himalayas for the remembrance of future generations. If they be not translated, India can never be civilized: This is the truth, this is the truth.' Shan Mohammad (ed.), *Writings and Speeches of Sir Sayyid Ahmad Khan*, pp. 231–32.

of the need to develop the vernacular as the vehicle for the propagation of their socio-religious ideas and the dissemination of scientific
knowledge, many of them were concerned with evolving a simple
style to reach out to a larger audience and the creation of a rich and
enlightened literature.[63] The most effective channel of communication of their ideas were the journals published in the vernacular
languages. Rammohun's *Sambad Kaumudi,* Young Bengal's *Gyan-
anveshan,* Debendranath and Akshay Kumar's *Tattwabodhini Patrika*
and Keshub's *Sulabh Samachar* in Bengal, Bal Shastri Jambekar's
Dig Darshan and *Bombay Darpun* (bilingual), Bhau Mahajan's
Prabhakar (in which Lokhitwadi's *Satpatre* were published) and
Dadabhai Naoroji's *Rast Goftar* in Bombay, Veeresalingam's
Vivekavardhini and Buchaiah Pantalu's *Hindu Jana Samskarini* in
Andhra Pradesh, were pioneering efforts in this direction. Some of
them, in spite of their English education, wrote exclusively in their
mother-tongue and members of associations like Sarbatatva Deepika
Sabha founded in 1833 took an oath to speak only in the mother-
tongue.[64]

The members of the 'Anglophile' Young Bengal were the first
to debate whether the mother-tongue should be made the medium of
instruction.[65] Uday Chandra Addhya, in a speech delivered to the

[63] The efforts of Vidyasagar and Veeresalingam, among others, are of
special significance in this attempt to evolve a modern prose. The primers
com-posed by Vidyasagar 'spelled out the elements to be used for shaping
the language to an order and a system to endow it with clear meaning and
correct form. The true Bengali prose had come to its own in the four major
literary works of Vidyasagar . . . Vidyasagar borrowed from Sanskrit and
English what could be harmoniously blended with Bengali and was necessary to strengthen and clarify its native genius. Close to common life, his
language was colloquial, and at the same time refined and elegant, lucid and
precise, and yet colourful and musical.' Asok Sen, *Ishwar Chandra Vidyasagar
and His Elusive Milestones,* Calcutta, 1977, p. 15. Also see S.K. De, *Bengali
Literature in the Nineteenth Century,* 1962, pp. 627–28 and V.R. Narla,
Veeresalingam, 1968, pp. 26–31. O. Chandu Menon, author of the
Malayalam novel *Indulekha,* published in 1889, ridiculed the highly
sanskritized language used by his contemporaries and wrote his social
novels in simple, almost colloquial, language.

[64] Chattopadhyaya (ed.), *Awakening in Bengal,* p. xxv.

[65] The intellectuals did not demand education exclusively in the English
language. The object of the Hindu College was 'the tuition of the respectable
Hindus in the English and Indian languages and in the literature and sciences
of Europe and Asia'.

Society for the Acquisition of General Knowledge in June 1833, made a passionate appeal for the proper cultivation of the Bengali language and the proper education of Bengalis by means of the mother-tongue. 'My heart bleeds and tears stream down my face', he said, 'when I think about the lack of the knowledge in the mother-tongue among the natives of this country.'[66] This lack of knowledge was seen as one of the major reasons for the misery and degradation of the country. A 'proper knowledge of the language of this country' was a necessary pre-requisite for progress and regeneration leading to political freedom.[67] The general belief that it would not be possible to prosper without the means of the English language was 'a mere illusion fostered by the vast wealth of the English'.[68] Even Krishna Mohan Bannerji, a prominent member of the Young Bengal group, who considered only those 'instructed in the literature, science and history of Europe' as 'educated' and all others as 'simply learned',[69] maintained that 'oriental classics or vernaculars were not to be excluded from any system of Indian education'.[70]

The vernacular languages found an equally ardent advocate in Akshay Kumar Dutt. He realized the consequences of the 'Macaulayian system' which was creating a group of emasculated people alienated from their national culture and from their own countrymen.[71] He was, therefore, totally opposed to education in English and instead, advocated the introduction of Bengali as the medium of instruction at all levels of schooling.[72] He asserted that English could never become the lingua franca of India.[73]

---

[66] Uday Chandra Addhya, 'A Proposal for the Proper Cultivation of the Bengali Language and its Necessity for the Natives of this Country', in Chattopadhyay (ed.), *Awakening in Bengal,* p. 26.

[67] 'The superiority of men lies in their efficiency. . . . Only when the people of this country learn properly the language of this country then and then alone will they acquire that efficiency which can enable them to shake off the present slavery and become the master of their own land.' Ibid., p. 27.

[68] Ibid., p. 26.

[69] Krishan Mohan Bannerji, *A Lecture on the Peculiar Responsibility of Indians,* n.d., p. 4.

[70] Krishna Mohan Bannerji, *The Proper Place of Oriental Literature in Indian Collegiate Education,* Calcutta, 1868, p. 18.

[71] *Tattwabodhini Patrika,* Shrawan, Saka 1768, No. 36, pp. 309–11.

[72] *Tattwabodhini Patrika,* Shrawan, Saka 1770, Vol. 2, No. 61, pp. 68–77.

[73] Ibid.

The central concern of Vidyasagar's educational programme too was the principle of adopting the mother-tongue as
the medium of instruction.[74] He believed that knowledge of Sanskrit
was primarily a means for the creation of 'an elegant, expressive and
idiomatic Bengali style'.[75] The reforms he introduced in Sanskrit
College were intended to raise a band of young students who would
be perfect masters of the Bengali language and who would help
disseminate sound knowledge among the people in the rural regions
of Bengal.[76] He also actively participated in the establishment and
running of vernacular schools.[77] Thus, in spite of the fact that English
education alone could ensure public appointments the need for
vernacular education was emphasized and advocated by the Indian
intellectuals.[78]

However, given the nature of socio-economic developments
during the nineteenth century which did not produce the necessary
preconditions for science and mass education, these ideas had no real
social relevance. They remained mere utopian dreams. Moreover, the
dependence of the intellectuals on the colonial state's initiative for the
implementation of their programme made this design a self-defeating

---

[74] Benoy Ghose, *Ishwar Chandra Vidyasagar*, 1971, p. 39.

[75] Mitra, *Karuna Sagar, Vidya Sagar*, p. 723.

[76] Ibid., pp. 732–33.

[77] In his letter to the Council of Public Instruction he wrote: 'Let us establish
a number of vernacular schools, let us prepare a series of vernacular class
books on useful and instructive subjects, let us raise up a band of men
qualified to undertake the responsible duty of teachers and the object is
accomplished'. Mitra, *Karuna Sagar, Vidya Sagar*, p. 732. He was, however, conscious of the fact that only English education ensured the students
public employment. He, therefore, appealed to the government to provide
vernacular students with suitable employment. Arabinda Guha (ed.),
Unpublished Letters of Vidyasagar, Calcutta, 1971, p. 29.

[78] Ranade, Veeresalingam and Sayyid Ahmad Khan held similar views on the
use of vernacular languages. Ranade, who was a member of the University
of Bombay, suggested that the students should be required to write an essay
in a vernacular language as a part of the university examination. Karve,
Ranade, The Liberated Prophet of India, p. 195. Sayyid Ahmad Khan, to
begin with, preferred English as the medium, but later advocated the
adoption of vernaculars also for higher education. Zobairic Riazuddin,
'Educational and Social Ideas of Sayyid Ahmad Khan', unpublished Ph. D.
thesis, Southern Illinois University, 1971, pp. 144, 152. Also see
Veeresalingam, 'Vernacular Languages', in *Vivekavardhini*, October 1881
and November 1886.

exercise. It was not within the logic of colonialism to promote a scheme of education which would eventually destroy its own foundations. The failure to recognize this reality led many intellectuals to entertain illusions about their ability to influence and change the policy of the government.

These illusions were linked to their understanding of the nature of British rule in India. Unlike in China, where the scholar-gentry debated the ways and means of saving their country from foreign conquest, the nineteenth-century intellectuals faced a political fait accompli, the colonial conquest being almost complete by the second quarter of the nineteenth century. They were not participants in or even witnesses to a struggle between a unified state and a foreign invader which could have aroused a high sense of patriotism and anti-foreignism. On the contrary, British rule was already placed on a sound footing with a well-organized administration, a strong army and police to support it. The attempt by the ideologues of colonial rule to project, on the one hand, the liberal ideals of which Britain was the source and inspiration, and on the other, the cruelty and licentiousness of Indian despots,[79] considerably coloured the intellectuals' perception of the political reality.

The intellectuals' understanding of pre-colonial political institutions in India underlined their despotic and arbitrary character. They believed that a system of 'arbitrary rule has been prevailing in the country for ages',[80] and that 'even those who were inclined towards liberal principles, at best, tempered it with a mild and conciliatory government' or by granting 'civil and religious liberty to his subjects', as in the case of Ranjit Singh[81] and Akbar[82] respectively.

---

[79] This is a very popular and recurring theme in colonial historiography. James Mill, John Malcolm, J.C. Marshman, Grant Duff, Henry Beveridge and a large number of others who wrote on the history of India gave currency to this idea.

[80] Ghose (ed.), *The English Works of Raja Rammohun Roy*, p. 234. Sayyid Ahmad Khan described the pre-colonial system as follows: 'The rule of the former emperors and rajas was neither in accordance with the Hindu nor the Mohammedan religion. It was based upon nothing but tyranny and oppression; the law of might was that of right; the voice of the people was not listened to.' Shan Mohammad, *Writings and Speeches of Sir Sayyid Ahmad Khan*, p.117.

[81] Ibid.

[82] Ibid., p. 359.

They believed that the idea of constitutional government was foreign to the Indian mind.[83] The rather fresh memory of the political and administrative anomie which immediately preceded the colonial rule seemed to reinforce these notions. The decline of the Mughal empire and the consequent emergence of autonomous states resulting in the absence of a strong political and military power over large parts of the country provided a golden opportunity to freebooters, both European and Indian, who plundered and ravaged the countryside in many areas. Before the avarice and rapacity of these plundering hordes—the Skinners and George Thomases, Amir Khans and Karim Khans, Chittus and Sindhias and Holkars—the country lay prostrate and helpless.[84] Minor chieftains who were unable to defend themselves applied for military and political protection to the East India Company, which had by then emerged as the de facto paramount power in India.[85] The concept of tyranny—Muslim in Bengal, Maratha in Rajasthan and Sikh in the Punjab—was an expression of this understanding of the political institutions and conditions during the precolonial period.[86]

[83] Ibid., p. 234.

[84] H.G. Keene, *Hindustan Under Free Lances, 1770–1820*, London, 1907; K.N. Panikkar, *British Diplomacy in North India*, New Delhi, 1968, pp. 43–49; and Edward Thompson, *Making of the Indian Princes*, London, 1943.

[85] It is interesting to note that the Rajput chiefs surrendered their independence without firing even a single shot.

[86] The references to 'Muslim yoke' and 'wretched oppressive Yavanas' and similar other descriptions of the Muslim rule have led to the supposition that 'the concept of Muslim tyranny was one of the most striking features of the nineteenth century renaissance'. Sumit Sarkar, 'Rammohun and the Break with the Past', in V.C. Joshi (ed.), *Rammohun Roy and the Process of Modernization in India*, 1975, p. 58, and 'The Complexities of Young Bengal', *Nineteenth Century Studies*, No. 4, 1973. See also Barun De, 'A Biographical Perspective on the Political and Economic Ideas of Rammohun Roy', in Joshi (ed.), *Rammohun Roy and the Process of Modernization in India*, p. 146. It will be useful to enquire whether this denunciation of Muslim rule was because it was Muslim or because it was tyrannous. In this connection it is pertinent to take into consideration Sayyid Ahmad Khan's description of the nature of the pre-colonial rule (see fn. 80; also Graham, *The Life and Work of Sayyid Ahmad Khan*, p. 89), the attitude of the Rajputs towards the Marathas and the sentiments in the Punjab about the Sikh rule. Even in Bengal, those who had talked about Muslim tyranny also recognized the common political privileges of Hindus and Muslims (see Ghose (ed.), *The English Works of Raja Rammohun Roy*, p. 465). Also, they do not seem to have displayed anti-Muslim sentiments in their

In contrast to this 'scene of violence, oppression and mis-rule'[87]—'a long period of mitigated slavery',[88] the changes brought about by the British—the rule of law, security to life and property and opportunity to acquire the arts and sciences of Europe, appeared 'truly astonishing'.[89] More important was the vision of a political future based on liberal and constitutional principles through the instrumentality of British rule. Democratic and constitutional institutions were the greatest ideals in their political perspective just as modern industrial development was the ideal in their economic perspective. Rammohun Roy gave a public dinner at the Town Hall of Calcutta to celebrate the establishment of constitutional rule in the Spanish colonies of South America[90] and he was greatly dejected when the constitutional government of Naples was overthrown in 1821.[91] 'Enemies to liberty and friends of despotism', he wrote, 'have never been and never will be ultimately successful.'[92] An equally ardent champion of democracy was Lokhitawadi. He asserted that only a democratic government could make the people happy and that 'the

---

attitude towards contemporaries. For instance, Rammohun Roy considered Mus-lim lawyers to be more honest than Hindus and pleaded for the appointment of Muslims as members of the jury. Vidyasagar extended his humanitarian activities to Muslims and Keshub Chandra Sen considered the members of all religious denominations his brethren. Ibid., pp. 245–62; Basu (compiled), *Life and Works of Brahmananda Keshav,* p. 273. Even Bankim Chandra, who is often at the centre of this controversy, did not categorize his characters as bad Muslims and good Hindus. Ayesha in *Raj Sinha* and Muhammad Ali in *Mirinalini* are obvious examples. At the conclusion of *Raj Sinha,* Bankim wrote: 'One is not good simply because he is a Hindu, nor bad because he is a Mohammedan. Nor can it be true to say that all Hindus are bad and all Mohammedans are good. . . . A man, whether he is a Hindu or a Muslim, who has no *Dharma* is inferior, no matter whether he is a Hindu or a Muslim.' S.K. Bose, *Bankim Chandra Chatterji,* New Delhi, 1974, pp. 99–100. However, this theme requires more detailed study.

[87] G.G. Jambhekar (ed.), *Memoirs and Writings of Acharya Bal Shastri Jambekar,* Vol. II, Pune, 1950, p. 8.

[88] Sayyid Ahmad Khan, 'Speech at the Scientific Society, Aligarh', in Shan Mohammed, *Writings and Speeches of Sir Sayyid Ahmad Khan,* p. 177.

[89] Jambhekar (ed.), *Memoirs and Writings of Acharya Bal Shastri Jambhekar,* p. 8.

[90] Collet, *Life and Letters of Rammohun Roy,* p. 162.

[91] Rammohun was so unhappy that he cancelled his engagement with Buckingham, the editor of *Calcutta Journal.*

[92] Collet, *Life and Letters of Rammohun Roy,* p. 131.

laws that are made for a country must have the consent of the people'.[93] England with her long unbroken record of constitutional government was not only the best ideal and example, where 'Indians could see for themselves how democracy functioned',[94] but was also 'the Liberator of Europe'[95] whenever freedom and liberty were endangered by despotic rulers. In their conception, England which held out the ideals of parliamentary democracy, civil liberties and modern economic development, would act as the instrument for their dispensation to other countries in the world.[96] England was 'a mirror of their own future'. 'All the refined and liberal ideas of the West', maintained Keshub Chandra Sen, 'came to India through England.'[97] British rule was, therefore, welcomed as the chosen instrument[98]—a divine dispensation—to bring about a total change,[99] a part of which was a change from arbitrary and despotic rule to a bourgeois–democratic political system.

The political and administrative reality in India, however, was sharply different from this ideal construct. The intellectuals

---

[93] Lokhitawadi, *Satpatre*, No. 54. Quoted by Biman Bihari Majumdar, *History of Indian Social and Political Ideas*, 1967, p. 202.

[94] Ibid., p. 201.

[95] Rammohun Roy, 'Appeal to the King in Council', in Ghose (ed.), *The English Works of Raja Rammohun Roy*, p. 467.

[96] *Keshub Chandra Sen in England*, p. 91.

[97] Rammohun Roy characterized England as a 'nation who not only are blessed with the enjoyment of civil and political liberty but also interest themselves in promoting liberty and social happiness, as well as free enquiry into literary and religious subjects, among these nations to which their influence extend'. Rammohun Roy, 'Final Appeal to the Christian Public', in Ghose (ed.), *The English Works of Raja Rammohun Roy*, p. 874.

[98] The British rule as divine dispensation was an idea commonly held by intellectuals in the nineteenth century. 'It is not a man's work, but a work which God is doing with his own hands, using the British nation as his instrument.' *Keshub Chandra Sen in England*, p. 90. Ranade saw the hand of God in the movement of the world and therefore believed that political changes were providentially arranged. T.V. Parvate, *Mahadev Govind Ranade*, 1963, p. 226. Also see Keshub Chandra Sen, *Lectures in India*, London, 1904, p. 320; Rammohun Roy, 'An Appeal to the King in Council', in Ghose (ed.), *The English Works of Raja Rammohun Roy*, pp. 446, 447; Veeresalingam, *Complete Works*, Vol. VIII, p. 9.

[99] Keshub Chandra Sen called it a 'Revolutionary Reform'. *Keshub Chandra Sen in England*, p. 89.

perceived the attempts to curb freedom of expression,[100] the 'notorious and shameless corruption' in the revenue, judicial and police administration,[101] the total absence of popular participation in legislative councils,[102] and the exploitation of Indian resources for British interests,[103] as glaring deviations, and severely criticized these. In an appeal to the King-in-Council and to the Supreme Court, Rammohun and his associates pointed out that if the Press Regulation was passed,

> they would be no longer justified in boasting that they are fortunately placed by Providence under the protection of the whole British Nation, or that the King of England and his Lords and Commons are their legislators, and that they are secured in the enjoyment of the same civil and religious privileges that every British is entitled to in England.[104]

In his evidence to the British Parliament during the renewal of the Charter Act Rammohun highlighted the inadequacies of the judicial and revenue administration of the East India Company.[105] The most devastating criticism of the Company's administration perhaps came from the members of Young Bengal.[106] In Rasik Krishan Mulick's estimate, the judicial administration 'was opposed to the just principles of government',[107] and Dakshina Ranjan Mukhopadhyaya denounced the police system as 'unworthy of reposing any confidence'.[108] Characterizing the government as aristocratic, the Hindu College boys deplored the fact that the people had no voice

---

[100] Rammohun and five others, 'Petition against the Press Regulation', and 'Appeal to the King in Council', in Ghose (ed.), *The English Works of Raja Rammohun Roy,* pp. 437–443, 445–67.

[101] Chattopadhyay (ed.), *Awakening in Bengal,* p. 390.

[102] B.B. Majumdar, *History of Indian Social and Political Ideas,* p. 53.

[103] Veeresalingam, *Vivekavardhini,* April 1880.

[104] Rammohun and five others, 'Petition against the Press Regulation', in Ghose (ed.), *The English Works of Raja Rammohun Roy,* p. 442.

[105] Rammohun Roy, 'Questions and Answers on the Judicial System of India', 'Revenue System of India' and 'A Paper on the Revenue System of India', in Ghose (ed.), *The English Works of Raja Rammohun Roy,* pp. 239–287.

[106] Sushoban Sarkar, *Bengal Renaissance and Other Essays,* New Delhi, 1970, p. 116.

[107] B.B. Majumdar, *History of Indian Social and Political Ideas,* p. 57.

[108] Chattopadhyay (ed.), *Awakening in Bengal,* p. 391.

in the council of legislature and no hand in framing the laws which
regulated their civil conduct.[109] Lokhitawadi objected to the dumping
of British manufactured goods in India,[110] Veeresalingam deplored
the drain of wealth from India to England,[111] and Keshub Chandra
Sen questioned the right of Englishmen to use 'the property, riches
and resources of India for selfish aggrandizement or enjoyment'.[112]
'You cannot hold India', Keshub said, 'for the interest of Manchester
nor for the welfare of any other section of the community here, nor
for the advantage of those merchants who go there. . . . If you desire
to hold India you can only do so for the good and welfare of India.'[113]
These reservations and criticisms did not amount to a disillusionment
with the ideals represented by the British; rather, they were because
of them.

The notion of divine dispensation—British rule was willed
by God—enabled the intellectuals to welcome and legitimize the
colonial presence and thus reflect the immediate, though not long-
term interests of the burgeoning bourgeoisie and petty-bourgeoisie
which were respectively tied up with the development of capitalism,
even if dependent, and the service sector. Yet, the notion of divine
dispensation was not devoid of a vision of a political future divorced
from colonial domination. That British rule could be an instument,
not so much of exploitation and oppression, but of socio-political
transformation, was an articulation of this consciousness.[114] It was in

---

[109] B.B. Majumdar, *History of Indian Social and Political Ideas*, p. 53.

[110] M.L. Apte, 'Lokhitawadi and V.K. Chiplunkar', *Modern Asian Studies*,
April 1973.

[111] Ramakrishna, *Veeresalingam and His Times*, pp. 127–28.

[112] Keshub Chandra Sen, 'England's Duties to India', in Basu (compiled), *Life
and Works of Brahmananda Keshav*, p. 214.

[113] Ibid.

[114] Rammohun's qualified approval of 'Europeans of character and capital'
settling in India was only as a means for improving 'the resources of the
country, and also the conditions of the native inhabitants, by showing them
superior methods of cultivation, and the proper modes of treating their
labourers and dependents'. He did not welcome Europeans of all descriptions to become settlers in India since 'such a measure could only be
regarded as adopted for the purpose of entirely supplanting the native
inhabitants, and expelling them from the country'. Rammohun Roy,
'Revenue System of India', in Ghose (ed.), *The English Works of Raja
Rammohun Roy*, p. 284. Also see 'Remarks on Settlement in India by
Europeans', ibid., pp. 315–20.

this sense that Englishmen were assigned the role of trustees[115] willed by God to rescue India from her miserable plight.[116] Once this mission was accomplished, the intellectuals believed that British rule would be terminated. This instrumentality was further emphasized when they argued that if the British misused this divine trust by attempting repression or passing legislation opposed to the people's interest, 'the people will declare themselves independent and tell the English to quit'.[117] Even if it took about two hundred years for Indians to free themselves from British domination, 'there was no doubt about the ultimate end'[118] and 'the transfer of power was inevitable'.[119]

However, the inability to grasp the contradiction between British imperialism and the interests of the Indian people led the intellectuals to believe that this transformation would occur within the colonial political framework—a false consciousness created primarily by the influence of the bourgeois–liberal ideologies disseminated by the colonial rulers and internalized by the intellectuals. Since their understanding of and attitude to British rule was partly dictated by this false consciousness, the fact that the reality of British rule was totally at variance with this premise escaped their notice. Their criticism was hence limited to the administrative lapses, to the restriction of civil liberties, and at best, to the infringement of the divine trust. The failure to transcend this ideological barrier accounts for the role they assigned themselves, namely, the creation of an ideological basis for a bourgeois order, 'with refined individuals, refined homes and refined society', within a colonially subject polity. This was in contrast to the nationalists whose ability to overcome this barrier and thus to perceive the contradiction with colonialism led to the national liberation struggle in India. The intellectual effort to create the ideological basis was itself subject to the limitations set by

[115] Keshub Chandra Sen, 'England's Duties to India', in Basu (compiled), *Life and Works of Brahmananda Keshav,* pp. 214, 271.

[116] *Keshub Chandra Sen in England* p. 90; Lokhitawadi, *Causes for Loss of Independence,* quoted by B.B. Majumdar, *History of Indian Social and Political Ideas,* p. 200; Veeresalingam, *Complete Works,* Vol. VIII, pp. 10–13.

[117] V.G. Dighe, 'Renaissance in Maharashtra', *The Journal of the Bombay Asiatic Society,* Vol. 36–37, 1961–62.

[118] Lokhitawadi's statement, ibid.

[119] Parvate, *Mahadev Govind Ranade,* p. 227.

the socio-economic formations under colonial rule. The fact that bourgeois–liberal ideas had no corresponding material basis to sustain them acted as an inhibiting factor in the development of ideas during the nineteenth century. It would be useful at this juncture to examine the limited and stunted nature of these ideas as they emerged and evolved during the course of the nineteenth century.

Rationalism and Religious Universalism

The two important intellectual and ideological strands in the nineteenth century were rationalism and religious universalism. Their sources of origin, channels of transmission and methods of application are yet unexplored areas of research; the present enquiry is limited to their development during the course of the nineteenth century.

The attitude towards socio-religious issues during the early part of the nineteenth century was highly influenced by rationalism. Rammohun's first extant work, *Tuhfat-ul Muwahhiddin,* published in 1803, in which he subjected the entire religious system—except theistic belief and faith in the soul and the other world—to an uncompromising rational critique, marked the beginning.[120] In a devastating attack on miracles and superstition, he upheld demonstrability and rational explanation as the only basis of truth.[121] To the members of Young Bengal, 'he who will not reason is a bigot; he who cannot is a fool and he who does not is a slave',[122] and to Akshay Kumar

---

[120] Rammohun's militant rationality in *Tuhfat* raises interesting questions about the formative influences on the nineteenth-century intellectuals. The source of Rammohun's rationalism of this period was primarily the Indian intellectual tradition since his familiarity with European philosophy and scientific thought was acquired only during the post-*Tuhfat* days. See K.N. Panikkar, 'Rationalism in the Religious Thought of Rammohun Roy', *The Indian History Congress Proceedings,* Chandigarh session, 1973. In this context, it is interesting to note that Akshay Kumar adopted the organic theory of society from western thought, whereas Veeresalingam reached the same conclusion from his reading of the Vedas. Akshay Kumar Dutt, *Dharamniti,* pp. 50–51 and Leonard, 'Kandukiri Veeresalingam', p. 207.

[121] 'How could a matter', he asked, 'which has no proof and which is inconsistent with reason be received and admitted by men of reason.' Rammohun Roy, *Tuhfat-ul Muwahhiddin,* in Ghose (ed.), *The English Works of Raja Rammohun Roy,* p. 956.

[122] Sushoban Sarkar, *Bengal Renaissance and Other Essays,* p. 111.

'pure rationalism is our teacher'.[123] According to Akshay Kumar, natural phenomena were not beyond human comprehension and the universe could be analysed and understood by purely mechanical processes without indulging in supernaturalism.[124] Keshub Chandra Sen during the early phase of his life totally rejected the authority of the scriptures[125] and ascribed to individual reason the power to determine what was rational and true and to individual conscience the power to determine what was right and wrong.[126] He did believe even at this stage in intuition as revelation from God, but he considered it as strictly subjective, the level of individual consciousness being the decisive factor.[127] In religious matters, rationality was the guiding principle for Sayyid Ahmad Khan;[128] Ranade considered 'our conscience and our reason the supreme, if not the sole guide, to our conduct';[129] and Lokhitawadi advocated rationality as the most important criterion of all social reforms.[130]

A retreat from this rationalist stand was clearly evident in the case of those who were involved in the actual process of socio-religious endeavour. Rammohun's rationalism of the *Tuhfat* days underwent a marked decline during his later life.[131] He abandoned his

---

[123] *Tattwabodhini Patrika*, Phalgun, Saka 1773.

[124] A.K. Bhattacharya, 'Akshay Dutt, Pioneer of Indian Rationalism', *Rationalist Annual*, 1962.

[125] A.C. Banerji, 'Brahmananda K.C. Sen', in A.C. Gupta (ed.), *Studies in Bengal Renaissance*, Jadavpur, 1958, p. 81; *The New Dispensation*, 11 June 1882.

[126] Ibid.

[127] Keshub Chandra Sen, 'Revelation', in Basu (compiled), *Life and Works of Brahmananda Keshav*, p. 32; Prosanto Kumar Sen, *Keshub Chandra Sen*, Calcutta, 1938, p. 23.

[128] Sayyid Ahmad Khan wrote: 'After all these considerations, I came to the conclusion that the only means of obtaining knowledge, conviction or faith is reason. But when knowledge or conviction of faith is not based on reason then their achievements in any age or period of time are impossible.' Quoted by Ali Ashraf, 'Sir Sayyid Ahmad Khan and the Tradition of Rationalism in Islam', *Islam and the Modern Age*, Vol. III, No. 3, August 1972. Also see M. Shah Din, *Sayyid Ahmad Khan as a Religious Reformer*, 1904, and Nizami, *Sayyid Ahmad Khan*, p. 121.

[129] M.G. Ranade, *The Miscellaneous Writings*, p. 193.

[130] B.B. Majumdar, *History of Indian Social and Political Ideas*, p. 199.

[131] See Panikkar, 'Rationalism in the Religious Thought of Rammohun Roy'.

deistic belief and accepted the Vedas as divine revelation.[132] Instead
of applying the critique of reason to the facts of the scriptures, he now
endeavoured to explain and reconcile the inconsistencies and contradictions in them.[133] In Keshub the change was more dramatic. The
young radical Brahmo who had launched a crusade to restore the
original non-conformism of the Brahmo Samaj, introduced *arti, puja*
and *sankirtan* in his prayers. Those who differed with him were
accused of being 'secularists, infidels, rationalists and men of little
faith'.[134] More significantly, as the high priest of the New Dispensation he extended his intuitive experience for universal acceptance.[135]
Ranade too faltered from his rationalist stand. Confronted with
social pressure, he abandoned his plan to marry a widow,[136] and in
spite of his conviction about its irrelevance he performed penance for
attending a tea-party hosted by Christian missionaries.[137] It is significant that individuals like Akshay Kumar Dutt who were not
directly involved in reform activities did not undergo this change.

The retreat was not limited to individuals alone, but was
applicable to movements as well. The theological rationalism of the
early Brahmo Samaj, in spite of internal struggles to uphold it, lost its
appeal with the second split in the Samaj and the establishment of the
New Dispensation. The spirit of rational criticism of the revealed
truth of the scriptures, a dominant feature of the early movements,

[132] Rammohun's later writings are replete with expressions like 'the Vedas
created by the Supreme Being', 'Divine guidance of the Vedas' and 'Vedas
is the law of God revealed and introduced for our rule and guidance'. See
Rammohun Roy, 'Abridgement of the Vedanta', 'A Second Defence of
the Monotheistic System of the Vedas' and 'Brahminical Magazine, IV',
in Ghose (ed.), *The English Works of Raja Rammohun Roy*, pp. 3–5, 105–
31, 181.
[133] See, for instance, his explanation for the plurality of gods and goddesses in
the scriptures and their mode of worship. He says in justification of idol
worship that it was 'inculcated for the sake of those whose limited
understanding rendered them incapable of comprehending and adoring the
invisible Supreme Being, so that such persons might not remain in a brutified
state, destitute of all religious principles.' Ibid., p. 36.
[134] Shivanath Shastri, *History of the Brahmo Samaj*, Calcutta, 1911, p. 269.
[135] Ibid., p. 268 and P.C. Mazumdar, *Life and Teachings of Keshub Chandra
Sen*, Calcutta, 1931, p. 180.
[136] James Kellock, *Mahadev Govind Ranade*, Bombay, 1926, pp. 57–60.
[137] Ramabai Ranade, *Ranade, His Wife's Reminiscences*, New Delhi, 1969,
pp. 138–41.

was conspicuously absent in the religious movements of the late nineteenth century. Dayanand and the Arya Samajists recognized not only divine revelation and the infallibility of the Vedas but also their universal and eternal relevance.[138] To them the role of reason was limited to that of an aid in understanding and interpreting the Vedas.[139] Ramakrishna accepted idolatry and justified all rituals and practices of traditional religion, and his disciple Vivekananda described the Vedas as 'the knowledge of God'.[140] Scriptural sanction and religious faith replaced the earlier emphasis on rational explanation and demonstrability.[141]

This process of decline and retreat was experienced in the realm of another important idea in the nineteenth century, namely, religious universalism. An enquiry into comparative religion and universal religious traits had marked the reformation in the nineteenth century, both among the Hindus and the Muslims. The idea of religious universalism as articulated by the reformers was rooted in this enquiry. The most striking feature of religious thought during the early phase of the reformation was a universal outlook based on the unity of Godhead and monotheism. For instance, a comprehensive study of the Hindu, Muslim and Christian scriptures convinced Rammohun that 'the core of religious truth, comprehending the unity of God as spirit, his worship in spirit and in truth, the immortality of the soul, and ethical discipline as the basis of spiritual life, formed the central teaching of the canonical scriptures of the historic religions.'[142] Keshub's position was not 'that truths are to be found in all religions',

---

[138] Dayanand Saraswati, *Satyarth Prakash*, pp. 565 and 196–200; Lala Lajpat Rai, *A History of the Arya Samaj*, p. 96; Vaidyanath Shastri, *The Arya Samaj: Its Cult and Creed*, New Delhi, 1967, pp. 19–20.

[139] An official publication of the Arya Samaj described the role of reason as follows: 'Human reason has only a limited amount of strength and needs divine help. It is quite rational to seek such aid because it is rational to realize the limitations of human reason.' Ganga Prasad Upadhyaya, *The Origin, Scope and Mission of Arya Samaj*, Allahabad, 1953, p. 36.

[140] Vivekananda, *Complete Works*, p. 11.

[141] I have argued elsewhere that the retreat in Rammohun's rationality was connected with the nature of Calcutta society, the problems of which Rammohun was involved with. Panikkar, 'Rationalism in the Religious Thought of Rammohun Roy', p. 14.

[142] Brijendranath Seal, *Rammohun Roy: The Universal Man*, Calcutta, n.d., p. 14.

but that 'all established religions of the world are true'.[143] Sayyid Ahmad Khan believed that all religions are essentially the same and all prophets had the same *Din*.[144] The differences in outward manifestation, in spite of this basic unity, were due to the differing needs of the society in which they flourished.[145] Rammohun believed that there was only one universal theism, the Hindu, Islamic and Christian theisms being its national embodiments.[146] It was this universalist outlook which led Rammohun to defend the monotheism of the Vedas and the unitarianism of Christianity, and at the same time to attack Hindu polytheism and Christian trinitarianism.[147] He defended basic religious principles, be they in Hinduism, Christianity or Islam, against attack by one another. Similarly, Keshub used his universalist concept of the 'Fatherhood of God' to imply the 'Brotherhood of man' and looked upon all around him—'whether Parsees, Hindus, Mohammadans or Europeans'—as his brethren.[148] Vivekananda was of the view that different religions were neither contradictory nor antagonistic.[149] In his concept, there was only one eternal religion which was applied to different planes of existence.[150]

The belief in religious unity formed the basis of an attempt at religious synthesis by Rammohun and Keshub Chandra Sen.

---

[143] 'Truth is no more European than Asiatic, no more Biblical than Vedic, no more Christian than Heathen: it is no more yours than mine.' Keshub Chandra Sen, *Lectures in India*, pp. 179–80.

[144] Sayyid Ahmad Khan, 'Islam and Tolerance', in Shan Mohammad (ed.), *Writings and Speeches of Sir Sayyid Ahmad Khan*, p. 60.

[145] *Tuhfat-ul Muwahhiddin*, in Ghose (ed.), *The English Works of Raja Rammohun Roy*, p. 947, and Apte, 'Lokhitawadi and V.K. Chiplunkar'.

[146] Seal, *Rammohun Roy: The Universal Man*, p. 19.

[147] Rammohun Roy, 'A Defence of Hindu Theism', 'A Second Defence of the Monotheistical System of the Vedas', 'The Precepts of Jesus, the Guide to Peace and Happiness', 'An Appeal to the Christian Public in Defence of the Precepts of Jesus' and 'The Brahminical Magazine', in Ghose (ed.), *The English Works of Raja Rammohun Roy*, pp. 87–101, 481–545, 143–99.

[148] Basu (compiled), *Life and Works of Brahmananda Keshav*, p. 273.

[149] Vivekananda, *Complete Works*, Vol. IV, p. 180.

[150] Vivekananda wrote: 'There never was my religion or yours, my national religion or your national religion, there never existed many religions, there is only one. One infinite religion existed all through eternity and will ever exist, and this religion is expressing itself in various countries in various ways. . . . Religions manifest themselves not only according to race and geographical position, but according to individual powers.' Ibid., p. 180.

Rammohun's postulate that all religions, through a process of synthesis, inevitably advanced towards a universal religion, did not imply that synthesis would lead to a merger of all religions and thus the establishment of a universal church.[151] On the other hand, it would only help the fuller development of universalist ideas in each religion without destroying the peculiar characteristics of national theisms. Keshub's New Dispensation tried to encompass the truth of all the scriptures in one unwritten scripture and to establish a universal church drawing upon the ideas and symbols of all established religions,[152] an attempt the Brahmo Samaj, in spite of its universalist commitment, had not made before. Although the Samaj was conceived on universalist principles, in practice it remained a Hindu theistic association.

During the later part of the nineteenth century this religious perspective underwent a sharp change. Religious universalism gave way to religious particularism. This change was perhaps first expressed by Bankim Chandra Chatterji, to whom 'the great principles of Hinduism were good for all ages and for all mankind'.[153] Dayanand Saraswati idealized the Vedas as the only revelation of God and the source of all knowledge, science and religion of mankind,[154] and Hinduism based on Vedic precepts as the only religion with universal application.[155] Unlike in the Brahmo Samaj, where Rammohun's concept of Vedic infallibility was challenged and abandoned under the influence of Akshay Kumar's rational arguments, the debate among the followers of Dayanand was whether the infallibility should be extended to the writings and pronouncements of Dayanand as well.[156] In spite of his emphasis on religious harmony, Vivekananda's ideal was a religion based on the findings of Vedic seers[157] and to him

---

[151] Seal, *Rammohun Roy: The Universal Man,* p. 19.

[152] 'Is Not the New Dispensation New', *The New Dispensation,* 2 September 1881.

[153] Bankim Chandra Chatterji, *Letters on Hinduism,* p. 12, and Rachel Rebecca Van Meter, 'Bankim Chandra Chatterji and the Bengali Renaissance', unpublished Ph.D. thesis, University of Pennsylvania, 1964, p. 242.

[154] Dayanand Saraswati, *Satyarth Prakash,* pp. 565, 196–200.

[155] Ibid., p. 265.

[156] Kenneth Jones, 'A Study of Social Reform and Religious Revivalism, 1877–1902', unpublished Ph.D. thesis, University of California, 1966, pp. 177–78.

[157] Binoy Roy, *Socio-Political Views of Vivekananda,* New Delhi, 1970, p. 9.

Hinduism was the mother of all religions which had taught the world the principle of universal tolerance and acceptance and to which he was proud to belong.[158] The emphasis on universal theism of Rammohun's days had clearly changed into a Hindu-centric theistic ideal. Thus, the universalist ideal died a premature death in the nineteenth century, aborting the possibility of the organic growth of a secular ideology from within it. It was replaced by religious particularism which considerably hampered the process of secularization, of which universalism was a necessary precursor in a multi-religious society. The decline to particularism became stronger in the twentieth century which, inter alia, contributed to the development of a communal ideology and the consequent communalization of society. It is paradoxical, but true, that the struggle for secularism in contemporary India does not go beyond the nineteenth-century struggle for the social and political acceptance of religious universalism. Although this ideological weakness was exploited by the colonial state and bureaucracy to promote and sharpen the communal divide in Indian society, the philosophically weak foundation of the reformation was no less responsible for it.

Ideology and Material Reality

It should be obvious that I am not making a plea for the 'autonomy' of intellectual history, divorced from the material reality of man's existence. Intellectual history, after all, is not the history of thought, but 'the history of man's thinking'. I therefore suggest that the complexities of intellectual developments may be properly understood only when placed in their specific historical context. For the modern period of our history, however, it would involve not simply a recognition of the constraints imposed upon intellectual developments by the objective conditions—the stultified and dependent form of capitalist development and the consequent character and course of class formations—but an effort to understand the inter-relationship between ideas and that objective reality by a detailed study and analysis of the ideas themselves. In other words, it would have to be a study of the dialectical relationship between the material base and

---

[158] Vivekananda, *Complete Works,* Vol. I, p. 3; Swami Nikhilananda, *Vivekananda,* Calcutta, 1971, p. 119.

the ideological system, with a proper appreciation of the role of the latter in the total structure. Only such an exercise will help clear the confusion that clouds our present understanding of the character and role of the intellectuals in nineteenth-century India. It is this constant interaction between the ideas and their material base which accounts for the limited and stunted character of the bourgeois–democratic ideas of the nineteenth-century intellectuals as well as their inability to struggle for them with fuller commitment. The colonial intellectuals were not 'organic' to a developing bourgeois order, but were those struggling for the acquisition, dissemination and acceptance of bourgeois ideas and values in a period of transition from a feudal society to a stultified and dependent form of capitalism under colonial domination. The roots of the crisis of identity referred to in the beginning lie in this contradiction: so also the failure, frustration and tragedy of nineteenth-century intellectuals as a whole, despite their individual radiance and endeavours.

The relationship between a class and its political and literary representatives was indicated by Karl Marx in relation to France during the rule of Louis Bonaparte, and captures the intellectual ambience in colonial India as well:

> What makes them [the democratic elements] representatives of the petty-bourgeoisie is the fact that in their minds they do not get beyond the limits which the latter do not get beyond in life, that they are consequently driven theoretically to the same problems and solutions to which material interest and social position drive the latter practically.[159]

This was the social limit that intellectual endeavour in colonial India was unable to transcend.

[159] Karl Marx and Frederick Engels, *Selected Works*, Vol. I, Moscow, 1955, p. 275.

2 Cultural Trends in Pre-Colonial India

The 'Dark Age'

Reflecting on the nature of society and polity in pre-colonial India, Rev. W. Tennant observed as follows:

> It may justly be questioned whether in any instance, the annals of nations can present to our contemplation a great community plunged into an abyss of anarchy, equally deep and gloomy, as that by which India was overwhelmed after the decline and fall of the Mughal Empire.[1]

That the eighteenth century was a 'dark age' for India has been a view held by several European administrator-historians and contemporary observers, by Henry Beveridge, James Mill and John Marshman among others. The pre-colonial political anarchy, intellectual stagnation and cultural backwardness, in contrast to the 'progress' under British benevolence, were to some an explanation and to others a justification for the conquest of India. This perspective was not limited to early colonial ideologues; it became an integral part of the later historical writings on eighteenth-century India. Thus, L.S.S. O'Malley, B.T. McCulley, Percival Spear, Jadunath Sarkar and Tarachand, either explicitly or implicitly, refer to the decline and decadence of pre-colonial Indian society.[2]

---

[1] Rev. W. Tennant, *Thoughts on the Effects of British Government on the State of Indostan,* London, 1807, pp. 78–79.

[2] L.S.S. O'Malley, *Modern India and the West,* London, 1968, pp. 54–66; B.T. McCulley, *English Education and the Origins of Indian Nationalism,* New Delhi, 1968, p. 160; Jadunath Sarkar, *The Decline and Fall of the Mughal Empire,* I, Calcutta, 1950, pp. 343–44; Tarachand, *History of Freedom Movement in India,* I, New Delhi, 1965, p. 5.

This gloomy picture was initially derived from a Delhi-centred view of the political conditions in India. The political anomie that followed the decline of Mughal authority, particularly in the heartland of the empire, not only led to almost continuous struggle between the various forces contending for political power, but also brought to the fore several military adventurers, both Indian and foreign, in quest of easy fortunes. The Pindarees and the Pathans under the leadership of Amirkhan, Karimkhan and Chittu ravaged and plundered central India,[3] and European freebooters like James Skinner and George Thomas looked for kingdoms in India.[4] The Marathas, as a part of their northward push, laid waste the states of Rajputana, made repeated incursions into Bengal and meddled in the politics of north India. The Mughal emperors who succeeded Aurangzeb lacked the efficiency and determination needed to deal with the decay that had set in in the administrative institutions, to contain the popular upsurge corroding the imperial foundations, and to restructure the economy to meet the new challenges. The power and authority of the empire was irretrievably lost and the emperor's right to the throne depended upon support from the Marathas, the Rohillas or the British. Viewed against this background, Gulam Hussain's characterization of the eighteenth century as 'an age of senseless, slothful princes, and of grandees, ignorant and meddling', seems well justified. He wrote:

> It is in consequence of such wretched administration that every part of Hind has gone to ruin, and every one of its discouraged inhabitants have broken their hearts. Life itself is become disgustful to most. So that, on comparing the present times with the past, one is apt to think that the world is overspread with blindness, and that the earth is totally overwhelmed with an everlasting darkness.[5]

There is no denying the fact that the decline of Mughal power was accompanied by political instability, administrative inefficiency

---

[3] K.N. Panikkar, *British Diplomacy in North India,* New Delhi, 1968, pp. 43–49.

[4] H.G. Keene, *Hindustan under Free Lances, 1770–1820,* London, 1907, and Edward Thompson, *The Making of the Indian Princes,* London, 1943.

[5] Quoted in V.P.S. Raghuvanshi, *Indian Society in the Eighteenth Century,* New Delhi, 1969, p. 8.

and social insecurity. But while the disintegration of the Mughal empire represented a political trend, the chaos, confusion and anarchy attendant upon it, did not. The alternate political trend that manifested itself in the eighteenth century was the emergence of autonomous states and their subsequent consolidation as independent states. In other words, the political process that followed the break-up of the Mughal empire was fragmentation of political power, not political disintegration. Disintegration of a centralized empire is not necessarily a misfortune, nor is it politically retrogressive. At any rate, the new political structure emerging in the eighteenth century was not devoid of vigour and vitality; the autonomous and independent states did not necessarily present a picture of anarchy and decadence. For instance, in Bengal under Murshid Kuli Khan and Alivardi Khan, though a realignment of forces was underway, the administration was as efficient as, if not better, than during the heyday of the empire.[6] So was perhaps Hyderabad and the Carnatic before the French intervention. Travancore, under the dynamic leadership of Marthanda Varma (1729–58), not only reorganized its administration and quelled internal dissensions but also became a powerful force in the region.[7] What would have been the nature of Indian polity if these tendencies were allowed to mature without colonial intervention is a futile speculation. At least one Indian ruler in the eighteenth century initiated steps, though unsuccessfully, to restructure the economy of his state, indicating a nebulous awareness of the needs of modernization.[8] While saying so, certain inherent weaknesses of the Indian political structure which could have adversely affected the emergence of new socio-economic formations are not to be overlooked. In Tipu Sultan's Mysore, for instance,

> The most prominent obstacle, speaking generically, was the ab-

---

[6] Philip Calkins, 'The Formation of Regional Elites in Bengal', *Journal of Asian Studies,* August 1970, pp. 799–806.

[7] A.P. Ibrahim Kunju, *Rise of Travancore: A Study of the Life and Times of Marthanda Varma,* Trivandrum, 1978, pp. 7, 99–122. P. Sankunni Menon, *Tiruvatancore Charitam* (translated by C.K. Kareem), Trivandrum, 1913, pp. 89–145, and R. Narayana Panikar, *The History of Travancore,* Part I, Trivandrum, 1933, pp. 84–150.

[8] Asok Sen, 'A Pre-British Economic Formation', in Barun De (ed.), *Perspectives in Social Sciences,* Calcutta, 1977, pp. 46–119.

sence of forces and perspective to work for the emergence of Civil Society and the whole complex of individualization of property and socio-economic change associated with the European experience of transition from feudalism to capitalism. Whether in respect of agriculture, or that of trade and industry, Tipu's means of striking an advance could not go beyond the elaborate manipulations of statecraft which continued and even accentuated the stranglehold of politics and bureaucracy on the process of appropriation and use of economic surplus.[9]

However, what Tipu Sultan represented was the willingness and ability of the Indian leadership to strike out on a new path and what the course of history denied to Indians was the chance to overcome the obstacles Tipu's efforts had encountered.

Cultural Decline?

Almost every work on eighteenth-century India posited a direct connection between political anarchy and socio-cultural development. 'Civilized life', wrote Raghuvanshi, 'cannot flourish amid conditions of insecurity and oppression. In the eighteenth century the break-up of the Mughal monarchy released forces of political disintegration and anarchical conditions which destroyed the creative and cooperative spirit of man. They caused deterioration in every phase of national life.'[10] Contemporary observers like Abu Dubois, Alexander Dow and Forbes have testified that Indian creativity had sunk to the lowest levels.[11] That political instability and economic crisis are necessarily accompanied by a void in artistic and literary creativity does not seem to have historical validity.[12] With respect to eighteenth-century India this point was first demonstrated by Hermann Goetz who argued that political instability did not lead to an overall decline in culture. He wrote:

For those symptoms of decadence which have been made a re-

---

[9] Ibid., p. 103.

[10] Raghuvanshi, *Indian Society in the Eighteenth Century*, p. 24.

[11] Ibid., p. 28.

[12] Robert S. Lopex, 'Hard Times and Investment in Culture', in Antony Molho, *Social and Economic Foundation of Italian Renaissance*, New York, 1969.

proach to eighteenth-century India, are clearly discernible in all those times which we consider as glorious periods in the history of other peoples. They have been, so to say, the inevitable shadow of the splendour, they have, no doubt, brought about the final collapse, but we generally overlook them because those dark sides have passed away whereas their splendour is still the living heritage of our culture. But a similar splendid side was inherent also in Indian civilization of the eighteenth and early nineteenth centuries. Can we overlook the fairy like palaces and gardens of Jaipur, Jodhpur, Dig, Udaipur, Lahore, Lucknow, Murshidabad, Poona, etc.? Can we deny the sweetness and the refined taste of the innumerable paintings of those times? Can we forget the Golden Age of Urdu, Bengali and Marathi literature? Can we doubt the high accomplishment of the music and dancing of those times? Or the refinement of social life and the important position of women in that society? Must we not come to the conclusion that the eighteenth and early nineteenth centuries have been a period not only of political and economic decline, but also of the highest refinement of Indian culture?[13]

Art

Detailed historical investigation into the nature of creativity in art and literature and the changing pattern of patronage in the eighteenth century is yet to be undertaken. Yet our existing knowledge about the painting, music and literature of that period does not indicate sterility and stagnation in these spheres. On the contrary, in certain fields creativity reached new heights and in some others it strove to attain new forms of expression. Did this have anything to do with the geographical shift in the centres of patronage and the new life experience of the artists? The puritanism of Aurangzeb and the financial crisis of the later Mughals led to the development of important regional centres of cultural activity. Lucknow, Hyderabad, the states of Rajputana and the Rajput states in the Punjab hill region became major sources of patronage during this period. Not that they did not exist as cultural centres before, but with the decline in

---

[13] Hermann Goetz, *The Crisis of Indian Civilization in the Eighteenth and Early Nineteenth Centuries*, London, 1938, pp. 6–7.

patronage of the imperial court and of the nobles attendant on it, the pull effect from the regional centres to the imperial capital ceased to exist. For instance, in the court of Akbar over a hundred painters were employed, mostly from Gujarat, Gwalior and Kashmir.[14] During the Aurangzeb and post-Aurangzeb periods this tendency was reversed. The painters and artists migrated to regional centres, one of the prominent examples being that of the family of Manak and Nainsukh in Kangra.[15] This had an important bearing on the development of regional cultural centres as well as on its spread effect across regions as a whole, drawing a larger number of territorial aristocrats into the network of patronage.

Miniature painting is a good example both of creative vitality and changes in patronage in the eighteenth century. Miniature painting had its origin in India in the eleventh-century Jain miniatures done on palm leaves which were used for illustrating religious texts. It flourished during Mughal rule with a marked Persian influence. Akbar had at his court two Persian artists, Abdus Samad and Mir Syed Ali, who trained painters assembled from all over India, and under the munificent patronage of Jahangir, Mughal miniature found its best expression.[16] During this period miniature painting became popular in the Rajput states as well, in all probability due to the Mughal influence.[17] But miniature painting thrived in Rajputana with a distinct character, style and content long after the Mughal school had passed its prime.[18] Some of the best creative efforts in this field, notably of the Kishangarh and Bundi schools, were spontaneous and innovative and possessed a style of romantic beauty which was unrivalled in Rajasthan painting.[19] 'The Bundi paintings', wrote Moti Chandra, 'are distinguished by a careful finish, brilliant colours, costumes, architectural settings and romantic landscapes.

[14] M.S. Randhawa, *Indian Miniature Painting*, New Delhi, 1981, p. 16.
[15] Mukund Lal, *Garhwal Painting*, New Delhi, 1968; Karl Khandalawala, *The Development of Style in Indian Painting*, Delhi, 1974, pp. 88–92; Jamila Brijbhushan, *The World of Indian Miniatures*, Tokyo, 1979, p.113; M.S. Randhawa, *Kangra Rangamala Paintings*, New Delhi, 1971, pp. 11–21.
[16] Percy Brown, *Indian Painting under the Mughals*, New York, 1975, pp. 69–71.
[17] Ananda Coomaraswamy, *Rajput Painting*, New York, 1975, pp. 11–16.
[18] Mario Bussagli, *Indian Miniatures*, London, 1966, p. 31.
[19] Randhawa, *Indian Miniature Painting*, p. 80, and Brijbhushan, *The World of Indian Miniatures*, p. 166.

The artists of Bundi were not slavish followers of any particular style; they seem to have fully imbibed the distinguished traits of other Rajput schools.'[20]

Similarly, the eighteenth century witnessed a flowering of miniature painting in the hill states of the Punjab.[21] Manak and Nainsukh in Kangra, Mola Ram in Garhwal and a host of other unidentified painters experimented with new styles, synthesizing the abstract and the natural. 'Painting begins to lean on the side of naturalism, a lyrical romantic quality comes into it and that search for delicacy of feeling begins.'[22]

The Rajput and hill paintings also mark a change in the objects of the painters' interest and the manner in which they are portrayed. Scenes from everyday life, religious festivals and ceremonies, mythological subjects, in particular episodes from the legend of Krishna, dominated their interest. The emphasis on religious themes was perhaps due to the continuing influence of the *bhakti* tradition, especially in Rajasthan.[23] But the tendency to identify living personalities with mythical characters could also be interpreted as the initial expression of the transitional process towards secular art. In Kishangarh, Sudhraj Nihalchand introduced the Savant Singh–Bani Thani love affair[24] into the Radha–Krishna theme. In Kangra paintings Krishna is often depicted as a *pahari* cowherd surrounded by *pahari* maidens in a hill setting.[25] From being an art confined to the experiences of courtly life under the Mughals, miniature painting during the eighteenth century was becoming sensitive to the larger social milieu. This was, in fact, indicative of an important shift in the creative realm as a whole in India at the time.

In the execution of paintings, the eighteenth-century minia-

---

[20] Moti Chandra, 'General Survey of Rajasthan Painting, Bundi', *Marg*, XI, March 1958.

[21] W.G. Archer, *Indian Paintings from the Punjab Hills*, Delhi, 1973.

[22] B.N. Goswami, *Pahari Paintings of the Nala-Damayanti Theme*, New Delhi, 1975, p. 2.

[23] The eighteenth-century Rajasthan literature which heavily drew upon *bhakti* was an indication of this influence.

[24] Savant Singh, the ruler of Kishangarh, fell in love with Bani Thani who was a highly accomplished slave girl. He married Bani Thani, abdicated the throne and retired to Mathura.

[25] Brijbhushan, *The World of Indian Miniatures*, p. 167.

tures of Rajasthan and Kangra maintained high aesthetic standards. Painstaking attention to detail, the use of soft and luminous colours, and tiny and delicate strokes which imparted a lifelike quality to the skin and hair and transparency to cloth characterized these paintings. This was also true of paintings in other areas like the Deccan and Oudh.[26] Signs of decadence appeared only in the nineteenth century: over-ornamentation, lack of proper proportions, clumsy drawings, strong colours laid with a heavy hand and filled-in surfaces which gave a solid and static appearance.[27]

Literature

Historians and literary critics have tended to view eighteenth-century Indian literature as pedantic, degenerate and decadent.

> The literature which was produced in these degenerate times suffered from all the ills society was heir to. Its poetry was dilettantish, weighed with euphemism and conceit. Its spirit was shackled by artificial limitations of rhyme, and its mood alternated between the sensuous and the spiritual, neither deeply experienced. Clouds of pessimism and despair hung over it. It sought rest in flight from reality.[28]

This view, echoed by several others,[29] overlooks the developing trends

---

[26] Several illustrations could be given for this. See, e.g., 'Marriage Procession of Dara Shikoh', Awadh, c. 1760, No. 58.58/38, National Museum, New Delhi; 'Ragini-Bhairavi', Deccan, c. 1725, No. 22.3292, Prince of Wales Museum, Bombay; and 'Maulavi with His Disciples', Deccan, early eighteenth century, No. 22.3427, Prince of Wales Museum, Bombay.

[27] E.g., see plates 67, 75 and 79 in Brijbushan, *The World of Indian Miniatures*.

[28] Tarachand, *History of Freedom Movement in India*, I, p. 192.

[29] About Tamil literature Varadarajan has written as follows: 'The literature of this period is full of rigid conceits and pedantic exercises of the grammarians and the simplicity, the directness and the restraint characteristic of the early literature are now lost. Most of the poets of this age seem imitative and repetitive not only in their narrative but also in their descriptions. Taste in poetry had become sophisticated and poets are judged by the jingle of their alliteration and the acrobatics of their metre. There is, in many works of this period, not so much of art as artificiality, and therefore many of these works have fallen into oblivion.' Nagendra (ed.), *Indian Literature*, Agra, 1959, p. 48; see also B.K.Barua, *History of Assamese Literature*, New Delhi, 1964, p. 102.

in Indian literature during the pre-colonial era. In fact, eighteenth-century literature registered a shift, both in form and content, towards popular literature from 'the painted, powdered and obsequious' sanskritist tradition of the earlier period. Mir and Sauda in Urdu, Brajanatha Bodajena in Oriya, Bharatchandra Ray in Bengali and Vemana in Telugu set new dimensions of literary experience for the people.[30] Brajanatha Bodajena (1730–95), the author of *Chatur Vinoda, Ambika Vilasa* and *Samaratarangana*, experimented with several styles of literary composition. *Chatur Vinoda* was written partly in prose and partly in blank verse, which was a novel attempt at a time when neither prose nor blank verse had been developed in Indian literature. 'This is the one prose work in the whole of old Oriya literature that is original, planned and complete. The style is strikingly fresh, untrammelled, conversational, and very near the modern.'[31] More important, the prose style of Bodajena was very close to the dialect of the common man. In Bengali the first half of the eighteenth century was a period of great literary activity,[32] and Rameswar Bhattacharya and Bharatchandra Ray represented the new tendency.[33] The latter, author of the trilogy, *Annapurnamangal*, is considered the most outstanding poet of Bengal before Tagore. *Vidyasunder*, part of the trilogy, continued to be influential among literary circles in Calcutta almost till the end of the nineteenth century.[34] An important feature of Bengali poetry during this period was the popular style of composition and an effort to portray gods in the image of common men which also characterized the miniature paintings of the eighteenth century. In Rameswar Bhattacharya's *Siva-Sankirtan* (1710), Siva is a petty and poor farmer and the

[30] Muhammad Sadiq, *A History of Urdu Literature*, New Delhi, 1964, pp. 66–116; Ram Babu Saxena, *A History of Urdu Literature*, Allahabad, 1940, pp. 54–66; George Bearse, 'Intellectual and Cultural Characteristics of India in a Changing Era, 1740–1800', *Journal of Asian Studies*, November 1965; W.H. Campbell, 'The One Great Poet of the People', in V.R. Narla (ed.), *Vemana through Western Eyes*, New Delhi, 1969, pp. 50–67; G.V. Sitapati, *History of Telugu Literature*, New Delhi, 1968, p. 36; Mayadhar Mansinha, *History of Oriya Literature*, New Delhi, 1962, pp. 155–62; and Sukumar Sen, *History of Bengali Literature*, New Delhi, 1960, pp. 151–62.

[31] Mansinha, *History of Oriya Literature*, pp. 156–57.

[32] J.C. Ghosh, *Bengali Literature*, London, 1948, p. 85.

[33] They both lived during the first half of the eighteenth century.

[34] Sen, *History of Bengali Literature*, p. 153.

heroine (Gauri) is the poor farmer's wife who is content with two square meals and a few yards of cloth.[35] The change in content became marked during the second half of the eighteenth century. The sad plight of forced labour and the protest of the ryots against the appointment of the dewan were some of the themes in ballads written in a folk style during this time.[36]

The eighteenth century was the heyday of Urdu literature which though romantic in content displayed a highly refined poetic imagination. It was the period of three outstanding poets in Urdu literature: Sauda (1713–80), Mir (1724–1810) and Dard (1719–85). They were sensitive to the declining fortunes of the imperial city and their poetry focussed on the tragedy engulfing the society. Symbolizing the tragedy of the common man toiling under feudal fatalism, their poetry reflected the cultural ethos of their age in an idiom at once intelligible to the masses.

In Oriya, Bengali, Telugu and Malayalam, and perhaps in all other literatures, the shift towards popular literature was clearly discernible in the eighteenth century. It marked a definite break, and in cases where the break had occurred earlier, a further advance, from the existing literary tradition which incorporated mainly upper-class themes in highly sanskritized diction. The process of vernacularization steadily gained ground during this period. Thematically too, as noted earlier, literature transcended the limits of princely courts and increasingly became sensitive to the stresses and strains of life outside. Purists have viewed this shift as decadence, whereas it should be considered a healthy tendency. This tendency, however, came to an end during the course of the nineteenth century when Indian literature lost its inherent vitality and became heavily imitative of the west.

Music

What has been said about painting and literature was also true of other realms of creativity. In Carnatic music the eighteenth century was the period of the famous trinity—Tyagaraja (1759–1847), Muthuswami Dikshitar (1775–1835) and Syama Shastri

[35] Ibid., p. 151.
[36] Ibid., pp. 158–59.

(1763–1827). Prolific in composition,[37] distinct in style and original in handling *ragas*, they brought about a marked change in the existing musical tradition and created a new era in the history of Carnatic music.[38] While the compositions of Syama Shastri and Muthuswami Dikshitar were learned and difficult to understand, Tyagaraja was a composer with great popular and emotional appeal. Muthuswami Dikshitar mainly composed in Sanskrit, but Syama Shastri and Tyagaraja used Telugu. All three were endowed with creative ability of a very high order; they composed new *ragas* and *talas* and their ability to introduce innovations within the same *raga* was remarkable.[39] Syama Shastri's compositions in *apurva ragas* like Manji Kalagada and Chintamani are evidence of his genius and originality in discovering new forms in fields which to others were apparently barren. His contest with Kesavayya of Bobbili was perhaps the best example of his creative ability. During the contest at the court of the Maharaja of Tanjore, Kesavayya rendered a *raga* and followed it with a *tana* in different *jatis* and *gatis*. To the sheer delight of the audience and to the great discomfiture of Kesavayya, Syama Shastri not only reproduced similar *tanas* with greater skill, but also rendered several sub-varieties which were not even known to Kesavayya.[40] The genius of Tyagaraja, the greatest composer in the annals of Carnatic music, lay not only in his originality and his innovative ability which gave to each composition even of the same *raga* a variant form (*rupa*) and nuance, but also in his capacity to take the music to the uninitiated masses. He was the originator of a new form and a new style of composition as represented by *geya natakam* (opera) and *ghana raga pancharatnam*.[41] He also created several new *ragas*; important among them are Devamrita Varshini, Saramati, Phalaranjani and Umabharanam.[42] Tyagaraja's compositions, particularly his devo-

---

[37] Tyagaraja had composed about 2,000 pieces and the other two 200 each. P. Sambamoorthy, *Syama Shastri and Other Famous Figures of South Indian Music*, Madras, 1934, p. 3.

[38] R. Rangaramanuja Ayyangar, *History of South Indian (Carnatic) Music*, Madras, 1972, pp. 219–39, and R. Seetha, *Tanjore as a Seat of Music*, Madras, 1981, pp. 200–14.

[39] P. Sambamoorthy, *Great Composers*, Book I, Madras, 1978, pp. 5–6.

[40] Sambamoorthy, *Syama Shastri and Other Famous Figures*, pp. 30–21.

[41] Sambamoorthy, *Great Composers*, Book I, pp. 5–6.

[42] Ibid., Book II, p. 13.

tional songs, drew a larger section of the population into a new cultural experience.

The era of the musical trinity was one of the most creative epochs in the cultural life of India. Assessing their contribution, S. Seetha has noted:

> The *kritis* of the Trinity happen to be the foremost definition of the *ragas* and the vivid portrayal of the melodic individuality of the 'abstract picture in the sound' helped in the standardization of their *lakshana*. This led to the development of *manodharma sangita* in all its varied aspects. The elaborate exposition of the *raga* through the different stages, the systematic *tana* and *ghanam* singing and the complicated *pallavi* expositions emerged.[43]

The contribution of Shah Walliullah to theological studies,[44] Maharaja Jai Singh's efforts in the field of astronomy and town planning,[45] and the development of architecture during the eighteenth century would also be significant areas to investigate.

Religion

In comparing the 'darkness' of the eighteenth century and the 'glory' of the nineteenth, religion and education have been the main areas of attention. It is argued that religion in the eighteenth century was characterized by obscurantist and superstitious prac-

---

[43] Seetha, *Tanjore as a Seat of Music,* pp. 200–14.

[44] S.A.A. Rizvi, *Shah Walliullah and His Times,* New Delhi, 1980.

[45] Jai Singh founded five astronomical observatories at Delhi, Jaipur, Ujjain, Mathura and Benaras. Astronomers from Bavaria, France and Portugal frequented his court to hold discussions and as a result Jai Singh was well posted with advances made in astronomy in Europe. It is an indication of how indigenous knowledge must have come to grips with the advances made in the west. It is also important that scholars from all parts of the country assembled in Jaipur. V.S. Bhatnagar, *Life and Times of Sawai Jai Singh,* Delhi, 1974, pp. 314, 343–46. Jai Singh was responsible for planning Jaipur city, which was in all probability the first planned city of India. It was not planned on the designs known in the *Shilpa Shastra,* but on Jai Singh's own design. Ashim Kumar Ray, *History of the Jaipur City,* New Delhi, 1978, p. xi, and Satya Prakash, 'Jaipur and Its Environs: A Study in Architecture', in J.N. Asopa (ed.), *Cultural Heritage of Jaipur,* Jaipur, 1979. See also Hermann Goetz, 'Later Mughal Architecture', *Marg,* Vol. XI, No. 4, September 1958, and Percy Brown, *Indian Architecture: Islamic Period,* Bombay, 1968, p. 113.

tices, and in contrast, the nineteenth-century reform movements inspired by European intellectual influences restored the pristine purity of religion. Similarly, to the intellectual stagnation and ignorance of the eighteenth century, western education brought enlightenment leading to political and social progress. This is a familiar theme in Indian historiography, worked out in great detail by historians ranging from J.N. Farquhar to R.C. Majumdar. Majumdar wrote:

> A new ideology suddenly burst forth upon the static life, moulded for centuries by a fixed set of religious ideas and social convention. It gave birth to a critical attitude towards religion and a spirit of enquiry into the origins of state and society with a view to determining the proper scope and function.[46]

The assumptions behind this contrast are the static nature of Indian social institutions, the moral and ethical degeneration, the educational and scientific backwardness, and above all, the inability of the Indian mind to come to grips with the problems of a 'decadent' society. Indeed, to the colonial ideologues and their modern historian-incarnations it is a convenient framework to impart a certain legitimacy to colonial rule, since they argued that but for the vistas opened up by European knowledge Indians would not even have become conscious of the ills of their society.

In the sect and caste-ridden eighteenth-century society, the popular Hindu religion had degenerated into a compound of magic, animism and superstition. While polytheism and idolatry turned religion into ceremonious ritualism, religious practices and rituals included physical torture and animal sacrifice. Exploiting the credulity and superstition of the ignorant laity, the priests converted religion into what Rammohun called 'a system of deception',[47] and religious worship became 'not worship of the god but coercion of the god, and invocation is not prayer but rather the exercise of magical formula'.[48] Once these maladies which vitiated the religious life of the

---

[46] R.C. Majumdar (ed.), *British Paramountcy and Indian Renaissance*, Vol. X, Pt. II, Bombay, 1965, p. 84.

[47] J.C. Ghosh (ed.), *The English Works of Rammohun Roy*, Allahabad, 1906, p. 496.

[48] Max Weber, *The Sociology of Religion*, London, 1971, p. 25.

people are noted, what is important to enquire is the manner in which society responded to this situation. Was there a general sense of resignation and acceptance, or was there any attempt to change and purify the religious life? The emergence of a large number of heterodox sects in almost all parts of India during the course of the eighteenth century indicates the latter response.

Education

Another commonly held assumption is the prevalence of an abject state of ignorance in eighteenth-century India. But for the emancipating role of western education, it is argued, the Indian mind would have continued to remain in a state of inertia. Surprisingly, in spite of the orientalist–anglicist controversy of the early nineteenth century, almost all discussions on educational progress in India do not take into account the indigenous system of education as well as the educational ideas developed by Indian intellectuals in the nineteenth century, which were distinct from the colonial system of education. They are dismissed either as non-existent or as inconsequential. Unfortunately, our knowledge of the state of education in the pre-colonial period is unsatisfactory; even the sources are limited and inadequate. Apart from incidental observations by European travellers and British official representatives, contemporary sources are almost non-existent. The only solution is to draw inferences from the reports on educational conditions during the early part of the nineteenth century which provide considerable insight into the organization, extent and content of the indigenous system. Thomas Munro's report in 1822 for Madras Presidency, Mountstuart Elphinstone's report in 1823 for Bombay Presidency and William Adam's report in 1835–38 for Bengal Presidency are the most important of them. Of these, Adam's report containing district-wise statistics is the most exhaustive and informative. His passionate involvement with indigenous education led him to undertake detailed investigations into the state of indigenous education. Such enthusiasm was lacking in Bombay and Madras in spite of Elphinstone's and Munro's respect for traditional institutions, and the reports for these two presidencies therefore remained sketchy and elementary.

General consciousness about the importance of education, particularly among the members of the upper strata of society, was quite evident. Scholars and teachers were held in high esteem both by the aristocracy and common men, and the educated were able to command a distinguished position in society. Adam observed:

> The teachers and students of Sanskrit schools constitute the culti-
> vated intellect of the Hindu people and they command that respect
> and exert that influence which cultivated intellect always enjoys.
> There is no class of persons that exercise a greater degree of
> influence in giving native society the tone, the form and the
> character which it actually possesses than the body of the learned.[49]

In the absence of direct control and direction by the state, educational institutions were maintained by voluntary efforts from within the society. The extensive contributions made by rulers and nobles formed an important source of patronage for arts and letters. On taking charge over the Maratha territory Elphinstone found that the Peshwa's charities amounted to Rs 15,00,000 and the custom of *dakshina* contributed to the encouragement of classical learning.[50] In Bengal Raja Kishan Chandra of Nadia and Rani Bhabani of Rajshahi took a keen interest in education. Krishna Chandra gave a stipend of Rs 200 to every student who reported at the tolls in Nadia and the Rani encouraged Sanskrit education by instituting endowments.[51] In the Carnatic, in Tanjore, Travancore, Cochin and almost all other states, the rulers and their subordinate chiefs contributed to the pursuit of knowledge.

The educational institutions may be broadly categorized as indigenous elementary schools and institutions of higher learning. Adam has identified two types of schools in the former category. The first derived their principal support from the patronage of a single wealthy family and the second depended upon the general support of the community in the town or village in which they were established. The primary object of the former was:

> the education of the children of the opulent Hindoos by whom they
> are chiefly supported, but as the teacher seldom receives more than

---

[49] William Adam, *Reports on the State of Education in Bengal*, edited by A.N. Basu, Calcutta, 1941, pp. 274, 429.

[50] Raghuvanshi, *Indian Society in the Eighteenth Century*, p. 172.

[51] Adam, *Reports on the State of Education in Bengal*, p. 166.

three rupees a month from that source, he is allowed to collect from the neighbourhood as many additional pupils as he can obtain or conveniently manage. They pay him at the rate of two rupees and eight annas per month, in addition to which each pupil gives him such a quantity of rice, pulse, oil, salt and vegetables at the end of each month as will suffice for one day's maintenance.[52]

This system, however, did not cater exclusively to the affluent families; children of the neighbourhood as a whole were also drawn to it.[53] Without taking into consideration this domestic system the educational facilities available in pre-colonial India cannot really be assessed.

The second category of schools were exclusively maintained by contributions made by the pupils. In addition to the monthly contribution by each pupil ranging from four annas to one rupee, the teacher was also entitled to receive one day's maintenance per month from each pupil. The *pathasalas* and *madrasas* run by individual teachers, or attached to temples and mosques, or maintained by charitable institutions belonged to this category.

Several centres of higher learning in Sanskrit, Arabic and Persian flourished during the eighteenth century. Forbes wrote:

> We contemplate the Hindu colleges and Brahmanical seminaries at Banaras and different parts of Hindustan, with pleasure; they are useful institutions; and however limited in their benefits to particular castes and descriptions of people they are the nurses of literature, medicine, and science as far as is deemed necessary among the Hindus.[54]

The major centres of Sanskrit learning were Benaras, Ujjain, Tirhut, Nadia, Rajshahi, Tanjore and Trivandrum. Calcutta had 28 seminaries of Sanskrit learning with 173 scholars in 1818; Twenty-four Parganas had 190 seminaries and Nadia had 31 with 747 scholars in 1801. In

[52] Ibid., p. 56.
[53] 'At Pandua in Hooghly district, it is said to have been the practice of the Musalman land proprietors to entertain teachers at their own private cost for the benefit of the children of their neighbourhood, *and it was a rare thing to find an opulent farmer or head of a village who had not a teacher in his employment for that purpose.*' Ibid., p. 57. Emphasis in the original.
[54] J. Forbes, *Oriental Memoirs,* Vol. I, London, 1834, p. 471.

Rajshahi in 1834–35 Adam found 38 colleges of Sanskrit education, 19 of Hindu law, 13 of general literature, two of logic and four of Vedanta, tantric, pauranic and medical learning.[55] According to him, the number of scholars engaged in the study and teaching of Sanskrit was 126,000 in Bengal.[56] The chief centres of Islamic learning were Jaunpur, Lucknow and Patna.

The extent of educational facilities available in pre-colonial India has been a point of controversy among scholars. Adam had estimated the existence of 100,000 indigenous elementary schools[57] in Bengal Presidency at the beginning of the nineteenth century. On the basis of the estimate that the population of the provinces was 40,000,000, Adam came to the conclusion that there was a village school for every 400 persons. He also calculated that there was on an average a village school for every 73 children of schoolgoing age and one for every 30 or 32 boys.[58]

> It will appear that the system of village schools is extensively prevalent, that desire to give education to their male children must be deeply seated in the minds of parents even of the humblest classes; and those are the institutions closely interwoven as they are with the habit of the people and the custom of the country.[59]

The ratio of one elementary school to every 400 persons or for every 73 children of schoolgoing age, in spite of the limited facilities and the nature of their organization, compares favourably with any country in the world. Philip Hartog has dismissed it as a myth and a fantastic exaggeration.[60] Was it really a myth and an exaggeration? According to the data collected by Adam, the districts of Murshidabad, Birbhum, Burdwan, South Bihar and Tirhut, with a total population of

---

[55] Adam, *Reports on the State of Education in Bengal,* pp. 175–83.

[56] Ibid., p. 17.

[57] By indigenous elementary schools Adam meant 'those schools in which instruction in the elements of knowledge is communicated, and which have been *originated and are supported by Natives themselves,* in contradistinction from those that are supported by religious or philanthropic societies'. Ibid., p. 6. Emphasis added.

[58] Ibid., pp. 6–7.

[59] Ibid., p. 7.

[60] Syed Nurullah and J.P. Naik, *History of Education in India,* London, 1962, p. 11.

5,679,778, had 2,567 elementary schools, whereas on the basis of the hypothetical ratio of 1:400 there should have been 14,200 schools.[61] Thus, Adam's calculation appears to be erroneous. But then, the figures for these five districts did not include the centres of domestic instruction which formed an important constituent of the institutional structure. The inclusion of domestic schools would considerably alter the picture. For instance, the six *thanas* of Murshidabad, Daulatbazar, Nanghia, Culna, Jehanabad and Bhasra with a population of 496,974, had 288 elementary schools, 80 schools of learning, 5 other schools and 1,747 schools of domestic instruction, making a total of 2,120 schools, whereas the ratio of 1:400 would need only 1,241 schools.[62] That 2,414 out of 6,786 students were receiving education in domestic centres underlines the importance of domestic education in pre-colonial India. Once domestic education is taken into consideration Adam's assessment ceases to be a myth and an exaggeration.

Though the available data for Bombay and Madras Presidencies are not as detailed as for Bengal, Adam's conclusions are equally true of these areas. In Madras Munro found one primary school in every village, for approximately 1,000 people. According to the reports received from the district collectors, there were 12,498 schools in the Presidency for a population of 12,850,941. The facilities for domestic instruction were not included here; the number of students receiving domestic instruction was five times as many as those in other schools. Munro's assessment was that one child out of every three of schoolgoing age received education.[63] In central India, Malcolm observed that every village with a hundred houses had an elementary school.[64]

The level of literacy in eighteenth-century India cannot be accurately ascertained in the absence of reliable data. However, the investigations of Buchanan in Purnia district of Bengal during the first decade of the nineteenth century provide some useful insights (see table on the following page).[65] The statistics would mean that about

[61] Ibid., pp. 14–16.
[62] Ibid.
[63] *Manual of the Administration of the Madras Presidency,* Madras, 1885, p. 568.
[64] John Malcolm, *Memoirs of Central India,* Vol. II, London, 1832, p. 190.
[65] Raghuvanshi, *Indian Society in the Eighteenth Century,* p. 196.

13 per cent of the total population could read and write, which does not compare unfavourably with the 'enlightenment' provided by British rule.

Total population	2,904,380
Number of teachers of vernacular schools	119
Teachers of Persian and Arabic schools	66
Sanskrit teachers	643
Men capable of keeping common accounts	18,650
Men who could sign their name	16,505
Men who could understand common poetry	1,830
Women who could understand common poetry	488
Total	38,301

The content of education, however, did not reflect the advance made in knowledge, particularly in science, technology and social thought, in other parts of the world nor was there an effort to further the traditional knowledge in mathematics and science. Instead, the emphasis was on memorizing literary texts, and on studying grammar and metaphysics. The study of grammar took up anything between two to twelve years and that of law and philosophy six to ten years. Education was more of an exercise in memory than excitement to the mind and the teacher–taught relationship induced a sense of conformity and hardly encouraged original thinking.[66] Discussing the defects of this system Adam felt that 'what was wanted was something to awaken and expand the mind, to unshackle it from the trammels of mere usage'.[67]

Nevertheless, the system was sensitive to the changing needs of society and had imbibed a certain utilitarian content. Apart from some knowledge of science and mathematics built into Arabic and Sanskrit education, training in correspondence, account-keeping, commercial accounts and agricultural accounts formed part of the curriculum in certain schools.[68] Adam remarked that 'my recollections of the village schools of Scotland do not enable me to pronounce

---

[66] Adam, *Reports on the State of Education in Bengal,* p. 18.
[67] Ibid., p. 147.
[68] Ibid., p. 252.

that the instruction given in them has a more direct bearing upon the daily interests of life than that which I find given or proposed to be given, in the humble village schools of Bengal.'[69]

That Indian society in the eighteenth century was not indifferent to its educational requirements needs no further elaboration. Whether the literary and classical education would have continued to engage the Indian mind and whether it would have remained impervious to the advances in knowledge in other parts of the world is inextricably linked to the nature of social change and progress. Yet Tipu Sultan's efforts to acquire scientific skills from France and Jai Singh's exchanges with European astronomers[70] indicate that Indians were not averse to the incorporation of knowledge developed in other societies. After colonial intervention, however, the choice did not rest with Indians.They had to receive the west through a process of filtration engendered by colonial domination. The dialogue of east and west would have been more meaningful and creative if colonial mediation had not occurred, since it would have imparted to Indians a sense of modernity, self-confidence and cultural rootedness.

While questioning some of the generally accepted assumptions on eighteenth-century society, the intention has not been to idealize pre-colonial India or to suggest that India was at the threshold of a transition when colonialism intervened. What is suggested is that in spite of the disintegration of the Mughal imperial polity and the disruption of economic life, dynamism and vitality in the intellectual and cultural realms were not sapped. The real disruption of creative ability occurred as a part of England's work in India.

[69] Ibid., p. 146.
[70] Bhatnagar, *Life and Times of Sawai Jai Singh,* p. 314.

3 Historiographical and Conceptual Questions

Intellectual history as a branch of history with a viable degree of autonomy or as an integrative tool is yet to become a part of Indian historiography. Till now it has remained confined to a study of the political, social or economic thought of a person or period, or of ideas in an ancient or medieval text.[1] Even biographies, until recently, have not been intellectual portraits of men in society or detailed life histories basic to the craft of prosopographers. The 'new history' initiated by James Harvey Robinson in the United States or the methodological innovation of Perry Miller in his *New England Mind,* which established 'intellectual history' as a distinct branch of the discipline, have had hardly any impact on Indian historiography. Not that the subject matter of this genre of history is new; in fact, problems which fall within the domain of intellectual history have always been the concern of historians. The departure is in the methodology employed. For instance, the influence of religious beliefs and attitudes on social life and social action did form the subject of several studies before Miller. But what distinguishes Miller's treatment from that of his predecessors, like Troeltsch, is its ability to demonstrate the interdependent character of intellectual activities and to show how changes in one intellectual domain lead to a realignment of thought in other realms as well.

Perry Miller and a host of others who followed him adopted an internal approach, an idealist view, of intellectual history, concerned mainly with the logical consistency of a sequence of thought, the

[1] Two early examples are U.N. Ghoshal's *History of Indian Political Ideas,* Madras, 1959, modelled on A.J. Carlyle's *A History of Medieval Political Theory in the West,* and B.B. Majumdar, *History of Indian Social and Political Ideas,* Calcutta, 1967.

elaboration of a world view or the influence of an idea in furthering intellectual advance. In essence, the focus was on the creative vitality of the human mind. It divorced ideas from events and social reality and systematized them only in the context of ideas. This method reduced intellectual history either to a history of intellectuals or to a history of ideas within a general theoretical and philosophical assumption of the primacy of ideas.

The external approach, the functional view of intellectual history, on the other hand, emphasized the connection between thought and deed. By treating ideas merely as a series of responses to given situations it tended to overlook the creative potential and innovative ability of the human mind. The emphasis here being on the dynamics of social activity, ideas were only of secondary importance. Functional utility was the yardstick for measuring the historical significance of ideas; therefore, their importance was judged by the deeds associated with them.

Admittedly, intellectual history cannot afford to overlook the notions inherent in both these approaches. What is required, however, is not an eclectic combination of both, but a methodology which, without being either idealistic or reductionist, would help to comprehend how individually differentiated thought emerges in the concrete setting of a historical–social situation. In other words, a methodology based on the conception that 'the production of ideas, of conceptions, of consciousness, is at first directly interwoven with the material activity and the material intercourse of men, the language of real life', and that 'consciousness can never be anything else than conscious existence, and the existence of men is their actual life process'.[2] To establish how ideas are 'directly interwoven' with, but are not *mere* reflections of or determined by 'the material activity and the material intercourse of men' is methodologically a difficult and challenging task. It forms a part of the theoretical considerations regarding the relationship between base and superstructure and of the various elements of the latter.

In the light of the general observations made above, this chapter suggests a conceptual framework for the study of some aspects

---

[2] Karl Marx and Frederick Engels, *The German Ideology*, Moscow, 1964, p. 37.

of the intellectual history of colonial India. Focussing on how reality was perceived, it seeks to explore the relationship between ideology and consciousness in the complex cultural–intellectual situation that came into being in the nineteenth century. Neither the nature of perception of reality nor the contours of consciousness, it is argued, may be explained solely by the political and economic contexts of colonial domination. Equally important are the cultural–intellectual processes, particularly those that emerged from the cultural–intellectual struggles engendered by the desire to create the ideological base of a modern society, distinct from the traditional and the colonial. Identifying the protagonists of these struggles as well as locating their social base and formative influences are crucial to an understanding of these processes.

A critique of the existing historiography forms the first part of this chapter, underlining issues which have so far remained outside the domain of the history of ideas in the nineteenth century.

The second section explores the formative influences, both intellectual and social, and examines the validity of the generally accepted notion of a direct relationship between the western influence and intellectual commitment as well as of characterizations like 'conservatives', 'reformers' and 'radicals' on the basis of intellectual make-up. Another aspect relevant to this discussion is the representative character of the intellectual, either of his own class or of the class which forms his social base. An exhaustive examination of this aspect has not been attempted, nor is it possible within the scope of this essay; yet it is suggested that the comprador–collaborator paradigm hardly suits the Indian situation.

The third section highlights the nature of perception of the social, political and economic reality and demonstrates how it contributed to the evolution of an anti-colonial consciousness. The basic assumption here is that intellectual endeavour in the nineteenth century was an integral part of the struggle to grasp the reality of subjection. As such, compartmentalization on the basis of dominant activity, either socio-religious or political, has to be dispensed with if the process by which the anti-colonial consciousness came into being is to be understood.

The final section is concerned with the role of cultural elements in the making of social and intellectual perspectives. The foray into the cultural terrain is impelled by unease with the notion that religious revivalism and conservatism were the motivating urge in the nineteenth-century effort to self-strengthen and revitalize social institutions. By recognizing the existence of a consciousness regarding other elements such as language and certain social practices, the concept of cultural defence has been suggested as an alternative. The implications of this concept for understanding intellectual attitudes would require very detailed consideration. What is offered here is only a preliminary statement.

Cultural Roots of Anti-Colonialism

The development of consciousness, dominant or contending, in a society forms one of the major themes of intellectual history. In colonial India, notwithstanding the existence of different streams of contending consciousnesses based on contradictions within the society, the dominant strand was the growth of an anti-colonial consciousness. The early manifestation of this consciousness was not necessarily in the realm of politics. In fact, given that the institutions of the colonial state were not more retrogressive than those of the pre-colonial, it found its initial expression in the realm of ideology and culture.[3] Whether this pre-political and overtly, but not inherently, non-political phase was an important link in the historical process which gave rise to an anti-colonial consciousness, and if so how, are issues that have not been within the focus of historical investigation. The manner in which the cultural–ideological struggle in the nineteenth century was a part of, and not distinct from or only contributory to, the dominant consciousness, seems to have escaped the notice of historians.

The cultural–ideological struggle in colonial India had two

[3] The importance of culture in national liberation movements finds forceful expression in Amilcar Cabral. He wrote: 'Study of the history of liberation struggles shows that they have generally been preceded by an upsurge of cultural manifestations, which progressively harden into an attempt, successful or not, to assert the cultural personality of the dominated people by an act of denial of the culture of the oppressor. Whatever the conditions of subjection of a people to foreign domination and the influence of economic, political and social factors in the exercise of this domination, *it is generally within the cultural factor that we find the germ of challenge which leads to the structuring and development of the liberation movement.*' *Unity and Struggle,* London, 1980, p. 143. Emphasis added.

mutually complementary facets. The first was directed against the backward elements of tradition, culture and ideology and was expressed in terms of the reformation and regeneration of socio-religious institutions. The second was an attempt to contend with colonial culture and ideology. The first formed a part of the second; what gave birth to the first was an awareness of the inadequacy of traditional institutions to cope with the new situation created by colonial intrusion. The intellectual debate in China, Japan and the West Asian countries articulated this awareness, and implicitly (during the early phase) so did the attitude of Indian intellectuals. While in countries such as China and Japan the question of revitalization of indigenous institutions was linked with their political destiny from the very beginning of the colonial thrust, in India the perception of this connection was slow in maturing. Yet the socio-cultural consciousness generated by revitalization movements was not altogether divorced from the evolving dominant consciousness, for the latter included within it the socio-cultural crisis created by colonial domination.

That European thought and knowledge were decisive factors in the cognition of socio-cultural reality and the idea of progress in colonial India is an assumption common to the bulk of the existing literature on the history of ideas. They are viewed as acculturative, arising from the contact of indigenous cultures or sub-cultures with the culture of industrial Europe, leading to cultural plasticity and creative syntheses. The analytical frameworks derived from this assumption do not seem to be sensitive to the fact that the difference in power was a major constraint on cultural–intellectual adaptation,[4] or to the fact that western ideas, once filtered through the medium of colonialism, did not have the same progressive function as at their source. Thus, to J.N. Farquhar, R.C. Majumdar and Charles Heimsath, English education and the western impact were key factors which brought about a socio-cultural and intellectual regeneration; to Salahuddin Ahmad and David Kopf, British institutions provided the necessary push. 'The stimulating forces', wrote Farquhar, 'are almost

---

[4] Von Grunebaum has demonstrated this in relation to Islamic civilization. G.E. Von Grunebaum, *Modern Islam: The Search for Cultural Identity*, New York, 1964, p. 32.

exclusively Western, viz. the British Government, English education and literature, Christianity, oriental research, European science and philosophy, and the material elements of Western Civilization'.[5] Charles Heimsath attributed not only ideas but even the methods of organization adopted by Indians to western inspiration.[6] David Kopf tried to demonstrate how Fort William College, an institution created for training British officials, played a decisive role in 'the social, cultural, psychological and intellectual changes' in Bengal in the nineteenth century. The Bengal renaissance to him was 'a result of the contact between British officials and missionaries on the one hand and the Hindu intelligentsia on the other'.[7] The social, intellectual and cultural regeneration is thus traced directly to western influences on the Indian mind through colonial rule. Most of the historical writings on nineteenth-century India which deal with social reform, the emergence of new ideas and the rise of nationalism follow this straitjacket explanation.

The image of the occident and what the occident meant to the Indian mind, as distinct from the general and descriptive terms 'western influences' and 'western impact', is of crucial significance in this context. European rational and humanist thought, scientific knowledge, economic development and political institutions were conceived by Indian intellectuals as progressive characteristics of the west. While these progressive attributes of western society were looked upon with admiration and approval and compared with conditions in India, there was no appreciation of the social and intellectual forces which made these advances possible. In other words, the point of interest was what was objectively superior and progressive in the west, not what led to that objective situation. Therefore the intellectual endeavour, at least to begin with, was to adopt and replicate these objectively superior and progressive attributes: no attempt was made to test their adaptability in the context

---

[5] J.N. Farquhar, *Modern Religious Movements in India,* Delhi, 1967, p. 433. Also see R.C. Majumdar (ed.), *British Paramountcy and Indian Renaissance,* Vol. X, II, Bombay, 1965, p. 89.

[6] Charles H. Heimsath, *Indian Nationalism and Hindu Social Reform,* Princeton, 1964, p. 46.

[7] David Kopf, *British Orientalism and Bengal Renaissance,* Berkeley, 1969, p. 1.

of the existing indigenous cultural and intellectual traditions. That the English-educated middle class, alienated from mass culture and placed almost totally outside the traditional intellectual milieu, formed the social base of this quest made it all the more restricted. Moreover, since the objective attributes of the west were divorced from the historical forces which went into their making, colonial power, as a representative of the west's progress and achievement, assumed ideological dimensions for Indians. What was objective about the west, in the context of colonialism, became an illusion, an ideology. This inversion negated the possible genesis of an indigenous body of thought to cope with the problems faced by Indian society. The scramble for Tom Paine in Calcutta, the intellectual's addiction to Mill, Spencer and Locke, the admiration for European political ideas and institutions, the approach to western science and technology, and a host of other examples right down to the shaping of the Indian constitution are indicative of this. How Indians in the nineteenth century arrived at this intellectual position can be appreciated only by a study of the role of colonial ideology.

What were the implications of the objectively advanced western knowledge, political ideas and social thought for the Indian mind labouring under the disadvantages inherent in a colonial situation? An unequal political relationship, along with the economic exploitation and stagnation that goes with it, is hardly ideal for creative intellectual adaptation of an enduring nature. Conventional historiography, mostly caught within the 'impact–response' syndrome —whether emphasizing the western impact or the Indian response— is not sensitive to this question. It merely follows the path chalked out by the ideologues of colonialism who saw Britain's role as a civilizing mission. An appreciation of the inherently different functions of western ideas at their source and in the colonies is the first necessary step for a departure from this trend. Recognition of the differences in the nature of social formation and the character of political institu-tions in the metropolis and the colony is equally vital. Given these differences, there can be no convergence in the socio-political role of the liberal principles and institutions upheld by the colonial ideol-ogues at home when superimposed on the colonies. This has two specific consequences: functional mutation and functional debility. The role of orientalism and utilitarianism in colonial societies, distinct from their basic intellectual quest, is an example of the first. The Indian intellectuals' efforts at modernization, which were blighted by the very weaknesses inherent in their historical situation, was indicative of the second. To certain aspects of these consequences attention was first drawn by D.P. Mukherjee in his seminal study of modern Indian culture.[8] A few years later Susobhan Sarkar's pioneering essays on the Bengal renaissance, while recognizing the role of the west in the Indian awakening, emphasized that 'foreign conquest and domination was bound to be a hindrance rather than a help to subject peoples' regeneration'.[9] In pointing out that imperialism 'raised barriers in the Indian mind against critical ideas from the West because these ideas came from the sources that were holding India down', A.K. Bhattacharya identified another important dimension.[10] More recent researches in this area by Marxist scholars have tried to place the intellectual developments within the context of the constraints and contradictions generated by colonialism.[11] Asok Sen's study of the life and work of Vidyasagar brings out admirably the consequences of this context:

> Vidyasagar was a victim of the illusions which he shared with his stage of history, about the prospects of modernization under colonial rule. The very process, which gave his genius a strong social commitment, imposed severe limits on effective social practice. Such limits were inherent in the economic directions of imperialism. This is where the colonial situation made a grievous

---

[8] D.P. Mukherjee, *Modern Indian Culture*, Bombay, 1948, pp. 25–28.

[9] Susobhan Sarkar, 'Rabindranath Tagore and Renaissance in Bengal', in *Bengal Renaissance and Other Essays*, New Delhi, 1970, p. 150.

[10] A.K. Bhattacharya, 'Akshay Dutt, Pioneer of Indian Renaissance', *The Rationalist Annual*, 1962, p. 29.

[11] Asok Sen, 'Rammohun and Bengal Economy', and Sumit Sarkar, 'Rammohun and the Break with the Past', in V.C. Joshi (ed.), *Rammohun and the Process of Modernization in India*, New Delhi, 1975; Barun De, 'A Historiographic Critique of Renaissance Analogues for Nineteenth Century India', in Barun De (ed.), *Perspectives in Social Sciences*, Calcutta, 1979, and 'The Colonial Context of Bengal Renaissance', in C.H. Philip and Mary Doreen Wainwright (eds.), *Indian Society and the Beginnings of Modernization c. 1830–1850*, London, 1976; Dipesh Chakrabarti, 'The Colonial Context of the Bengal Renaissance: A Note on Early Railway Thinking in Bengal', *The Indian Economic and Social History Review*, May 1974; Asok Sen, *Iswarchandra Vidyasagar and His Elusive Milestones*, Calcutta, 1977.

anomaly of Iswarchandra Vidyasagar, a significant individual
among our first 'moderns', of his existential need for social integrity
of self-development.[12]

Marxist historiography has primarily attempted to demonstrate how politico-economic structures warped intellectual developments in nineteenth-century India. Though tending towards reduc-
tionism and determinism at times, it does define the parameters of
intellectual endeavour and thus explains why intellectuals in the
nineteenth century had to face certain defeat and tragedy in their
socio-cultural efforts. While it marked a distinct departure from
earlier colonial and liberal historiographical trends and assumptions,
it does not delineate how intellectual perceptions and positions were
arrived at. This can be seen only when the analytical focus is on
processes within the given historical context. The context as such
does not explain the essentials of a particular phenomenon, it only
defines its general character. The emphasis on context, though
important, has tended to blur this distinction.

Formative Influences
The ideas articulated by intellectuals are not the only concern of intellectual history. It embraces the moods, beliefs, values and
thoughts of members of all social strata. For instance, a peasant's or
an industrial worker's perception of his situation in society as well as
the way in which the rationalization of primordial beliefs or the
internalization of a given ideology contributes to the making of his
consciousness and to his ability to struggle for emancipation, are very
much within the domain of intellectual history. They are, however,
not counterposed to the hitherto popular emphasis on the creators,
reproducers and propagators of relatively enduring and effective
ideas in society. Nor do they, by mere virtue of being the object of
investigation, provide a methodological advance or fuller understanding of the historical process. Therefore, although the intellectual history of a society is not the history of its intellectuals alone,
given their hegemonic role, an enquiry into their social and intellectual
formation, their socio-political function and their ideas does form an

---

[12] Sen, *Iswarchandra Vidyasagar*, p. 154.

important and integral part of intellectual history.

Who constituted intellectuals in colonial India? How did they come into being socially and intellectually, and what function did they perform in the given social and political situation? In describing the creators and propagators of ideas as well as early social and political activists, several categorizations have been employed: social reformers, marginal men, cultural brokers, westernizers and compradors are some of them. These are based on either partial or false perceptions of their role in society. Basically they were non-conformists, critical of existing social conditions and performing the social function of generation or adoption and propagation of ideas with a view to ushering in socio-political progress and advancement. They were not limited to a handful of activists but comprised a large number of lesser known people engaged in the elaboration and dissemination of ideas. What distinguished them from intellectual workers in general was the specific social function they performed, which Gramsci has characterized as follows:

> The problem of creating a new stratum of intellectuals consists in the critical elaboration of the intellectual activity that exists in everyone at a certain degree of development, modifying its relationship with the muscular-nervous effort towards a new equilibrium, and ensuring that the muscular-nervous effort itself, in so far as it is an element of a general practical activity, which is perpetually innovating the physical and social world, becomes the foundation of a new and integral conception of the world.[13]

In identifying intellectuals as a distinct social stratum the emphasis on their specific social function—what Gramsci calls the creation of a new equilibrium and the perpetual innovation of the physical and social world—has been a central concern in most studies on intellectual development.[14] The distinction between the 'cultural objective' and 'philosophic subjective' intelligentsia by Richard

---

[13] Antonio Gramsci, *Selections from the Prison Notebooks*, New York, 1971, p. 9.

[14] A notable exception to this is Edward Shills who uses the term to include 'the independent man of letters, the scientist, pure and applied, the scholar, the university professor, the journalist, the highly educated administrator, judge or parliamentarian'. *The Intellectual between Tradition and*

Pipes,[15] between the educated and the intelligentsia by Theodor Geiger and Boris Elkin, the concept of concentric circles for differentiating intellectuals from the intelligentsia by Milnikov,[16] and Edgar Morin's definition of intellectuals based on 'a profession that is culturally validated, a role that is socio-political and consciousness that relates to universals',[17] are some examples.

The distinctions drawn above raise several questions, of which the more important for our purpose are: what enables the 'critical elaboration of intellectual activity', thus arriving at a commitment to a specific social function, and to what extent do ideological and cultural systems and the nature and direction of social formations influence or determine cognitive ability? In attempting to answer the first, formative educational influences have been generally identified as the decisive factor, almost fully excluding the role of social experience: how social factors mediate in the formation of intellectuals and the growth of consciousness. One reason for this emphasis is the intellectual historian's concern with identifying factors which contribute to the making of cognitive ability. Richard Pipes on Russia, Joseph Levinson on China and Edward Shills on India are representative of this perspective. The bulk of the literature on social reform and the emergence of nationalism in India shares this point of view, as evidenced by Charles Heimsath, David Kopf and R.C. Majumdar on reform and regeneration in the nineteenth century, and David MacCulley, Anil Seal and Tarachand on the national movement. The biography of Rammohun Roy by S.D. Collet, of Keshub Chandra Sen by Meredith Borthwick and of Dayanand Saraswati by J.T.F Jordens fall into the same category. This is not a viewpoint

---

Modernity: The Indian Situation, Hague, 1961, p. 9. Shills, however, recognizes the existence of a group with a different social function in advanced countries, but not in newly independent countries. 'Political Development in the New States', *Comparative Studies in Society and History*, II, 1960.

[15] Richard Pipes, 'The Historical Evolution of the Russian Intelligentsia', in Richard Pipes (ed.), *The Russian Intelligentsia*, New York, 1961, p. 48.

[16] Martin Malia, 'What is Intelligentsia', and Boris Elkin, 'The Russian Intelligentsia on the Eve of the Revolution', in Richard Pipes (ed.), *The Russian Intelligentsia*, pp. 1–18, 32.

[17] Quoted in Philip Rieff (ed.), *On Intellectual–Theoretical Studies, Case Studies*, New York, p. 81. Also see Syed Hussein Alatas, *Intellectuals in Developing Societies*, London, 1977, pp. 8–9.

limited to colonial, liberal and nationalist historians; most Marxist historians also seem to follow a similar path. Such an approach has been detrimental to the formulation of a methodology which draws intellectual history closer to the sociology of knowledge.

An assumption inherent in this approach is that western knowledge and philosophical notions were fundamental to the development of a critical attitude and cognition of reality. Is this supposition true of colonial India? In terms of formative educational influences, two broad categories may be identified among Indian intellectuals: one nurtured on traditional knowledge and the other on a combination of the western and the traditional. Radhakanta Deb, Dayanand Saraswati and Narayana Guru belonged to the first category; Rammohun Roy, Vivekananda, Bal Gangadhar Tilak and Jawaharlal Nehru belonged to the second.

The available biographical information on several nineteenth-century intellectuals is not exhaustive enough to enable their intellectual evaluation with accuracy. Therefore, qualitative changes in their consciousness and the consequent changes in their sensitivity to social problems remain obscure and inexplicable. Even elementary biographical sketches are wanting in many cases, and where they do exist there are far too many areas of darkness. For instance, the intellectual influences on and the social experience of Rammohun during the pre-1815 period are yet to be carefully chronicled; what led to Dayanand's transition from a Vedic scholar to a social reformer is unknown; how Ranade reconciled himself to that which by conviction he did not approve is not entirely clear, in spite of the illuminating reminiscences of his wife. These are only a few examples; similar gaps exist almost everywhere.

Despite these limitations, certain broad generalizations about formative influences can still be advanced by referring briefly to the intellectual evolution of Rammohun and Dayanand. Rammohun was born in all probability in 1772 in a devout Vaishnava family, but the Vaishnava influence, if any, was negative.[18] Information about Rammohun's life between 1772 and 1776 is scanty. One of his earliest biographers, Sophia Dobson Collet, gives us hardly any

[18] Barun De, 'A Biographical Perspective on the Political and Economic Ideas of Rammohun Roy', in V.C. Joshi (ed.), *Rammohun and the Process of Modernization*, p. 14.

information about this phase and those who followed her have not been able to go much further. Yet it seems fairly certain that by 1800 Rammohun had acquired a good knowledge of Islamic theology, particularly of the teachings of the rationalist school of *mutazillas* and of the Hindu scriptures.[19] Whether he was associated with any particular *madrasa* in Patna, and if so what its curriculum was, is unknown. But the influence of Islamic theology was certainly dominant during his early life, as is evident from his first extant work, *Tuhfat-ul Muwahhiddin*, written around 1800.[20] In the absence of any specific information about the source of this influence, a textual analysis of *Tuhfat* in the context of the knowledge of the Islamic tradition would be a useful exercise. The manner in which he came to acquire knowledge of Hindu philosophy and scriptures is equally unknown. It has been suggested that his knowledge of Hindu philosophy was through his connection with Hariharananda Tirthaswami, a *tantrik,* at Rangpur. It would be worth investigating whether his trip to Varanasi was motivated by a desire to acquire closer familiarity with the *shastras* and, if so, information on the pundits with whom he came into contact would help to establish an important link in his intellectual evolution—particularly as *Tuhfat* is almost entirely of Islamic inspiration and bereft of any Hindu influence. At any rate, it is certain that Rammohun's first exposure was

---

[19] Lant Capenter, a friend and admirer of Rammohun, has recorded: 'Under his father's roof he received the elements of native education, and also acquired the Persian language. He was afterwards sent to Patna to learn Arabic; and lastly to Benares to obtain a knowledge of Sanscrit, the sacred language of the Hindoos. His masters at Patna sent him to study Arabic translations of some of the writings of Aristotle and Euclid; it is probable that the training thus given strengthened his mind in acuteness and close reasoning; while the knowledge which he acquired of the Mahommadan religion from Mussulamen whom he esteemed, contributed to cause that searching examination of the faith in which he was educated, which led him eventually to the important efforts he made to restore it to its early simplicity.' Rama Prasad Chanda and Jatindra Kumar Majumdar (eds.), *Selection from Official Letters and Documents Relating to the Life of Raja Rammohun Roy,* Calcutta, 1938, p. xxx.

[20] In *Tuhfat* Rammohun dealt with the origin of religion and the nature of religious system at an abstract and general level. He quoted profusely from the Qoran and his arguments were in keeping with the rationalist critique within Islamic tradition. J.C. Ghose (ed.), *The English Works of Raja Rammohun Roy,* Allahabad, 1906, pp. 941–58.

to Indian tradition, both Hindu and Muslim, and his familiarity with European languages, thought and philosophy came at a later stage.[21] Thus, traditional Indian knowledge was a decisive factor in the make-up of Rammohun's intellectual world and the east–west synthesis for which he is generally lauded was attempted from strong indigenous moorings. Several others, such as Vivekananda, Bal Gangadhar Tilak and Jawaharlal Nehru, seem to have undergone an intellectual process in the reverse order: they were initially exposed to western knowledge and philosophy and at a later stage returned to their own sources.[22] After initial intoxication with European philosophy, Vivekananda sought enlightenment in the spirituality of Ramakrishna Paramahamsa. Bal Gangadhar Tilak, in spite of his knowledge of western political praxis, took to the *Gita* for guidance. Jawaharlal Nehru, whose training at Harrow and Cambridge made him something of a misfit both in the east and the west, had to attempt a discovery of India to discover himself. These examples strongly suggest the importance of the indigenous tradition in the make-up of an intellectual and his ability to perform his socio-political function. In fact, those who were unable to relate to their own tradition failed to rise to the level of intellectuals who could assume social and political leadership: they could engage themselves only in the elaboration of middle-class values. The bulk of the literature which explains the rise of social and political consciousness out of the contradictions inherent in English education in India seems to overlook this dimension.

In contrast, Dayanand Saraswati, like Radhakanta Deb and Narayana Guru, was a product almost exclusively of the Indian intellectual tradition. All that Mula Sankara, the precocious young

---

[21] Rammohun started learning English only in 1796 and when William Digby met him in 1801 'he could speak it well enough to be understood . . . but could not write it with any degree of correctness'. Sophia Dobson Collet, *Life and Letters of Raja Rammohun Roy*, Calcutta, 1962, p. 24.

[22] 'Return to the source' is a concept used by Cabral to explain the response to colonial culture and domination. 'The "return to the source" is not and cannot in itself be an *act of struggle* against foreign domination (colonial and racist), and it no longer necessarily means a return to tradition. It is the denial by the petite bourgeoisie of the pretended supremacy of the culture of the dominant power over that of the dominated people with which it must identify itself.' *Return to the Source: Selected Speeches of Amilcar Cabral*, New York, 1973, p. 63.

boy from Kathiawar born into a Shaivite family, received by way of education before becoming Dayanand, the reformer, was knowledge of Vedanta, Sanskrit grammar, tantrism, yoga and practical experience of social conditions in the country through extensive travel. He had no knowledge of European thought and philosophy, nor did he, like many of his contemporaries, make an effort to acquire it. This intellectual make-up did not adversely affect his cognitive ability; rather, it seems to have equipped him to test through experimentation the very sources of the knowledge he had acquired.[23] It also provided him with the intellectual drive necessary for confronting social problems.

As in the case of Rammohun, there are several gaps in the biographical information on Dayanand. The three years from 1860 to 1863 which he spent at Mathura under the guidance of Swami Virjananda, and the subsequent four years during which he travelled extensively through various parts of the country, seem to have been crucial for his intellectual evolution and the development of his social vision. He reached Mathura as a *sanyasi* in quest of the path to *moksha*, but at the end of these seven years he emerged as a reformer impatient with the existing social and religious practices. The process through which this transformation took place has not been a point of enquiry in his innumerable biographies, except in the latest, and thus far the best, by J.T.F. Jordens. Jordens has posited Virjananda's involvement with the regeneration of Hinduism, his advice to his disciple to propagate the books of the *rishis* and the Vedic religion, and Dayanand's own reaction to Hinduism as he saw it around him at Mathura, as possible factors.[24] The extent to which his social experience during his journey through various parts of the country contributed to this transformation would be a rewarding investigation.

It is important to emphasize that, in spite of the differences in

---

[23] In order to verify the information on human anatomy contained in some religious works, he dissected a corpse at Garhmukteshwar. When he found that the description given in the books did not tally at all with the actual details, he tore the books into pieces and threw them into the river along with the corpse. K.C. Yadav (ed.), *Autobiography of Dayanand Saraswati,* Delhi, 1976, p. 38.

[24] J.T.F. Jordens, *Dayanand Saraswati: His Life and Ideas,* Delhi, 1978, pp. 33–39.

the formative educational influences on the members of these two groups, their perception of reality and vision of social transformation seem remarkably similar. In their understanding of the connection between social and religious practices, in their perception of British rule as divine dispensation, and in their attitude towards caste, idolatry and polytheism, this similarity was clearly manifest. In fact there was no direct correlation between their formative influences and their specific position on various social questions. Stereotypical labels such as 'conservatives', 'radicals' and 'reformers', commonly employed in the existing historiography on the basis of traditional, western and synthetic intellectual influences, respectively, are therefore of doubtful validity. Just as western influences did not automatically lead to 'progressive' social and political consciousness, traditional influences did not invariably create conservative attitudes. In fact, some who were rooted in traditional knowledge and culture held more advanced views on several social questions than their western-educated contemporaries. The attitude of Radhakanata Deb towards female education and of Narayana Guru towards caste are cases in point. It would be interesting to examine whether a traditional intellectual milieu had the potential to stimulate ideas which had already made their appearance in western societies. The sources from which Akshay Kumar Dutt and Veeresalingam derived the idea of an organic theory of society and Rammohun and Narayana Guru evolved the idea of religious universalism are interesting pointers.

This enquiry into the intellectual evolution of Rammohun and Dayanand suggests that the formative educational influence, though important, was not the only determinant in the formation of Indian intellectuals in the nineteenth century. It also suggests that differences in the nature of formative educational influences did not prevent an identical mediation in the social process. Conversely, it may also be argued that similarity in intellectual influences did not lead to identical cognitive ability or social mediation. Access to knowledge is an essential but not a sufficient pre-requisite, since it only creates the basic ability to internalize social experience which plays a crucial role in the formation of intellectuals. The arrangement of the known epistemological components or the articulation of qualitatively new ideas are not necessarily of any social consequence. Only when those ideas are related to socio-cultural and political interests or dissent, at least potentially, do they assume social significance. The ability to establish such a relationship is a crucial component in the making of an intellectual. What underlined the role of Rammohun in Bengal, Dayanand in Punjab, Veeresalingam in Andhra and Narayana Guru in Travancore was that their ideas suited the social requirements of the new classes trying to break away from certain existing social norms. Although the dynamics of these classes set the parameters of their socio-political action and effectively mediated in their transition from an academic to an intellectual position, it did not limit their socio-political vision to the interests of these classes. Instead, their efforts were to develop a consciousness which was progressive at the given historical juncture. The role and character as well as the 'organicity' of the intellectuals in nineteenth-century India has to be located within this context. The tendency to characterize them as 'compradors' or 'almost compradors' and representatives of a particular class or caste misses this all-important point. What Karl Marx said about Ricardo is pertinent here:

> Ricardo's conception is, on the whole, in the interest of the *industrial bourgeoisie*, only *because* and in so far as, their interests coincide with that of production or the productive development of human labour. Where the bourgeoisie comes to conflict with this, he [Ricardo] is just as ruthless towards it as he is at other times towards the proletariat and the aristocracy.[25]

Perception of Colonial Reality

A study of the nature of perception of reality is a necessary prelude to an understanding of the evolution of consciousness in society. The existing literature on the history of ideas in the nineteenth century focuses mainly on movements and the ideas propagated by them; the perceptions of reality which generated these movements are only incidental to this central concern. The inter-relationship between perception and consciousness is also relegated to the background. They are treated either in isolation, or perception is considered to be synonymous with consciousness.

The recent interest in the differences between objective

---

[25] Karl Marx, *Theories of Surplus Value*, Vol. 2, pp. 117–18.

reality and perceived reality is integral to studies concerning the impact of colonialism on Indian social development. Why intellectuals in the nineteenth century failed to realize the true nature of colonial rule has been the focus of this interest. False consciousness, compradorism and class interest are some of the explanations offered. That colonial ideology and the character of the colonial state and state institutions influenced the nature of perception of reality seems too general and perhaps too obvious an observation. Nevertheless, the manner in which colonial state apparatuses functioned as instruments of ideological dissemination, and the way colonial state institutions (which were 'overdeveloped in relation to the structure' in the colony[26]) functioned as ideological instruments aiding political control, have remained unexplored areas.

While ideological dissemination was inherent in almost every policy pursued by the British in India, the principles on which the state institutions were organized tended to mystify the reality of colonial domination. In pursuit of cultural hegemony the colonial state and its ideologues endeavoured to create and propagate several myths about the character and capacity of the colonised which in course of time the colonised themselves began to believe.[27] Moreover, the character of the institutions created by the British in India

---

[26] Hamza Alavi, 'The State in Post-Colonial Societies: Pakistan and Bangladesh', *New Left Review*, No. 74, July–August 1972, p. 61.

[27] Syed Hussein Alatas has demonstrated how the myth of the lazy native came into currency in Malaysia during colonial rule. Syed Hussein Alatas, *The Myth of the Lazy Native*, London, 1977. Jose Rizal, the well-known Filipino patriot and martyr and a leading intellectual of the time, was one of the first to call attention to this. He argued that the indolence of the Filipinos was not hereditary but due to historical reasons. E. Alazona (ed.), *Selected Essays and Letters of Jose Rizal*, Manila, 1964. In India also, deception, dishonesty and undependability as characteristics of Indians became a part of its self-image only during the colonial era. Today the English-educated elite readily ascribe these qualities to the masses. Rammohun was sensitive to how Indians came to acquire these qualities. Pointing out that 'the peasants or villagers who reside at a distance from large towns and headstations and courts of law, are as innocent, temperate and moral in their conduct as the people of any country whatsoever', he observed: 'The inhabitants of the cities, towns or stations who have much intercourse with persons employed about the courts of law, by Zamindars etc. and with foreigners and others in a different state of civilization, generally imbibe their habits and opinions. Hence their religious opinions are shaken without any other principles being implanted to supply their place. Consequently a

imparted to it certain ideological dimensions. For, these institutions, based on principles which informed an advanced polity and economy, were quite overdeveloped in the given political and social context of the colony. The effort of the colonial state to establish hegemonic control over the colonised society was aided by this objective reality. The nature of perception was, at least partly, contingent on these factors, what Francis Bacon called 'the idols that rule the minds of men'.[28] Indeed, the idols also came from the traditional ideology and culture.

In perceiving the reality of colonial rule the intellectuals in nineteenth-century India adopted an idealized view of the state, without making any distinction between an alien and a native government. Conscious of the economy that had preceded the colonial conquest, and faced with a well-established state system based on liberal principles, most of them accepted and even welcomed British rule as divine dispensation.[29] This attitude arose not out of any personal profit from collaboration but from a belief in the instrumentality of British rule for realizing a political future based on liberal and constitutional principles.[30] That Britain in the first half of the nineteenth century represented the most advanced polity and economy in the world, and was the 'liberator of Europe' whenever freedom and liberty were endangered by despotic rulers, reinforced this belief.[31]

---

great proportion of these are inferior in point of character to the former class (villagers and peasantry) and are very often even made tools of in the nefarious work of perjury and forgery.' Ghose (ed.), *The English Works of Raja Rammohun Roy*, pp. 296–97. For an interesting study of colonial stereotypes in India, see Gyanendra Pandey, 'The Bigoted Julaha', *Economic and Political Weekly*, Vol. XVIII, No. 5, 29 January 1983; a later version of this paper is included in his *The Construction of Communalism in Co-lonial North India*, New Delhi, 1990.

[28] E. Curtis and John W. Petras (eds.), *The Sociology of Knowledge: A Reader*, London, 1970, p. 7.

[29] Rammohun Roy, 'An Appeal to the King in Council', in Ghose (ed.), *The English Works of Raja Rammohun Roy*, pp. 446–47; Veeresalingam, *Complete Works* (Telugu), Rajamandri, 1951, p. 9; Keshub Chandra Sen, *Lectures in India*, London, 1904, p. 320; and T.V. Parvate, *Mahadev Govind Ranade: A Biography*, Bombay, 1963, p. 226.

[30] For instance, Keshub Chandra Sen observed: 'it is not a man's work, but a work which God is doing with His own hands, using British nation as His instrument'. *Keshub Chandra Sen in England*, Calcutta, 1938, p. 90.

British rule was therefore looked upon as the 'chosen instrument' for leading India to the path of political and economic modernization. Rammohun characterized England as a nation of people who not only are 'blessed with the enjoyment of civil and political liberty but [who] also interest themselves in promoting liberty and social happiness, as well as free enquiry into literary and religious subjects among those nations to which their influence extends'.[32] The attitude towards British rule during its early phase was integrally a part of this notion of instrumentality.

When asked whether it would be beneficial to allow Europeans of capital to purchase estates in India and settle on them, Rammohun favoured Europeans of *character and capital* to do so, since 'it would generally improve the resources of the country, and also the condition of the native inhabitants, by showing them superior methods of cultivation, and the proper mode of treating their labourers and dependents'.[33] He also felt that if Europeans returning home were encouraged to settle in India with their families, it would greatly improve the resources of the country.[34] However, he was opposed to the idea of admitting Europeans of all descriptions to become settlers, as 'such a measure could only be regarded as adopted for the purpose of entirely supplanting the native inhabitants and expelling them from the country'.[35] Rammohun was evidently concerned with the preconditions necessary for industrialization, namely capital and technology. The lack of capital and the backwardness of technology occupied an important place in nineteenth-century economic thought. A solution was sought through the British connection.

However, a different perception of the nature of British rule was developing simultaneously in the nineteenth century. This was an outcome of the intellectual quest to understand the economically exploitative and politically dominating nature of colonial rule. Evolving from within and not parallel to the perception of the British as 'the chosen instrument' of Indian regeneration, what gave rise to it

[31] Ghose (ed.), *The English Works of Raja Rammohun Roy*, p. 367.
[32] Rammohun Roy, 'Final Appeal to the Christian Public', in ibid., p. 284.
[33] Ibid., p. 284.
[34] Ibid., p. 285.
[35] Ibid., p. 284.

was the contradiction inherent in the very nature of colonial rule. Beginning as a vague sense of patriotism and national pride and as abstract discussion on the disadvantages of dependence, it culminated in a definite vision of a future free from British domination. The poems of Kashi Prasad Ghose, the speeches and articles of Kylash Chunder Dutta, Sharada Prasad Ghose, Prasanna Kumar Tagore, Shama Charan Dutt, several anonymous contributions to contemporary journals in Bengal, the articles of Bhaskar Pandurang Tarkadkar and of anonymous pamphleteers in the *Bombay Gazette* in Maharashtra, were indicative of the early attempts to grapple with political reality. A letter published in *Reformer*, a journal edited by Prasanna Kumar Tagore, while discussing the connection between England and India, drew the following conclusions:

> Without her [India's] dependence on England as her conqueror and possessor, her political situation would be more respectable and her inhabitants would be more wealthy and prosperous. The example of America which shows what she was when subjected to England and what she has been since her freedom, most naturally lead us to such a conclusion.[36]

This was not an isolated instance. Sharada Prasad Ghose considered 'the deprivation of the enjoyment of political liberty as the cause of our misery and degradation'.[37] Kylash Chunder Dutta, in an essay on the India of his dreams a hundred years hence, conjured up an armed rebellion for the overthrow of British rule.[38] Akshay Kumar Dutt was concerned with dependence itself which he considered a terrible suffering, worse than *naraka* of the Hindus, hell of the Christians and *jahannam* of the Musalmans.[39]

The growing consciousness about the new political situation was also reflected in periodicals published in Maharashtra. In a series of letters written in the *Bombay Gazette* in 1841 under the pseudonym 'A Hindoo', Bhaskar Pandurang Tarkadkar not only focused

[36] Gautam Chattopadhyay (ed.), *Awakening in Bengal in the Early Nineteenth Century,* Calcutta, 1965, p. xiv.

[37] *Bengal Harkaru,* October 1841, quoted in Gautam Chattopadhyay (ed.), *Bengal: Early Nineteenth Century,* Calcutta, 1978, p. xii.

[38] Kylash Chunder Dutta, 'A Journal of 48 Hours of the Year 1945', *Calcutta Literary Gazette,* 6 June 1835, in ibid., p. xi.

[39] Majumdar, *History of Indian Social and Political Ideas,* p. 74.

attention on administrative lapses and injustice, like many of his predecessors, but also tried to comprehend the nature and consequences of British rule.[40] At the very outset he tried to demonstrate how British rule was alien and different from that of earlier conquerors who had established their empires in India. In drawing this distinction two criteria were employed: the administrative and the economic. In administrative matters like employment and the dispensation of justice, Muslim rulers did not discriminate on religious grounds whereas the British clearly favoured their countrymen.[41] Citing instances to show how the British were partial to Europeans in the dispensation of justice, the disparity between the principle of the rule of law and its practice was highlighted.[42] More important, however, was the perception of the role of the law and judiciary in promoting colonial interests. 'Whenever', Tarkadkar wrote, 'you [the British] have to establish a new act of oppression, your first precaution is to insert it in your Indian code of laws and give it the colour of justice and equality.'[43]

The second criterion used by Tarkadkar to identify the alien character of British rule was its economic activity, which was geared to the transfer of wealth to England 'at the sad expense of the prosperity and happiness of the poor and inoffensive inhabitants' of India.[44] He contrasted this with the lack of any such intent by earlier rulers, thus displaying his sensitivity to a crucial element which distinguished British rule. He was also conscious of the fact that the British did not identify themselves with the socio-cultural life of the country.

The perception of economic conditions and the consequent

[40] For a general survey of Bhaskar Pandurang Tarkadkar's ideas, see J.V. Naik, 'An Early Appraisal of the British Colonial Policy', *Journal of the University of Bombay,* Vols. XLIV and XLV, Nos. 80–81, 1975–76.

[41] 'A Letter from a Hindoo', 28 July 1841, *Bombay Gazette,* 30 July 1841, Vol. LIII, new series, No. 25, p. 103.

[42] 'Your partiality to your countrymen is extreme and it is not very seldom that we witness your sacrificing your conscience and trampling underfoot your law and casting aside every other consideration to preserve the life of your countryman or lighten his punishment however extremely heinous his crime may be and however deserved he may be to very harsh punishment.' *Bombay Gazette,* 30 July 1841, No. 25, p. 103.

[43] *Bombay Gazette,* 10 August 1841, No. 37, p. 138.

[44] Ibid.

involvement with economic problems was limited during the first three quarters of the nineteenth century. Yet the intellectuals were neither indifferent to the general economic condition of the country nor insensitive to the economic implications of colonial rule. The poverty of the masses, inequality in society, the conditions of the peasantry, the destruction of the handicraft industry and the drain of wealth through trade attracted their attention. Almost everyone from Rammohun to Vivekananda was concerned with poverty and inequality. Some only bemoaned the misery of the people, but others reflected on the causes which produced this misery. While Rammohun sought an explanation in administrative practice,[45] Akshay Kumar Dutt and Bankim Chandra Chatterji posited it within the existing socio-economic relations in society.[46] Bankim Chandra's *Samya,* which, like Rammohun's *Tuhfat,* is a landmark in the intellectual history of India, was the most significant literary effort in the nineteenth century to deal with the problem of inequality. Borrowing from a variety of European thinkers and thus eclectic in content, *Samya* is a good index of the strength and weakness of intellectual development in colonial and modern India.[47] While it indicated a certain penchant for philosophical speculation and abstract discussion that was almost non-existent in nineteenth-century India, it tended to rely heavily on an alien intellectual tradition, a tendency which has almost become a debility in our contemporary intellectual life.

That the economic consequences of British domination, particularly the drain of wealth and the decline of handicrafts, were within the focus of the nineteenth-century perception of reality, has not received adequate notice in existing historical writings. Rammohun was conscious of the drain of wealth from India through salary remittances, savings from the professional incomes of English civilians as well as from the earnings of English merchants, agents and

---

[45] Susobhan Sarkar (ed.), *Rammohun on Indian Economy,* Calcutta, 1965, p. 9.

[46] Majumdar, *History of Indian Social and Political Ideas,* p. 74, and M. K. Haldar, *Renaissance and Reaction in Nineteenth Century Bengal,* Calcutta, 1915. The title of Haldar's book is misleading. It is a translation of Bankim's *Samya,* with an introduction by the author.

[47] For a good discussion of Bankim's ideas see B.N. Ganguli, *Concept of Equality: The Nineteenth Century Indian Debate,* Simla, 1975.

planters, and through Indian revenues expended in England. On the authority of 'a very able servant of the Company, holding a responsible situation in Bengal', he estimated 'the aggregate of tribute, public and private, so withdrawn from India from 1765 to 1820 at £110 million'.[48] In course of time, attention came to be further focused on this question. The central argument in Tarkadkar's critique of British rule was the drain of wealth. In fact, the very purpose of his letters was 'to show how rigorous the present policy of the British has been in operation in regard to draining India of its wealth and reducing it to poverty'.[49] He recognized British trade as the main channel of the drain and argued that it had 'more effectively emptied our purses in a few years than the predatory excursions of these tribes [Pindaries and Ramosies] could do in some five or six hundred years'.[50] To Rammohun the main consequence of the drain was the lack of capital necessary for economic development, but Tarkadkar saw it as an important reason for poverty.[51]

The impact of British economic policies on indigenous handicraft industries also formed a part of the emerging consciousness in the nineteenth century. Rammohun and his contemporaries and several others soon after him were not alive to the sad plight of the artisans whose 'bones lay bleached in the plains of Bengal', and to the changing patterns of consumption and the market. That they were unaware is not altogether surprising, given their perspective of industrialization. Yet the import of this change was not entirely overlooked, particularly by intellectuals in Maharashtra. A letter published in the *Bombay Gazette* under the pseudonym 'Philanthropy' attributed the main cause of the misery of the inhabitants of Konkan and the Deccan to the destruction of indigenous industry owing to the import from Great Britain of 'almost all the necessaries and luxuries of life, entirely superseding those produced in the country'.[52] Citing the example of the weavers of Konkan, it argued that artisans were losing their source of livelihood and were forced to

---

[48] Rammohun Roy, Appendix to 'Questions and Answers on the Revenue System of India', in Ghose (ed.), *The English Works of Raja Rammohun Roy*, p. 311.

[49] *Bombay Gazette*, 30 July 1841, No. 25, p. 103.

[50] *Bombay Gazette*, 20 August 1841, No. 46, pp. 174–75.

[51] *Bombay Gazette*, 10 August 1841, No. 37, pp. 138–39.

[52] Quoted in Naik, 'An Early Appraisal'.

take to cultivation and tillage.[53] This idea found further elaboration in Gopal Hari Deshmukh, who advocated swadeshi and boycott of foreign manufactured goods and opposed the export of raw materials:

> Our people should make a firm determination jointly not to buy foreign goods; they should buy only home-made articles, although inferior in quality. We should use our own cloth, our own umbrellas and so on. Thus we will be able to retain our money in our country. All the merchants and producers should resolve to sell to the British people only the finished Indian goods and not the raw materials.[54]

The existing literature on nineteenth-century India overlooks almost entirely the connections between these early gropings and the growth of anti-colonial consciousness. Treating the pre-nationalist and nationalist phases as separate and independent, the former is assigned socio-religious reform and the latter the more 'progressive' nationalist political activity. Such analyses miss the vital point that pre-nationalist intellectuals were the heralds of the cultural and ideological struggle, and thus were participants in and contributors to the emerging dominant consciousness in colonial India. The burden of their endeavour was to elaborate an ideology which would counter both the traditional and the colonial. Their ambivalence is explained by the necessity to draw upon elements represented by both. Viewed from this perspective, the socio-cultural manifestations in colonial India call for a re-examination.

Defence of the Indigenous Tradition

Compared to their perception of the political and economic reality, nineteenth-century Indian intellectuals had a clearer vision of the country's socio-religious conditions. The interdependence and interconnection of religion and social life, religious beliefs and social evils, the distortions and misrepresentations of religious scriptures and knowledge, the social implications of some prevalent forms of worship, and the adverse influences of social institutions such as caste, were a part of this perception. Reformation in this sphere, which

---

[53] Ibid.
[54] Majumdar, *History of Indian Social and Political Ideas*, p. 202.

was the main task undertaken by intellectuals in the nineteenth century, was induced not solely by these objective conditions but by their perceived linkages with the destiny of society. The early expression of the cultural–ideological struggle in colonial India was within this ambit. This idea, namely that socio-religious reformation was not an end in itself, is a point missing in most of the innumerable studies on the subject.[55]

Almost simultaneous with this awareness, Indian society witnessed the emergence of a consciousness about the cultural–ideological implications of colonialism. Since the destruction or denigration of indigenous culture was integral to the methods of domination and control, and because colonial rule did not bring about a sharp retrogression in the form of government and the nature of state institutions, the initial expression of the struggle against alien domination manifested itself in the realm of culture. The intellectual quest to realize the potential inherent in traditional culture was a part of this struggle.

These two tendencies, the first marked by struggle against the backward elements of traditional culture and ideology to modernize society, and the second by reliance on the strength of traditional culture and ideology to shape the future, have been characterized as reformist and revivalist respectively. Is it possible to locate both these strands within the same process which contributed to the making of an anti-colonial consciousness through a dual struggle against traditional and colonial cultures and ideologies? The classes (the petty-bourgeoisie and the bourgeoisie) which formed the social base of this struggle, initiated and furthered by the intellectuals, experienced a dual alienation from the corresponding cultural–intellectual milieu,

---

[55] It has even been argued that intellectuals in the nineteenth century considered religion the basis of society. S.N. Mukherjee, 'The Social Implication of the Political Thought of Raja Rammohun Roy', in R.S. Sharma and V. Jha (eds.), *Indian Society: Historical Probings*, New Delhi, 1974, p. 372. Mukherjee has based his argument on a wrong reading of Rammohun. Rammohun in fact was pointing out how religion originated from the social necessity to preserve property rights and relations. Rammohun Roy, *Tuhfat-ul Muwahhiddin*, in Ghose (ed.), *The English Works of Raja Rammohun Roy*, p. 947. The interpretation and use of religious texts and ideas in the nineteenth century, particularly by Rammohun, Vidyasagar, Bankim Chandra and Vivekananda, are also important in this context.

to begin with from the traditional and later from the colonial. It was within the world of these classes in the Presidency towns of Calcutta, Bombay and Madras that the reformist urge first made its appearance. So also was the attempt to 'return to the sources', which was not a return to tradition *per se* but rather an attempt to challenge and deny the pretended supremacy of the culture of the coloniser as well as to reassert the cultural identity of the colonised. This was 'not a voluntary step, but the only possible reply to the demand of concrete need, historically determined, and enforced by the inescapable contradiction between the colonised society and the colonial power'.[56] The socio-cultural regeneration in colonial India, which is generally but not altogether appropriately termed 'renaissance', was a consequence of this dual alienation and struggle.[57]

Amilcar Cabral, one of the few political activists to pay attention to the role of culture in liberation struggles, locates it in the dual alienation of the petty-bourgeoisie,[58] which provided the social base for the intellectual–cultural struggle leading to regeneration in colonial societies. Since the aspects of this struggle have not been worked out in detail, at this stage it can only be suggested as a possible alternative to the existing typologies based either on western inspiration or internal dynamics.

Colonial domination, which inevitably impinged upon the cultural existence of the colonised culture, is viewed as 'a whole way of life' embracing all 'signifying practices' such as language, religion, arts, philosophy, etc. Two important areas in which cultural sensitivity found articulation were language and religion. The perception of language as an important component led intellectuals in the nineteenth century to realize the consequences of the use of English

---

[56] Amilcar Cabral, 'The Role of Culture in the Struggle for Independence', paper presented at the UNESCO conference on the Concept of Race, Identity and Dignity, Paris, 3–7 July 1972.

[57] The discussion of the socio-cultural regeneration in colonial India has tended to draw heavily on the renaissance model. How far this model is applicable to the Indian situation has recently attracted some attention. See Barun De, *Perspectives in Social Sciences*, and Rajat Ray, 'Man, Woman and the Novel: The Rise of a New Consciousness in Bengal, 1858–1947', *The Indian Economic and Social History Review*, Vol. XVI, No. 1, January–March 1979.

[58] Cabral, *Return to the Source*, p. 63.

as the medium of instruction in education. English, they asserted, was creating a group of people alienated from their national culture and consequently from their countrymen.[59] They were conscious of the gulf that separated the English-educated—superficially educated to Bankim, and spineless creatures to Vivekananda—and the uneducated masses in ideas, thought, feeling and manner of living. Cultivation of the vernacular languages, therefore, occupied an important place in their programme of national regeneration. Beginning with 'Young Bengal' and Akshay Kumar Dutt, up to Sayyid Ahmad Khan and the Dawn Society, it was a continuous and progressively developing consciousness. Making a passionate appeal for education in the mother-tongue, Uday Chandra Adhya emphasized 'a proper knowledge of the language of the country' as a necessary pre-requisite for progress and regeneration leading to political freedom.[60] About four decades later, Sayyid Ahmad Khan expressed this in more emphatic terms:

> The cause of England's civilization is that all the arts and sciences are in the language of the country. Those who are bent on improving and bettering India must remember that the only way of compassing this is by having the whole of the arts and sciences translated into their own language. I should like to have this written in gigantic letters on the Himalayas for the remembrance of future generations.[61]

This emphasis on enriching the vernaculars should not be viewed in isolation. It was in fact a response to the cultural, social and intellectual consequences of colonial education, as evident from the conscious use of the vernaculars in preference to English and from the endeavour to develop an alternate system of education.[62] The large number of vernacular journals and periodicals were indicative of this

---

[59] Akshay Kumar Dutt in *Tattwabodhini Patrika*, Saka 1768, No. 36, pp. 309–11.

[60] Uday Chandra Adhya, 'A Proposal for the Proper Cultivation of the Bengali Language and its Necessity for the Natives of the Country', in Chattopadhyay (ed.), *Awakening in Bengal*, p. 26.

[61] Shan Mohammad (ed.), *Writings and Speeches of Sir Sayyid Ahmad Khan*, Bombay, 1972, pp. 231–32.

[62] For a discussion of educational ideas in the nineteenth century and their implications, see the chapter 'An Overview' in this volume.

preference, as also the fact that several associations decided to conduct their proceedings in the vernaculars. For instance the members of the *Sarbatatva Deepika Sabha* founded in 1833 resolved to hold their discussions and speak only in the mother-tongue.[63] So did Raj Narain Bose's Society for the Promotion of National Feeling among the Educated Natives of Bengal, which advocated learning the mother-tongue in place of English, the cultivation of Sanskrit, publication of the results of research into Indian antiquities in Bengali, and conversation and proceedings of meetings in Bengali.[64] Nabha Gopal Mitra, Bhudev Mukherjee, Pandit Guru Dutt and a host of others vigorously pursued this ideal, which culminated in the ideas and activities of the National Educational Council[65] and the Society for a Uniform Script.[66] Attempts to revitalize the Indian system of medicine, to probe into the potentialities of pre-colonial technology and to reconstruct traditional knowledge should be viewed in this cultural context.[67]

The cultural concern was most strongly expressed whenever religious beliefs and practices were perceived to be violated by the administrative measures undertaken by the colonial state or by the evangelizing efforts of Christian missionaries. Legislative interventions in social matters were interpreted as interference in ancient usages and customs, as reflected in the memorials against the abolition of sati and the Lex Loci Act.[68] A circular issued by the Hindus of Calcutta argued that the Act would prove a 'weapon of destruction to the Hindoo race and eradicate the tree of Hinduism';[69] it would

---

[63] Chattopadhyay (ed.), *Awakening in Bengal,* p. xxv.

[64] David Kopf, *Brahmo Samaj and the Shaping of the Modern Indian Mind,* Princeton, 1979.

[65] The object of the Council was 'to impart Education—Literary as well as Scientific and Technical—on National lines and exclusively under national control, *not in opposition to, but standing apart from,* the existing system of Primary, Secondary and Universal Education'. Uma and Haridas Mukherjee, *The Origins of the National Education Movement,* Calcutta, 1959, p. 44.

[66] Ibid., p. 230.

[67] For a brief survey of these attempts see Kopf, *Brahmo Samaj.*

[68] Muhammad Mohar Ali, *The Bengali Reaction to Christian Missionary Activities,* Chittagong, 1965, pp. 117–36, and S.R. Mehrotra, *The Emergence of the Indian National Congress,* Delhi, 1971, pp. 47–50.

'sap the foundation of their religion'.[70] A memorial signed by 14,000 Hindus of Calcutta expressed this fear in no uncertain terms and gave vent to their disenchantment with the British government, which, they feared, was aiding and abetting evangelization. *Hindu Intelligencer* recorded that 'it appears that [the] Indian Government as well as the authorities in Leadenhall Street have identified themselves with the missionaries and their cause'.[71] Apprehension about the purpose of the Act and its possible consequences was shared by the Hindus in other Presidencies as well. In fact, attempts were made to organize protest and opposition simultaneously in all the three Presidencies, including a call to desist from cultivation of land and payment of revenue.[72]

There was a growing suspicion that British officials were actively supporting evangelizing efforts. The close social intercourse between officials and missionaries in district towns, the partiality of officials to missionaries and converts in disputes,[73] the attempts to introduce a Christian content in education[74] and the conversion of students receiving English education reinforced this suspicion. Judgements in cases relating to the custody of converts, wives and children and other related matters made even the judiciary appear

---

[69] Ibid., p. 47.

[70] Mohar Ali, *The Bengali Reaction*, p. 130.

[71] Quoted in Mehrotra, *Emergence of the Indian National Congress*, p. 44.

[72] Ibid., p. 48.

[73] The Tinnelvelli riot case is a good example. About a hundred Hindus who had allegedly participated in the anti-missionary riot were jailed by the local magistrate but were acquitted on appeal by the sessions judge. The Governor of Madras disapproved of the action of the judge and transferred him from Tinnelvelli. See Robert Eric Frykenberg, 'The Impact of Conversion and Social Reform upon Society in South India during the Late Company Period: Questions Concerning Hindu-Christian Encounters with Special Reference to Tinnelvelly', in Philip and Mainwright (eds.), *Indian Society and the Beginnings of Modernization*, pp. 187–243.

[74] Several officials advocated the introduction of Bible classes as a part of the curriculum in schools. Lord Tweeddale, who implemented it by making the Bible a textbook of English, observed in his controversial 'Bible Minute': 'It is the only means I know of giving to the natives a practical knowledge of the sciences from which rise all those high qualities which they admire so much in the character of those whom Providence had placed to rule over them.' Quoted in Mehrotra, *Emergence of the Indian National Congress*, p. 40.

partisan.[75] Consciousness of the cultural implications of the colonial presence and of the need to preserve the Hindu way of life was a result of these perceptions. The opposition to the Bible Minute, in which not only orthodox Hindus such as Radhakanta Deb and Ashutosh Deb, but also liberals like Devendranath Tagore participated,[76] and the mammoth memorandum from Madras signed by 70,000 people remonstrating against the use of education for religious propaganda and demanding that education be imparted without interference in religious beliefs, were indicative of this awareness.[77]

The defence of indigenous culture and institutions and an introspective study of their strength and past glory were thus a consequence of colonial cultural intrusion. It was not, to repeat an earlier argument, a voluntary act, but was forced by historical circumstances which necessitated a redefinition of identity. Rejecting all that colonialism represented, it led to a search for identity in indigenous tradition. This tendency, although it originated in the colonial conquest, became manifest only during the second half of the nineteenth century with the maturing of cultural and ideological contradictions with colonialism. Shared both by Hindu and Muslim intellectuals, it made religious particularism and even communalism possible. However, its origins lay not in the perception of communal differences or communal antagonism but in the reaction to colonial culture and ideology. Viewed in this light, the invocation and reinterpretation of the past was not inherently retrogressive; it was only a means for self-strengthening and not a basis for a vision of the future. The tendency to rely on the vitality of traditional culture and to reinterpret it to meet the requirements of contemporary society— as expressed in the thought of Bankim, Dayanand, Raj Narain Bose, Bhudev Mukherjee, Pandit Guru Dutt, Syed Alavi and Makti Tangal— was a part of this quest. It represented not cultural revivalism, but cultural defence. This was not an end in itself but a component in the growth of dominant consciousness in colonial India. That it possibly

---

[75] Mohar Ali, *The Bengali Reaction,* pp. 101–16.

[76] *Harkaru,* 13 December 1847.

[77] Memorandum to John Elphinstone, Governor of Fort St George, 11 November 1839, in P.J. Thomas, *The Growth of Higher Education in Southern India,* Madras, n.d., p. 5.

hindered the growth of a secular ethos was a part of the general failure to effectively combine the cultural–ideological and political struggles.

4 Culture and Ideology

Central to the changes in the intellectual domain in colonial India were the cultural–ideological struggles occurring simultaneously at two planes: against the ideological basis of the traditional order on the one hand, and against colonial hegemonization on the other. The colonial conquest underlined the weaknesses of the traditional order and the need for reform and regeneration of its institutions. An alternative, however, was not envisaged entirely in the western model presented by colonial rule, mainly because of the apprehension aroused in the Indian mind by the cultural and intellectual engineering of the colonial state as a part of its strategy of political control. While traditional culture appeared inadequate to meet the challenge posed by the west, colonial hegemonization tended to destroy the tradition itself. Hence a struggle ensued against both which shaped the intellectual situation in colonial India.

The intellectual quest to shape the future of Indian society, which was based on this dual struggle, remained ambivalent, often contradictory, in its attitude towards tradition and modernity. The endeavour of a subjected people to reclaim the uninterrupted development of their history cannot but be based on the strength of their tradition. Therefore, an emphasis on the past, 'a return to the sources', as Amilcar Cabral called it,[1] did not necessarily mean an attempt to resurrect the past in opposition to contemporary forces of progress. Nor did modernity involve a rejection of the past, since tradition served as a powerful tool in the effort to realize modernity.

[1] Amilcar Cabral, *Return to the Source: Selected Speeches of Amilcar Cabral,* New York, 1973, p. 63.

In fact, to a colonised people, history did not present the possibility of making a clearcut demarcation between the past and the future. Consequently, their conception of the past and of the future tended to be mutually intrusive. The course and character of cultural–ideological struggles were influenced by the ambiguity and uncertainty generated by this intrusiveness; so also the intellectual transformation which drew upon these struggles.

Formation of an Intellectual Community

In the development of cultural–ideological struggles the formation of a community of intellectuals distinct from the intelligentsia, and cutting across regional, religious and caste barriers, was of crucial importance.[2] While the objective conditions created by colonial rule facilitated its formation, it was integrated into an active community only through commonly shared socio-political endeavours. Bonds within the community were finally forged only during the politically active phase of the national liberation struggle; however, the process of its formation had begun much earlier, almost at the beginning of the nineteenth century, as socio-cultural undertakings wore down individual isolation and established communication links at the regional level, to begin with, and at a national plane later. This integration was not brought about by identical socio-cultural perspectives; differences in views contributed equally to this process, for the intellectuals shared the common objective of social regeneration. Hence, even while conducting debates with differing views they were becoming part of a community committed to the transformation of their society.

During the course of the nineteenth century the intellectuals were brought together, either in opposition or in unity, in a series of struggles over socio-cultural issues. Between the debate over the abolition of sati in Bengal in the early part of the nineteenth century and the national controversy over the Age of Consent Bill during its

[2] The distinction between intellectuals and intellectual workers in general, or the intelligentsia, is based on the specific social function they performed which Antonio Gramsci characterized as the creation of a new equilibrium and the perpetual innovation of the physical and social world. Antonio Gramsci, *Selections from the Prison Notebooks,* New York, 1971, p. 9. For a discussion of this distinction in colonial India see the chapter titled 'Historiographical and Conceptual Questions' in this volume.

closing decades, a number of public issues became their common concern—the Anti-Conversion Petition, the Anti-Idolatry Memorial, the Lex Loci Act, the Widow Marriage Act and the Civil Marriage Act, to mention a few. The formation of local and regional intellectual communities and their eventual transition to a national community may be discerned during the course of agitation over these issues.

The early formation of the community of intellectuals was around socio-cultural organizations and voluntary associations which reflected the initial intellectual ferment in colonial India. Apart from the well-known organizations involved in socio-religious reforms, there were several other associations, small and often shortlived, nevertheless important, in forging bonds at local levels. The Academic Association and the Society for the Acquisition of General Knowledge in Calcutta, the Students' Literary and Scientific Society and Dnyanprasarak Sabha in Bombay and the Literary Society in Madras were the more important of them.

There were also a large number of voluntary associations established by colonial officials and ideologues which served as channels of dissemination of colonial culture and ideology in which Indian intellectuals participated. Unlike those promoted by Indians, these associations made inter-communal intercourse possible. For instance, in the Calcutta School Book Society there were four Hindus and four Muslims in 1818.[3] This was true of public societies of specialized interest like the Horticultural Society, and several others. Participation in these societies, however, brought home to the Indian members their subordinate position, even when working on a seemingly equal footing with Englishmen. The treatment meted out to Ram Gopal Ghose in the Horticultural Society and to Rajendralal Mitra in the Photographic Society are good examples. Ram Gopal was removed from the Society for opposing the views of Englishmen and Rajendralal Mitra was asked to retire from the Society for criticizing the activities of non-official Europeans in India.[4] The Europeans in

---

[3] The Hindus were Babu Tarni Charan Mitra, Mrityunjay Vidyalankar, Babu Radhakanta Deb and Babu Ram Kamal Sen. The Muslims were Maulavi Abdul Wahid, Maulavi Kareem Hussain, Maulavi Abdul Hamid and Maulavi Muhammad Rashid. *The First Report of the Calcutta School Book Society,* Calcutta, 1818.

[4] Ram Gopal Ghose, *A Short Sketch of His Life and Speeches,* Calcutta, 1868, p. 12, and *Bombay Gazette,* 30 July 1857.

India also took interest in establishing and promoting 'native' libraries with the active participation of Indians.[5] Despite being conduits for the dissemination of colonial ideology, these institutions provided a useful platform for intellectual exchange. In fact, many who became active, either socially or politically, had their baptism in public work in these organizations.

Although these associations were important in providing opportunity for mutual contact, what was more significant in the formation of the intellectual community were the actual campaigns and agitations over socio-cultural issues. The earliest example of this in colonial India was the well-known controversy over the abolition of sati. This brought two important intellectuals of early nineteenth-century India, Radhakanta Deb and Rammohun Roy, and their supporters, generally but not altogether appropriately termed 'conservatives' and 'reformers' respectively, into open confrontation. The campaign initiated by Rammohun in 1818 through two tracts in which he set out the religious and social issues in the form of a dialogue between an advocate and an opponent of sati, was the beginning of an unprecendented debate among the Calcutta intelligentsia.[6] In advocating the abolition of sati, Rammohun based his arguments on scriptural authority as well as on humanitarian considerations.[7] The opponents appeared to be more concerned with the changes sought to be introduced in traditional practices. It is, however, significant that the 'conservative' leaders did not observe the rite of concremation in their own families. The suggestion that Radhakanta Deb, like Tilak later, was more concerned with the changes introduced through external intervention is worth consideration, particularly because he was a champion of progressive measures like female education.[8] Several of his supporters disapproved

---

[5] See the discussion on 'native' libraries in Bombay in *Bombay Times*, 9 August to 20 September 1843.

[6] Amitabha Mukherjee, *Reform and Regeneration in Bengal, 1774–1823*, Calcutta, 1968, pp. 276–82.

[7] J.C. Ghose (ed.), *The English Works of Raja Rammohun Roy*, Allahabad, 1906, pp. 325–29 and 360–62.

[8] Radhakanta Deb's biographer, J.C. Bagal, has suggested that he was apprehensive that the interference of the alien government would lead to complete disintegration of the Hindu society. Mukherjee, *Reform and Regeneration in Bengal*, p. 282.

of his stand on female education and had deserted his *dal*.[9] Rammohun himself, despite his utilitarian leanings, preferred the changes to come from within.

The mobilizing potential of the agitation over sati was largely confined to Bengal; nevertheless, it raised certain fundamental issues of social transformation which became the general concern of intellectuals all over India. In this sense the debate over sati was the beginning not only of a regional but also of a 'national' intellectual community. It raised two questions—first, the relevance of scriptural sanction as a precondition for changing the social norms in vogue; second, the desirability of state intervention in socio-cultural matters.

During the course of the nineteenth century both these questions became part of a debate in all the three presidencies over issues relating to the marriage of widows and the legislation conferring the right to inherit ancestral property on Hindus converted to Christianity.

Although the widow marriage movement was not organized on an all-India basis,[10] the debate about it did assume an all-India character. The discussion, in Bombay, Bengal and Madras took place through newspapers, enabling supporters and opponents of the cause to share common arguments.[11] Much before Vidyasagar's celebrated treatise, 'Marriage of Hindu Widows', appeared in 1856, two tracts written by Subaji Bapu of Sehore in Bhopal and a brahmin pandit of Pune were published in Marathi. Subaji Bapu's essay was written in response to a series of letters which appeared in *The Bombay Darpun*, a weekly edited by Bal Shastri Jambekar, in August 1835.[12] Bapu saw widow marriage as a part of the general emancipation of women and hence emphasized the importance of female education.[13] In favouring widow marriage the pandit from Pune was mainly persuaded by humanitarian considerations.[14] In the public discussion that ensued on these tracts the question of scriptural sanction was invoked.

---

[9] *Hindu Intelligencer*, 2 July 1849.

[10] Charles Heimsath, *Indian Nationalism and Hindu Social Reform*, Princeton, 1964, p. 89.

[11] *Bombay Gazette* for 1851–54 contains several examples of this exchange.

[12] G.G. Jambhekar (ed.), *Memoirs and Writings of Acharya Bal Shastri Jambekar*, Vol. II, Poona, 1950, p. 76.

[13] *The Bombay Darpun*, 8 September 1837.

[14] Ibid.

Referring to the pandit's arguments *Darpun* noted:

> We are constrained to say that in all his essay he does not adduce
> a single authority from the Shastras to support his view. . . . One
> solid injunction of the Shastras would have been a hundred times
> more valuable than all these quotations. . . . We ought to have
> authorities from the Shastras, and since these cannot be produced,
> the question must be begged in the way the learned shastree has
> done on the ground of the hardship and inconvenience of the
> custom. No one admires the learning and research of this author
> more than ourselves; and we are aware that the deficiency we have
> been noticing arises rather from want of authorities in support of
> his opinion than from any other cause.[15]

The main point of dispute between the advocates and opponents of
widow marriage was whether it had the sanction of the *shastras*. The
advocates—Vidyasagar and Debendranath Tagore in Bengal,
Vishnushastri Pandit and Vishnubawa Brahmachari in Maharashtra
and Raghunath Rao and Veeresalingam in Madras—argued that
they were not trying to introduce a measure which had no religious
approval.[16] This was precisely what the opponents contested and they
strove to prove that there was nothing in the Hindu scriptures to
admit of the reformers' contention.[17] The authority of the scriptures
was thus accepted by both; they only differed in their interpretation
of it.

There was also considerable agreement over the need to
bring about mental and material changes, if the reform in existing
social practices had to be really effective. Rammohun had already
argued that no substantial improvement in the condition of women
can be brought about without giving them the right to property.[18] He
had also identified lack of education as the principal reason for their

---

[15] Ibid.

[16] 'I had not taken up my pen in defence of widow marriage', wrote Vidyasagar,
'till I was convinced that it had the approval of the *shastras*.'

[17] 'Discussion on Widow Marriage in Ahmednagar Debating Society', *Bombay
Gazette*, 23 February and 8 June 1855.

[18] 'Brief Remarks Regarding Modern Encroachments on the Ancient Rights
of Females, According to the Hindu Law of Inheritance', in Ghose (ed.), *The
English Works of Raja Rammohun Roy*, pp 375–84.

'inferiority'.[19] Thus a general perspective on emancipation, although within a bourgeois–patriarchal framework, was held by the reformers as a whole. The *Hindoo Patriot,* underlining the importance of education as a precondition for introducing changes in social customs, wrote: 'We are only for having this extremely desirable measure [widow marriage] grow out of education and result from the dissemination of knowledge amongst our country women.'[20]

The opposition to widow marriage was based on the same premises: individual reforms to be effective and successful had to have a favourable social climate, as otherwise they would prove to be premature attempts, producing 'much uneasiness and discord among the domestic circle'.[21] The *Hindu Intelligencer* which did not approve of the demand for widow marriage legislation expressed this opinion in unambiguous terms:

> The text of Parasara quoted by the learned Pandit [Vidyasagar], which admits of such different interpretation as it has already received, cannot be expected to set aside at once the established custom of some thousand years. To produce any effect, it must fall upon a proper soil. Public opinion must be ripe for the change. . . . It appears to us that the way for the remarriage of our widows can only be gradually prepared by first educating and enlightening our females; and this must be done silently and in private without noise or uproar. Without this preliminary step being taken and the minds of the fair sex being first enlightened, it is vain to attempt effecting so great a revolution in our social economy, as is necessarily involved in the remarriage of our widows.[22]

The opinion of both the 'reformers' and the 'conservatives' thus converged on the task of 'preparing the soil'. That was why Radhakanta

---

[19] 'As to their inferiority in point of undertaking when did you ever afford them a fair opportunity of exhibiting their natural capacity? How then can you accuse them of want of understanding? If after instruction in knowledge and wisdom, a person cannot comprehend or retain what has been taught him we may consider him deficient; but if you keep women generally void of education and acquirements, you cannot, therefore, in justice pronounce on their inferiority.' Ibid., pp. 360–61.

[20] *Hindoo Patriot,* February 1853.

[21] *Hindu Intelligencer,* 19 February 1855.

[22] Ibid.

Deb, while opposing the movement for widow marriage, supported Bethune's efforts to promote female education.[23]

The discussion on widow marriage addressed the fundamental question of women's emancipation and the methods to be adopted for it in the conditions prevalent in colonial India. Although the movement was organized on regional and caste lines, the problem was perceived as common to all Hindus and the intellectuals in the three Presidencies borrowed arguments and counter-arguments from one another. The debate on widow marriage also indicated an attempt to construct a Hindu community at a national plane, drawing on the authority of common scriptures. While the *Darpun* pointed out in 1837 that widow marriage was prohibited only among the upper castes, the debate during the second half of the century did not refer to any such distinctions.[24]

The introduction of a bill in 1845 to provide for the inheritance of ancestral property to Hindus converted to Christianity and its eventual legislation as the Lex Loci Act in 1851 occasioned simultaneous agitations in all the three Presidencies. Soon after the bill was introduced the intellectuals got in touch with each other to oppose the proposed legislation which was looked upon as a motivated attempt to interfere in their cultural life.[25] Meetings were organized and memorials drawn up opposing the bill.[26] The memorials were prepared in mutual consultation and a countrywide agitation, including non-payment of revenue and non-cultivation of land, was envisaged. In an open letter to the Governor-General, 'a Brahmin' from Madras asserted: 'I am confident that my countrymen in the three Presidencies will join in one compact for their own interests, and translate this letter into the common languages of the country for its better circulation among our community here and elsewhere.'[27] Through participation in these struggles, an intellectual community committed to the transformation of society came into being at the national plane during the course of the nineteenth century. This

---

[23] *Hindu Intelligencer*, 2 July 1849.

[24] *The Bombay Darpun*, 18 August 1837.

[25] S.R. Mehrotra, *The Emergence of the Indian National Congress*, Delhi, 1971, p. 44.

[26] *Bombay Witness*, 5 June 1845 and *Bombay Gazette*, 10 July 1845.

[27] Quoted in Mehrotra, *Emergence of the Indian National Congress*, p. 48.

community was the vehicle of the cultural–ideological struggle referred to earlier as well as the vanguard of the national liberation struggle. Although the members of this community did not share common views on many social and cultural issues, their ideological premises were remarkably similar.

Ideological Premises

The intellectual community in colonial India functioned within the parameters of bourgeois–liberal ideology, except in the second quarter of the twentieth century when a section of it was drawn towards Marxism. In their choice of the nature of polity, economy and society the imprint of bourgeois liberalism was quite marked. This choice was to a great extent influenced by the ideological system created by colonial rule and the western ideas filtering through its ideological apparatuses. Yet it was not solely contingent on them but was integral to the transition to a capitalist order, even if stunted and distorted, taking place under the colonial aegis.

The political perspectives and activities in colonial India were based on the ideal of gradual realization of a bourgeois–democratic order. The character of pre-colonial political institutions and of the colonial state was understood and assessed within this framework. Hence the early critique of the pre-colonial political system and the acceptance of British rule as divine dispensation. Dosabhoy Framjee's views in a pamphlet entitled 'The British Raj Contrasted with Its Predecessors' were representative of this understanding:

> This steady expansion of English dominion has been followed by the establishment of peace in all the borders of the land; by a firm and upright administration of the laws, and by a security of life and property to which India had been unhappily a stranger from the remotest times. The children have forgotten the adversities of their fathers—the true character of that bloody and lawless tyranny from which England has emancipated the people of India; and the object of the author was to recall the fading memories of the unhappy past and contrast them vividly with the peaceful experience of British rule.[28]

---

[28] *Bombay Gazette*, 5 November 1857.

This stark contrast between the conditions that prevailed in the two systems reflected the differences in the nature of polity—one, despotic arbitrary and tyrannous, and the other, liberal and democratic.[29] The idea of a constitutional government did not form a part of pre-colonial polity and hence 'the voice of the people', as Sayyid Ahmad Khan said, 'was not listened to'.[30]

While liberalism formed the criterion for rejecting the pre-colonial system, colonial rule was welcomed for the same reason, for colonialism was seen as a carrier of liberal, democratic and constitutional principles as well as of social and scientific knowledge.[31]

Mill, Spencer, Rousseau and Tom Paine were heady wine for 'Young India', who envisioned the political future of their society on the lines adumbrated by these thinkers. The Indian intellectuals believed that these principles were best embodied in the political system then prevailing in Britain. More importantly, Britain was viewed as the champion of these principles: 'A nation of people not only blessed with the enjoyment of civil and political liberty but [who] also interest themselves in promoting liberty and social happiness, as well as free inquiry into literary and religious subjects among those nations to which their influence extends.'[32]

A bourgeois order was therefore believed to be the logical outcome of British rule. It was this conviction about the political process that informed the public endeavours of Indian intellectuals. Rammohun's protest against the Press Regulation and Dadabhai Naoroji's characterization of colonial rule as un-British were expressions of these premises. In their appeal to the Supreme Court Rammohun and his co-petitioners pointed out that

> the inhabitants of Calcutta would be no longer justified in boasting, that they are fortunately placed by providence under the protection of the whole British Nation, or that the King of England and his Lords and Commons are their Legislators, and they are secured in

---

[29] Ghose (ed.), *The English Works of Raja Rammohun Roy*, p. 234; *The Bengal Spectator*, May 1842; *Bombay Times*, 12 June 1838.

[30] Shan Mohammad (ed.), *Writings and Speeches of Sri Sayyid Ahmad Khan*, Bombay, 1972, p. 117.

[31] 'Discussion in Ahmednagar Debating Society', *Bombay Gazette*, 1 February and 23 February 1855.

[32] Ghose (ed.), *The English Works of Raja Rammohun Roy*, p. 284.

the enjoyment of the same civil and religious privilege that every Briton is entitled to in England.[33]

In the sphere of the economy and society too the changes envisaged were firmly within a bourgeois perspective. The basic assumption of economic thinking, even when anchored on opposition to colonial exploitation, was the development of a capitalist order. The critique of the revenue administration and the system of inheritance which facilitated fragmentation of property and hence hampered accumulation of capital, the emphasis on import of capital and technology, the opposition to drain of wealth and export of raw material, and a passionate commitment to industrialization were all part of a bourgeois vision. Although most of these ideas developed as a critique of colonialism, their inherent ideological and class character were quite evident.

The influence of liberal–democratic premises was also manifest in social thought and action which by and large remained within the parameters of bourgeois humanism. The main thrust of the efforts at social and religious regeneration was to create a new ethos which would complement the emerging bourgeois order. The 'refined individuals, refined homes and refined society' that the reform movements sought to create reflected this new ethos. Behind the attempts to oppose oppressive social institutions, to abolish social practices which militated against human dignity and to deny the monopoly of scriptural knowledge to priests by making the scriptures easily available and by simplifying rituals, lay the forces of fundamental change occurring in Indian society. Mahadev Govind Ranade summed up the main features of these changes: 'The changes we should all seek is thus change from constraint to freedom, from credulity to faith, from status to contract, from authority to reason, from unorganized to organized life, from bigotry to toleration, from blind fatalism to a sense of human dignity.'[34]

If Ranade's conception of change is read in the context of the general socio-economic ideas which underlined thrift and economy, individual liberty and enterprise, and change from otherworldliness to the pleasures of worldly existence, the unmistakable urge for

[33] Ibid., p. 442.
[34] M.G. Ranade, *The Miscellaneous Writings,* Bombay, 1915, p. 116.

creating the ideological superstructure of a bourgeois society can be seen.

Two aspects of the humanist ideas that developed in colonial India would help to emphasize further the bourgeois premises of the intellectual community. First, there was a shift of emphasis from otherworldliness and supernaturalism to the problems of worldly existence in religious thought. The religious protest and reform movements during the pre-colonial period—beginning with Buddhism to the heterodox sects in the eighteenth century—were invariably concerned with the ways and means of salvation. In contrast, religious reform in colonial India was almost indifferent to this earlier preoccupation. More important, even those who assigned a dominant role to religion, like Bankim Chandra Chatterji and Vivekananda, were not indifferent to the needs of material existence over religious demands.[35] Vivekananda, the high priest of neo-Hinduism, consistently tried to make spirituality take cognizance of material needs.[36]

Integral to this shift of focus from otherworldliness was the civil use of religion. The interpretation of religious scriptures and personalities so as to serve contemporary social and political needs and the invocation of religious ideas to eradicate institutions incompatible with social progress were part of this pragmatic function. Rammohun's and Vidyasagar's appeal to Vedic sanction for the emancipation of women, Keshub Chandra Sen's application of monotheism to construct a casteless society, Bankim's interpretation of Krishna, and Tilak's reading of the *Gita* are examples. To illustrate, Keshub Chandra Sen's prescription for a casteless society reads as follows:

> To believe in the fatherhood of God is to believe in the brotherhood of man; and whoever, therefore, in his own heart and in his own house worships the True god daily must learn to recognize all his fellow countrymen as brethren. Caste would vanish in such a state of society.[37]

---

[35] Bankim posed this question rather dramatically: 'How could there be religion, if people did not get two meals a day?'

[36] Swami Vivekananda, *The Complete Works*, Vol. IV, Calcutta, 1971, p. 362.

[37] P.S. Basu (ed.), *Life and Works of Brahmananda Keshav*, Calcutta, 1940, p. 142.

The above perspective, relatively indifferent to the problems of soul and salvation and at the same time responsive to the immediate, was indicative of a new ethos, seeking to release the individual from the various bonds which restricted his freedom of action. By questioning religious superstition and priestly control, associated with the quest for salvation, it paved the way for the restoration of human dignity and the development of individualism.

The second area in which humanism found expression was in an enquiry into the nature of inequality and its consequences, particularly, poverty and human suffering. Akshay Kumar Dutt, an ardent rationalist and a pathfinder in many ways, was perhaps the first to devote attention to this problem. He tried to demonstrate that poverty was caused by the appropriation of the fruits of labour of one section of society by another.[38] Keshub Chandra Sen went a step further in his powerful essay, significantly entitled 'Men of Conse-quence', in which he argued that wealth was created by the poor classes, but enjoyed by the rich. Addressing the poor, whom he described as 'men of consequence', he exhorted them to act in their self-interest:

> Those of you who are farmers or artisans, do you unite and stand up. Exert yourselves to the utmost to improve your condition, to forcibly stop outrage, cruelty and oppression to the tenantry . . . sleep no more. It is time, wake up. No one is there to speak for you.[39]

A more complex exposition of inequality was undertaken by Bankim in his essay, *Samya,* which is a milestone in the intellectual history of modern India. Drawing upon a variety of sources—Rousseau, Proudhon and Mill, on the one hand, and Louis Blanc, Robert Owen and Saint Simon, on the other—Bankim set out to locate the causes of inequality and the nature of its manifestation in Indian society. He accepted and justified inequality based on natural differences, but considered inequality engendered by unnatural dif-ferences 'unjust and harmful' to mankind.[40] In the Indian context he

---

[38] B.B. Majumdar, *History of Indian Social and Political Ideas,* Calcutta, 1967, p. 74.

[39] Basu (ed.), *Life and Works of Brahmananda Keshav,* p. 277.

[40] Bankim Chandra Chatterji, *Samya,* in M.K. Haldar, *Renaissance and Re-action in Nineteenth Century Bengal,* Calcutta, 1977, p. 166.

identified three kinds of unnatural inequality: between the brahmin and the sudra, between the foreigner and the Indian, and above all, between the rich and the poor. These unnatural inequalities were considered responsible for India's social backwardness and retrogression.[41] After elucidating his rather radical views on inheritance of property, emancipation of women and exploitation of peasantry, Bankim's conclusion was as follows:

> We do not intend to give such explications of egalitarianism as would imply that all men should be in the same condition. That can never be. Where there is a natural difference in intelligence mental powers, education, strength, etc., there will be differences in conditions—no one will be willing to resist this. But the equality of rights is necessary. If one has the power, he should not be disappointed on the plea that he has no right.[42]

Despite the rhetoric in favour of the poor, the general critique of inequality and poverty was enclosed within a bourgeois perspective, for it was more concerned with ways to reinforce the system which generated inequality, rather than transforming it. However, the misery of the common man was rhetorically described and graphically detailed; remedy was sought in either enlightenment or class compromise. For instance, after exhorting the peasants and workers to rise in self-defence, Keshub Chandra Sen offered the following remedy:

> In advanced countries there has already begun a class war. . . . We do not desire that the Proletarians should commit outrages. But we do certainly wish that they should without committing unlawful deeds bring the land-owners to their senses. . . . Did not god equip you with consciousness and understanding when he created you? Why then do you continue in ignorant slumber. . . . Exert yourselves; put forth effort; receive enlightenment.[43]

---

[41] B.N. Ganguly, *Concept of Equality: The Nineteenth Century Indian Debate,* Simla, 1975, pp. 94–95.

[42] Bankim Chandra Chatterji, *Samya,* in Haldar (ed.), *Renaissance and Reaction in Bengal,* p. 203. This is an almost exact formulation of Voltaire and Voltairian liberals; see Ganguli, *Concept of Equality,* p.102

[43] Basu (ed.), *Life and Works of Brahmananda Keshav,* p. 277.

Similarly, Vivekananda, despite his vision of the future as belonging
to the sudras and identifying God with the poor, repeatedly came
back to the acquisition of knowledge and spiritual enlightment as
the solution to poverty.[44] The radical sections of *Samya,* particularly
those on peasant exploitation, were deleted by Bankim in subsequent
editions.

That the intellectuals in colonial India were concerned with
the problem of poverty is in itself not very significant; given the
prevalent conditions, they could not have remained insensitive to it.
What is important, however, is how they viewed this problem:
whether their approach was from the standpoint of the poor or that
of the privileged. Generally, it was the latter; therefore, while poverty
was decried the system and structure which created it was not
denounced. The emphasis was on amelioration and trusteeship and
on providing opportunities to the poor to improve their condition, as
otherwise the privileged themselves would be adversely affected.
Such sentiments in different forms can be traced in the social thought
of almost every intellectual in nineteenth-century India. Akshay
Kumar's *Dharamniti,* although part of a plea for organic growth in
society, quite explicitly pointed out the adverse effects of poverty on
the privileged.[45] This class partisan perspective, among others, indicated the bourgeois ideological hegemony over the intellectuals in
colonial India.

The bourgeois–liberal premises had no direct correlation
with the nature of the formative influences. Neither were the English-
educated the exclusive carriers of this ideology; the vernacular-
educated did not fall outside the pale of its influence.[46] The different
strategies for social change, like 'reform' and 'revival', were also
enclosed within the same ideological spectrum. Thus, a 'reformist'
Rammohun Roy and a 'conservative' Radhakanta Deb, or a rationalist Akshay Kumar Dutt and a 'revivalist' Dayanand Saraswati, or an
English-educated Ranade and a vernacular-educated Narayana Guru,

---

[44] Vivekananda, *The Complete Works,* Vol. II, pp. 362–63, 460–69; Vol. V,
pp. 222–23.

[45] Majumdar, *History of Indian Social and Political Ideas,* p. 67.

[46] For a discussion of formative influence on Indian intellectuals and their
social implications, see the chapter titled 'Historiographical and Conceptual Questions' in this volume.

had broad areas of agreement over several issues of the ideological and structural transformation of society. This was because they were all ideologues of a developing bourgeois order and their social and political premises were liberal–democratic. In course of time, the liberal intelligentsia played an active role in the reproduction of bourgeois ideology and its eventual hegemony.

Despite the historical antecedent of a bourgeois society in the west, the social transformation envisaged in India was not a replication of the western model, divorced from the cultural specificity of the Indian civilization. The cultural tradition, on the other hand, became an important factor in the intellectual transformation of colonial society.

Culture and Intellectual Transformation

The relationship between the indigenous cultural tradition and intellectual transformation in colonial India was mediated by a process of acculturation, taking place through the active intervention of state institutions, voluntary organizations and religious orders. It was not, therefore, an organic relationship, based on uninterrupted interaction. External cultural elements intervened very decisively in this relationship to influence the course and nature of intellectual transformation.

Colonial cultural hegemonization, of which acculturation was an inevitable component, tended to be denigrative of indigenous culture. Therefore the subjected increasingly took to the defence of indigenous institutions and traditional culture. Resurrection of the past, identification of modernity in tradition, an inquiry to establish the superiority of traditional knowledge and achievements—a nativitistic tendency in general—were the chief characteristics of this response. Intellectual transformation was inevitably curbed by this historical necessity, which induced the development of externally stimulated thought, defence of culture and eventually even sectarian perspectives. The areas in which the colonial cultural enterprise met with immediate reaction were religion, language and education.

One of the early expressions of cultural response in colonial India was related to the implication of the colonial presence for the religions of the subjected people. Various legislative measures undertaken by the state which impinged upon the religious sensibilities of the people aroused considerable apprehension. The reaction was particularly sharp against the evangelizing endeavours of Christian missionaries.

Indian society generally favoured fair play in religious matters, so that the different religious denominations enjoyed considerable freedom in projecting the principles of their faith. In fact, theological disputations formed an important component of Indian intellectual quest. Hence the activities of Christian missionaries had gone on for centuries without attracting any serious opposition. An entirely different dimension was introduced, however, during the course of the nineteenth century. Although Christianization was not on the colonial agenda, a nexus between government officials and missionaries came to be established during this period. Within the government a strong lobby favoured encouragement to missionary pursuits, not only as a religious enterprise but also as a possible prop for the permanence of the empire, as they believed that evangelization would help ensure loyalty. The conduct of some of these officials gave the impression that the missionaries were acting in collaboration with the government. The intervention of British officials to ensure the right of converted Christians to use public wells in Bombay, Pune and Ahmednagar,[47] the partiality of officials to missionaries and converts in public disputes[48] and the attempts to introduce a Christian content in education[49] were convincing examples of this connection. Court judgments in which converts were favoured with the custody of their wives and children made even the judiciary look partisan.[50] The colonial system of education itself was viewed as an attempt to indirectly help Christianization.[51] A letter to the editor in the *Bombay*

---

[47] *Bombay Gazette*, 8 April 1857; *Poona Observer*, 17 January, 6 April 1861.

[48] See the chapter 'Historiographical and Conceptual Questions' in this volume.

[49] *Bombay Gazette*, 8 April 1857, and Mehrotra, *The Emergence of the Indian National Congress*, p. 40.

[50] Muhammad Mohar Ali, *The Bengali Reaction to Christian Missionary Activities*, Chittagong, 1965, pp. 101–16.

[51] 'There is not a single book in the English language used in our Indian schools, which does not more or less inculcate the saving truths of the Gospels of Christ. The Hindu student, though nominally secured against a Christianizing education, cannot fail to be influenced by Christianity revealed to his mind through the medium of his textbook.' Kylash Chunder Ghose, *A Brief Memoir of Baboo Durga Churan Banerjee*, Calcutta, 1871,

Gazette clearly underlined the connection between the government and the missionaries.

> It is better to have an open enemy than one under the garb of friendship. In fact the English Government acts in the latter capacity with its subjects. It superficially claims against any sort of interference in religious matters, and inwardly assists its cause with a persecuting spirit. A few years back no missionary could dare entice a lad underage to Christianity, but this is done with perfect impunity now-a-days, with the assistance of the police.[52]

In the light of this link with the government, the Christian missionaries came to be looked upon as propagandists who denigrated indigenous culture as part of a design to undermine, if not destroy, existing religious beliefs in order to facilitate conversion to Christianity. This inevitably led to virulent opposition to missionary propaganda and activities as well as a defence of indigenous culture and institutions. Muthukutty Swami in Tamil Nadu, Debendranath Tagore in Bengal, Vishnubawa Brahmachari in Maharashtra, Makti Tangal in Kerala and a large number of relatively unknown social activists in various parts of the country gave expression to this cultural quest.

The initial response was to disprove the missionary propaganda at the religious plane first, by pointing out its fallacy in relation to Christian doctrines themselves and second, by highlighting the religious truths contained either in Hinduism or Islam. In Bengal the initiative was taken by the Tattwabodhini Sabha under the leadership of Debendranath Tagore and Akshay Kumar Dutt. The vigorous campaign mounted by its members against the missionaries was so effective that Alexander Duff described the Sabha as 'the grand counter antagonist of an aggressive Christianity'.[53] The members of the Sabha undertook clarification and defence of the basic tenets of

---

p. 4.

[52] *Bombay Gazette,* 8 April 1857.

[53] For a study of the ideas and attitudes of the Tattwabodhini Sabha see Arundhati Mukhopadhyaya, 'Attitudes towards Religion and Culture in Nineteenth Century Bengal: Tattwabodhini Sabha, 1839–59', in K.N. Panikkar (ed.), *Studies in History,* Special Number on 'Intellectual History

Hinduism by publishing several pamphlets, of which the most important and influential was 'Vaidantic Doctrines Vindicated'.[54]

The missionary propaganda against Hinduism drew equally strong reaction in Maharashtra. John Wilson's interpretations of Hindu theology and religious practices did not go unchallenged and several tracts were written to highlight the distortions contained in them and to convey the real essence of Hinduism as propounded by the *shastras*. A society was formed and a monthly journal started in Bombay for the defence of Hinduism.[55]

Vishnubawa Brahmachari, a brahmin ascetic, author of 'An Essay on Beneficient Government' which has been hailed as a project for the establishment of a casteless and classless society, tried to create a more popular base to this religious response. Every Saturday evening he held lectures and discussions at Chowpatty which attracted very large audiences. Reporting on one of his meetings, the *Bombay Gazette* noted that 'the place was densely thronged, not, as one might suppose, by old Hindus, but by the more enlightened and awakened classes of the community'.[56] In these lectures he referred to the attacks made upon Hinduism by the Christian missionaries, to the existence of mission schools, to the defections that had taken place, the ignorance of their own religion among Hindus, their consequent inability to defend it when it was assailed, and then demonstrated evidence to defend it against arguments that were made against it. He distinguished between knowledge of the arts and sciences and of God. While conceding the superiority of European knowledge in the former, Hinduism was projected as the true religion, superior to Christianity.[57] Later he systematized his ideas and arguments in a book entitled *Vodokta Dharma Prakasa,* published in 1859.[58]

Vishnubawa's campaign created a stir in Bombay and the missionaries sought to refute his arguments through public discourses, pamphlets and articles in newspapers. The American

---

of Colonial India', Vol. 3, No. 1, January–June 1987.

[54] Dilip Kumar biswas, 'Maharshi Debendranath Tagore and the Tattwabodhini Sabha', in Atulchandra Gupta (ed.), *Studies in the Bengal Renaissance,* Jadavpur, 1958, p. 41. Also, *Tattwobodhini Patrika,* Phalgun, Saka 1766, No. 19 and Chaitra, Saka 1766, No. 20

[55] *Bombay Gazette,* 9 May, 26 July and 23 December 1851.

[56] *Bombay Gazette,* 6 October 1856.

[57] Ibid.

missions published a book entitled *Discussions on the Seaside* to si-
lence the Bawa.[59] In open debates, however, the Hindu audiences
carried with them the impression that the missionaries were no match
for the Bawa and that they had no answers to his arguments.[60]

The reaction in other communities was almost similar. Haji
Muhammad Hashim, Makti Tangal and several others rose to the
defence of the Islamic faith.[61] Makti Tangal travelled throughout
Kerala to counter the missionary propaganda and to educate Muslims about the real nature of their religious faith.

The cultural defence implicit in the religious response embraced almost all spheres of culture during the course of the nineteenth
century, particularly during its latter half when the consequences of
the colonial cultural intrusion was more strongly felt. It was expressed
in two ways: first, the creation of an alternative to colonial cultural
practices, and second, the revitalization of traditional institutions.
While concern about education and language underlined the former,
inquiry into traditional knowledge and an effort to translate it into
contemporary practice formed a part of the latter.

The ideas on education held by Indian intellectuals were
qualitatively different in their basic premises and purpose from those
of the colonial system.[62] An important dimension of these ideas was
sensitivity to the cultural implications of colonial education with
English as the medium of instruction. The influence of colonial
education which drew upon the elements of an alien culture and upon
the historical experience of a different civilization was primarily
denationalizing, as it alienated the members of the educated middle
class from their cultural moorings and made them 'blindly imitate
what others have done'.[63] This was not conducive to cultivation of the
mind and therefore was a stumbling block in the way of national
progress. An essay on 'The Present Condition of Education', published

---

[58] Majumdar, *History of Indian Social and Political Ideas*, p. 206.
[59] *Bombay Gazette*, 31 October 1857.
[60] *Bombay Gazette*, 1 and 22 October 1856.
[61] *The Oriental Christian Spectator*, May 1833, and K.K. Muhamad Abdul
   Kareem (ed.), *Makti Tangalude Sampurna Kritikal* (Malayalam), Tirur, 1981.
[62] For a discussion of these ideas see K.N. Panikkar, Presidential Address,
   Modern Indian History Section, *Indian History Congress Proceedings*, 1975.
[63] *Tattwabodhini Patrika*, Agrahayan, Saka 1798, No. 440. Also *Somprakash*,
   Kartik 16, Bikram Samvat 1293, and *Bengal Spectator*, Vol. 1, June 1842,

in *Tattwabodhini Patrika,* was representative of this widely shared sentiment:

> Our faculties would have developed freely and our national progress would have commenced, if our thoughts were not influenced by English. The books that are being prescribed in the schools and colleges are completely devoid of any national feeling. . . . The books on ancient Indian history are written by foreigners who are biased towards their own race and therefore unnecessarily criticize the people of this country. The students who study these books hardly learn about their real past.[64]

The effort to develop and enrich the vernacular languages was a part of this national–cultural perspective. One of the reasons cited for the backwardness of this country and its 'present degraded condition' was the neglect of the vernacular languages and the lack of knowledge in them.[65] That Indians would not be able to realize their intellectual and creative potential unless instructed in the mother-tongue was a widely held conviction.[66] Enrichment of the vernaculars was therefore undertaken as a cultural project to counter the 'baneful influences' of English education.

The emphasis on the vernacular represented an attempt to redirect attention from the progressive qualities attributed to various components of the colonial cultural complex to the elements of indigenous culture, seen as being crucial to socio-political advancement. An inquiry into the inherent qualities of traditional institutions, which was not devoid of glorification and romanticization, was integral to this attempt. Knowledge about the past produced by Asiatic researches, though conducted in 'obscurely organized

pp. 42–44.
[64] *Tattwabodhini Patrika,* Magh, Saka 1798, No. 402. For a discussion of cultural bias in English textbooks see *Bengal Spectator,* Vol. II, 24 October 1843, pp. 4–5.
[65] Uday Chandra Adhya, A Proposal for the Proper Cultivation of the Bengali Language and its Necessity for the Natives of this Country', in Gautam Chattopadhyay (ed.), *Awakening in Bengal in the Nineteenth Century,* Calcutta, 1965, p. 26.
[66] *Hindu Intelligencer,* 9 January 1854; *The Reformer,* 24 March 1833; *Tattwabodhini Patrika,* Shrawan, Saka 1770, No. 61; and *Somprakash,*

political circumstances',[67] opened up possibilities. The Tattwabodhini Sabha promoted inquiry into Indian history and culture, with a perspective different from that of the orientalists. Its aim was to demonstrate how 'India was a symbol of righteousness and greatness and among all countrymen Hindus were given a superior position'.[68] Rajendralal Mitra and Bhudev Mukherjee in Bengal, Vishnu Shastri Pandit and Vishnu Narayan Mandalik in Maharashtra, Dayanand Saraswati and Pandit Guru Datt in Punjab, and several others in various parts of the country pursued this ideal.

Strongly influenced by 'nativism', this cultural defence was a complex phenomenon. It was not just an attempt at religious revival and glorification, but an intellectual inquiry into the past, embracing almost every field of social, cultural and political endeavour: the Indian system of medicine, the potentialities of pre-colonial technology, Indian music, Hindu drama, the political system, the condition of women, and so on. The attempt was to prove Indian superiority in all these fields and thus to suggest that the present was not an index of what Indians were capable of. Implicit in this was the assumption that regeneration and restructuring of the existing cultural complex were necessary pre-requisites for the realization of this potential.[69] Hence the Indian mind increasingly turned inward.

The manner in which culture and ideology thus came into play engendered a contradiction in the nature of intellectual transformation in colonial India. The dual character of the cultural struggle, inevitably brought about by the colonial presence, impinged upon the construction of a vision fully incorporating either the bourgeois ideology or traditional culture. Uninhibited interaction between the two was also negated by the mediation of colonial culture. The intellectual transformation of colonial society reflected the ambiguities and contradictions inherent in this historical process.

Badra 12, Bikram Samvat 1271, No. 43.

[67] Edward W. Said, *Orientalism*, London, 1978, p. 10.

[68] *Tattwabodhini Patrika*, Jaishta, Saka 1770, No. 58.

[69] Bhudev Mukherjee, *Achar Prabhanda* (Bengali), Hugli, Bikram Samvat 1301, p. 3.

5 Search for Alternatives: Meaning of the Past in Colonial India

The past figured prominently in the quest for modernization in colonial India, be it of the coloniser or of the indigenous elite. What constituted the past or how it would influence the modernizing process was difficult to determine; yet, the need to confront the past was compelling. For, without being sensitive to the past, no effective social intervention was possible in a society that was heir to a long cultural tradition. The intellectual quest in colonial India, engaged in an enquiry into the meaning of the past and thus in an assessment of its relevance to contemporary society, was an outcome of this awareness. Although articulated differently at different points of time, introspection into the essence of tradition was a common feature. This chapter is concerned with the implications of this introspection for the struggle for hegemony in colonial India.

Colonial Construction of the Past

The context in which Indian intellectuals interrogated the past was created by colonial intervention and the path of 'progress' that it charted for Indian society. Confronted by one of the oldest civilizations in human history, the colonial rulers could hardly ignore its past. Intellectual curiosity apart, the sheer compulsions of rule dictated the need to contend with the past. The colonial concern with the past, however, was not merely an exercise in 'knowing', it was an effort in constructing it anew as well.

A corpus of literature, beginning with the reports of the commissions entrusted with the task of enquiring into the conditions of the conquered territories, to the innumerable histories of India and its regions penned by colonial administrators, and the memoirs and travelogues recorded by unofficial Englishmen, constructed, *inter alia*, the history and tradition of the colonised. The 'native' society and its past thus constructed by colonial rule and its ideologues were substantially different from what the 'natives' knew about themselves. This construction not only provided the rationale for colonial social engineering, but also laid the ground for a colonial perception of the self by the 'natives'.

The colonial construction was informed by a comparison between the history of the coloniser and the colonised. The 'native' obviously suffered in comparison, despite the orientalist admiration for the ancient Indian civilization. Even the orientalists seem to have been impressed more by its simplicity than its achievements. After all, William Jones attributed his excitement on approaching the shores of India to its inhabitants being the closest to nature! In a sense, philosophical and pragmatic differences notwithstanding, colonialism had an overarching view of the native past which in all accounts was inferior to its own. The past, however, was a surrogate for the present. What colonialism did through the construction of the past was to justify and legitimize the present.

The nexus between the past and the present in colonial practice was evident in the rationale sought for administrative actions. Nothing illustrates this better than the changing interpretation of proprietorship in land. For instance, when the British took over Malabar in 1792 from the Sultan of Mysore, past practice was invoked to invest the landlords with proprietorship, as they were then conceived as the natural leaders of society and as a possible social base of colonial rule.[1] This view remained in force till the last quarter of the nineteenth century when, troubled by recurring peasant uprisings, the colonial state was forced to revise its earlier notion about the position of the landlord. Whether the officials had erred initially in their assessment of customary practices was subjected to close scrutiny. The consequent proposal to alter the existing land relations drew upon evidence from the past to rectify the mistake.[2] The reading of the past thus influenced administrative practice, though constructed differently each time, to suit the changing needs.

[1] C.A. Innes and F.B. Evans, *Malabar*, Madras, 1951, p. 307.
[2] William Logan, *Report of the Malabar Special Commission*, Vol. I, Madras, 1882. Also see K.N. Panikkar, *Against Lord and State*, Delhi, 1989, p. 106.

What was central to the colonial attitude towards the native past, however, was not appropriation, but the denial of a valid history to the colonised. One of the many examples of this wilful denial is the myth of a changeless Indian society initially propagated by colonial administrators and later authenticated by imperialist historians.

Bankim Chandra Chatterji who was the first to propose an agenda for an Indian historiography drew attention to this:

> In our opinion there is not a single work in English that is a true history of Bengal. What has been written is not the history of Bengal, not even the merest fragment of it. It has nothing at all to do with the history of the Bengal nation in it. A Bengali who accepts this kind of writing as the history of Bengal is not a true Bengali.[3]

By the time Bankim warned his countrymen about colonially constructed history, it had already become part of the intellectual make-up of the educated middle class. James Mill's periodization of Indian history, Marshman's description of social customs, Henry Beveridge's account of religious practices, and Robert Orme's explanation for the British military success had become integral to middle-class vocabulary. The Indian intelligentsia thus viewed its own history through the colonial prism.

Examples of the Indian intelligentsia's internalization of colonised history and its dissemination are many. One obvious fall-out was the concept of 'divine dispensation' used by the intelligentsia for rationalizing the colonial conquest.[4] According to this concept, what occasioned God to will British conquest was the pre-colonial past, characterized by social degradation, religious superstition and political anarchy. This recurring theme, advanced in colonial historiography as the justification for conquest, also became the guilt-ridden intelligentsia's rationale for their own subjection.

A more specific instance may be cited for elucidation—the influence of James Mill's multi-volume *History of British India*. Going

---

[3] Quoted in Ranajit Guha, *An Indian Historiography of India: A Nineteenth Century Agenda and Its Implications*, Calcutta, 1988.

[4] For an elaboration of the notion of 'divine dispensation' see the chapter titled 'An Overview' in this volume.

far beyond its title, it attempted an estimate of the Hindu and Muslim civilizations and indulged in a sweeping condemnation of Indian history. Used as a textbook at Haileybury College where the East India Company's civil servants were trained, Mill's *History* had an abiding influence on British administrators in India. Hayman Wilson who edited and updated Mill's *History* in 1844 observed:

> In the effects which Mill's *History* is likely to exercise upon the connection between the people of England and the people of India . . . its tendency is evil: it is calculated to destroy all sympathy between the ruler and the ruled; to preoccupy the minds of those who issue annually from Great Britain to monopolize the post of honour and power in Hindustan, with an unfounded aversion towards those over whom they exercise that power. . . . There is reason to fear that a harsh and illiberal spirit has of late years prevailed in the conduct and councils of the rising service in India which owes its origin to impressions imbibed in early life from the *History* of Mr Mill.[5]

Mill's influence was not limited to the Company's administrators; the Indian intelligentsia also fell victim to Mill's *History*. For quite some time the intelligentsia's notions of pre-colonial political institutions and social organization were derived from Mill. Rammohun Roy has used almost the same vocabulary as that of Mill to describe the despotism of Indian rulers.[6]

An idea which persisted for long was Mill's periodization of Indian history in terms of Hindu and Muslim civilizations. Emphasizing the separateness of each of those periods the periodization led to a communal view of India's past, as it assumed that the separateness was innate to Indian society and that it began with the coming of the Muslims to India, terminating the earlier 'glorious' period of Hindu rule. It also 'encouraged the notion of distinct religious communities which were projected as the units of Indian society for political and

---

[5] C.H. Philips, 'James Mill, Mountstuart Elphistone, and the History of India', in C.H. Philips (ed.), *Historians of India, Pakistan and Ceylon*, London, 1961, pp. 225–26.

[6] J.C. Ghose (ed.), *The English Works of Raja Rammohun Roy*, Allahabad, 1906, p. 234.

socio-legal purposes'.[7] Its effects are still to be seen in contemporary India in terms of providing substance to communal ideologies.

Retrieving History

Given the colonial expropriation of India's historical past, retrieval of history became an important aspect of the anti-colonial agenda. Initially the retrieval was not manifested in a consciously constructed alternate historiography, but as an integral part of the modernizing social movements in the nineteenth century. An alternate historical construction of the past questioning the premises of colonial historiography took a long time to mature, and when it did occur it was more in the nature of a nationalist reaction which sought to establish either parity with or superiority over the west.

The intellectual and social movements of the pre-nationalist phase contended with the past in a different manner. The main thrust of these movements being the transformation of the present, the question of continuity and break with tradition became a contentious issue. To what extent can the present be different from the past and what are the elements of tradition which should persist in the present? There was no consensual view on this question, not even within the same social movement. Therefore, internal schisms developed as in the case of two major socio-religious movements of the nineteenth century, the Brahmo Samaj and the Arya Samaj.[8]

Debates within the modernizing movements on the meaning of history revolved around what constituted the authentic tradition. There was hardly any social issue in which the question of past practice, and scriptural sanction for it, did not become a matter of dispute. At the time of abolition of sati in 1829, and later during the campaign for widow marriage and for raising the age of consent, both the supporters and opponents of change invoked the past in defence of their positions. In the case of sati, while Rammohun drew upon the Hindu scriptures to justify reform, his opponents invoked the same

---

[7] Romila Thapar, 'Communalism and the Historical Legacy: Some Facets', in K.N. Panikkar (ed.), *Communalism in India: History, Politics and Culture*, New Delhi, 1991, p. 19.

[8] See for details Shivanath Shastri, *History of Brahmo Samaj,* and Kenneth W. Jones, *Arya Dharma*, Berkeley, 1976.

sources to maintain the status quo.[9] Both were seeking to establish continuity with the past and thus to use the past as a legitimizing force.

Whether invoked by the supporters of change or of the status quo, the debate over the past had two characteristics. First, it was qualitatively different from the colonial construction of history. Neither of them, unlike the colonial ideologues, was engaged in expropriating the past; on the contrary, they were exploring its strength, establishing its authenticity. Second, the conception of tradition was brahminical and textual, seeking to invent homogeneous traditions applicable to all Hindus. During the debate over sati the arguments about scriptural sanction appeared to gain precedence over the issue for which the past was being invoked. This emphasis on the scriptures led a scholar to remark: 'Tradition was not the ground on which the status of women was being contested. Rather the reverse was true: women in fact became the site on which tradition was debated and reformulated. What was at stake was not women but tradition.'[10]

What constituted the authentic tradition was indeed central to the debate. Yet, the debate was spurred not by concern with the past, but by the condition of the present. The aim was not the revival of tradition; tradition was invoked only for instrumentalist and pragmatic reasons.

The second feature of the debate, the brahminical–textual view of tradition, overlooked the existence of multiple traditions even among followers of Hinduism. A majority of the Hindus were outside 'the great tradition' which in essence was ideology of upper-caste domination. The construction of scripture-based Hinduism by upper-caste reformers during the colonial period was in effect an attempt to universalize the brahminical tradition. At the same time, a search for traditions outside the brahminical and the textual and an attempt to forge movements of reform within them, distinct from the upper-caste movements, were also afoot. The movements initiated by Narayana Guru in Keralam, Jotiba Phule in Maharashtra, and

---

[9] Ghose (ed.), *The English Works of Raja Rammohun Roy*, pp. 321–65.
[10] Lata Mani, 'Contentious Traditions: The Debate on Sati inColonial India', in Kumkum Sangari and Sudesh Vaid (eds.), *Recasting Women*, New Delhi, 1989, p. 118.

Ramaswami Naicker in Tamil Nadu were indicative of this trend. Rejecting the upper-caste literate tradition, they tried to create social and religious practices without seeking legitimacy from brahminical scriptures. Narayana Guru, an untouchable, himself consecrated idols in the temples he set up without performing rituals. By doing so he not only challenged the brahminical tradition, but also contributed to the subversion of the upper-caste religious ideology. At the time of the first consecration he just picked up a stone from a nearby stream and installed it as the idol; subsequently, he used a piece of mirror as the object of worship.[11] Although a champion of the universalist idea of 'one god, one religion, one caste', he was sensitive to the cultural implications of the incorporation of lower castes into brahminical modes of worship. That was perhaps the reason why he sought to create new places of worship rather than initiate a movement for the entry of untouchables into upper-caste temples. In fact, his response to the Gandhi-led temple entry movement was lukewarm, almost indifferent.[12]

The search for an authentic tradition also suffered from a religion-centred view. Linked as it was to community-based reform, the conception of the past inevitably revolved around the religious tenets of the community. A 'Hindu' and a 'Muslim' tradition were thus constructed and appropriated. Consequently, the Vedas and the Upanishads became prescriptive texts for the Hindus and the Qoran and the Hadiths for the Muslims. This particularistic tendency continued through the entire colonial period and has gained further ground in contemporary India. The syncretic tradition of the medieval Bhakti movement invoked during the nationalist struggle did not succeed in off-setting the particularistic consciousness. An identity between tradition and religion therefore got embedded in social consciousness.

Alternatives to Liberalism
The search for an authentic tradition, though inward-look-

---

[11] Thomas Samuel, *One Caste, One Religion, One God,* New Delhi, 1977, pp. 49–50.
[12] During the Vaikkom Satyagraha Narayana Guru did visit the satyagraha camp, but did not participate in the satyagraha. His attitude did not betray much enthusiasm for the movement.

ing, also gave rise to the quest for an alternative to the path of development charted by colonial modernization. Social and political change, limited and controlled by colonial needs, was linked with colonial hegemonization. A counter-hegemony therefore needed to rest upon a different notion of progress than the one posited by the 'benevolent' colonial rule. In constructing such a notion the expropriated past became the terrain of enquiry, particularly with a view to realize the potential of traditional institutions and ideas for the transformation of contemporary society. The three decades following the failure of the revolt of 1857 was the period when, through this introspection, Indian intellectuals tried to relate the understanding of their own history to the needs of the present.[13]

In the path to progress presented to the Indian mind by colonial rule, the concept of a liberal polity was the most influential. The political vision of the intelligentsia became so rooted in liberal principles that liberalism became the sole criterion for testing political institutions, be they of colonial rule or of Indian rulers. The hegemonic influence of liberalism was such that the quest for an alternative in the field of political institutions and practices was the least articulated.

Early colonial Indian political thought was set forth either in an exposition of liberal ideas or in a critique of colonial political practice. The latter, though it helped transcend the belief in the theory of divine dispensation, was firmly grounded in liberal principles. However, efforts to seek out different forms of polity and social organization were not altogether wanting in colonial India, as reflected in the treatise on government entitled *Sukhadayaka Rajyapraharani Nibandha* (An Essay on Beneficient Government), written by Vishnubawa Brahmachari in 1867 in Marathi and translated into English in 1869.

Vishnu Bhikaji Gokhale, popularly known as Vishnubawa Brahmachari, was born in 1825 in a Konkanastha brahmin family in Thane district of Bombay Presidency. He did not have the advantage of a proper education, either traditional or modern. After spending a few years in a village school, possibly due to the poverty of his family, he took up a job in the shop of a grain merchant and later with the customs department. He resigned from his job, reportedly in

---

[13] See the chapter titled 'Culture and Ideology' in this volume.

response to divine calling, and retired to the Saptashringiri hills to spend several years as a religious recluse in meditation. Although the details of his intellectual interest are difficult to ascertain, he emerged from the sojourn fairly well-equipped with Hindu religious knowledge and with a determination to propagate and defend *dharma*. After brief visits to different places in western Maharashtra—Sangli, Miraj, Kolhapur, Wai, Satara, Pune and Ahmadnagar—Vishnubawa reached Bombay in 1856, which became the centre of his activities till he died in 1871.[14] Vishnubawa was neither a reformer nor a revivalist in the nineteenth-century mould. Unlike Rammohun and Dayanand, he did not initiate a movement or set up an organization. The imperative of his mission, as aptly stated by Frank Conlon, 'was coloured fundamentally by Christian challenge to Indian religions'.[15]

After the East India Company lifted the ban on missionary activities in 1813, an aggressive and multipronged campaign for evangelization was mounted in Maharashtra. It was no longer limited to street-corner preachings; more abiding propaganda was carried out through newspapers, journals, tracts and school textbooks. The belief that Christianizing India should be part of the colonial agenda found forceful articulation in newspaper columns. The increasing incidence of conversions bore testimony to the success of the missionary efforts.

The Hindu intelligentsia was alarmed by the missionary onslaught. Theological disputation was not alien to them. In fact, it was an integral part of the Indian intellectual tradition. Even with the Christian missionaries, it had gone on for a long time, particularly after the arrival of the Portuguese. What alarmed them now was the possibility of political support to the missionaries and the consequent disadvantage to Hinduism in its defence against Christianity.[16] The Hindu intelligentsia was, therefore, stirred to activity; it submitted memorials against conversions to the government,

---

[14] This life-sketch is based on Frank F. Conlon, 'The Polemic Process in Nineteenth Century Maharashtra: Vishnubawa Brahmachari and Hindu Revival', in Kenneth W. Jones (ed.), *Religious Controversy in British India*, New York, 1992, and B.B. Mazumdar, *History of Indian Social and Political Ideas*, Calcutta. 1967.

[15] Conlon, 'The Polemic Process', p. 11.

[16] See Letters to the Editor, *Bombay Gazette*, 8 April and 15 June 1857.

established societies for the defence of Hinduism, published tracts and journals, and entered into public debate with the missionaries.

Vishnubawa's entry into public life was similarly motivated by the need to counter the missionary efforts to undermine Hinduism and to promote Christian evangelization. Hinduism had already found in Maharashtra defenders like Gangadhar Shastri, Morobhat Dandekar and Lakshman Shastri. They publicly disputed the missionary propaganda and published tracts in vindication of Hinduism.[17] But the 'counter attack against Christian doctrines' unleashed by Vishnubawa in a series of lectures was the most effective.[18] The *Bombay Guardian* reported that 'Hindus, zealous for the honour of their religion . . . hailed his advent with great joy' and that his lecture-hall was 'densely thronged, not by old Hindus, but by the more enlightened and awakened classes of the community'.[19] The popular perception of these lectures was that Vishnubawa, referred to by his followers as the 'hermit', was able to develop the truth of the Hindu faith and 'argumentatively defeat the chaplains of Christianity'.[20]

Vishnubawa's confrontation with the missionaries proved to be a precursor to his intellectual quest to envision an alternative to the then existing political and social order. His ideas in this respect are contained in his seminal work, *Vedokta Dharma Prakasha* (1859) and in the pamphlet *Sukhadayaka Rajyaprakarani Nibandha* (1867).[21]

Sukhadayaka Rajyaprakarani Nibandha, called 'an essay on the right form or constitution of happiness yielding Government' by Vishnubawa, is a landmark in Indian intellectual history. It is divided

---

[17] *Bombay Gazette,* 9 May, 26 July and 23 December 1851. Also Conlon, 'The Polemic Process', pp. 11–12.

[18] The gist of these lectures was published in the missionary newspaper, *Bombay Guardian,* and later as a tract by George Bowen, entitled *Discussions by the Seaside,* Bombay, 1867.

[19] *Bombay Guardian,* 4 October 1856.

[20] *Bombay Gazette,* 1 October 1856.

[21] The essay was translated into English in 1869 by Capt. A. Philip, Deputy Assistant Commissioner General, Aden. The first edition had 10,000 copies. His other writings are *Bhayartha Sindhu* (1856), *Chaturshloki Bagawata Yacha Artha* (1857), *Sahajsthiticha Nibandha* (An Essay on the Natural State) (1868), *Narayanbawakruta Bodha Sagarche Rahasya* (undated), and *Setubandhani Tika* (1890)

into fifteen sections or 'These' and a conclusion titled 'Finis'.[22] Described as 'a specimen of what the Hindu mind would this day be, if there had been no educational work carried on here by the men of the West' and dismissed as a 'Hindu Utopia',[23] it conceptualized the framework of a social and political order which would ensure the necessary production and equitable distribution of agricultural and industrial goods. The object of the essay was to constitute a society in which 'the whole of mankind would be prone, in a disinterested manner, to speak about truth, and to cherish feelings of friendship, humanity, forgiveness, and tranquility, in their intercourse with one another'.[24]

The keywords employed in the essay are family and king Society is conceived as a large family with the king as its head. 'The King of a country should regard the whole of the subjects residing within that country as constituting his own family, and himself, as the sole master of that family of subjects.'[25] The subjects, on their part, should submit to 'the righteous King a respectful assurance that they would be loyal and prompt to execute his orders'.[26] The duty of the king was to ensure the material and spiritual well-being of his subjects. Society would thus function on the principle of mutual cooperation of the ruler and the ruled.

The responsibility for the production and distribution of food, clothes and other necessities of life devolved on the king. He 'should consider the whole of the land in his charge, as constituting one garden, and should therefore do all that is necessary, to the best of his powers, to make the said garden, that is the country, yield as much as may be sufficient to the said family of subjects.'[27]

In order to ensure the continuous cultivation of this land by the 'governed', he should also construct embankments across rivers as well as reservoirs and tanks.[28] The king was also expected to set up manufactories for the production of clothes, ornaments and other necessary products. These were recognized as specialized areas of

[22] *Essay on Beneficient Government,* Bombay, 1869, p. 2.
[23] *Bombay Guardian,* 18 May 1867.
[24] *Essay on Beneficient Government,* p. 3.
[25] Ibid.
[26] Ibid.
[27] Ibid., p. 4.
[28] Ibid., p. 13.

work which could be undertaken only by those with training and expertise, for which educational establishments were envisaged, to be provided for by the king.[29]

The system of production and distribution was conceived on the principle of communal ownership. Therefore, land and other means of production were to be jointly owned and all products were to be shared by all members of the society according to individual needs. Everyone, including the king, would 'use the same kind of food but no flesh of any description; the said food being removed from one common mess which should be kept for and consumed by all.' Similarly, a large stock of clothes should be kept at village depots from which 'everyone should be allowed to make cloth of any description as might be agreeable to him'.[30]

The system of production and distribution under the overall control of the king, as envisaged by Vishnubawa, would usher in a society in which people would be provided with all their necessities and luxuries. The best possible food and the most plentiful clothing and ornaments would be at the disposal of the people without any discrimination. They would have ample opportunities for enjoyment: dances, festivals and other amusements. Similarly, palanquins, chariots and horses would be available to everyone for trans-portation.[31]

The outcome of this system would be a harmonious society, 'enemy-free, passionless, and happy quietude'.[32] For, 'the desires and affections of everybody would be fully satisfied, and there would be no cause for ill-will which is produced, when men find that some of their desires remain unfulfilled. No excitement existing, there would be nothing like a grudge likely to draw one to the commission of offences.'[33]

While envisioning a primitive, egalitarian utopia, Vishnubawa was sensitive to at least some of its possible inherent problems. One of them was regarding an acceptable criterion for the distribution of work in a society in which everyone had equal rights and opportunities. Who would, for instance, perform menial jobs like cleaning the

[29] Ibid.
[30] Ibid., p. 4.
[31] Ibid., p. 11.
[32] Ibid., p. 19.
[33] Ibid., p. 11.

prives and spittoons or discharge conservation duties like cleaning
roads? The solution, in Vishnubawa's scheme, was through a recognition of the natural inequality of individuals. 'Men are not', he
argues, 'all endowed with the same kind and extent of taste, and are
consequently not habituated to the performance of the same kind of
duties.'[34] By taking into account these inherent differences in individual
ability the king should groom his subjects to discharge different
duties in society. This, however would not apply to hereditary
professions, as the children of each generation would be trained in the
professions for which they are best suited.[35]

Influence of the Past

Vishnubawa's essay cannot be commended for internal
consistency or logically constructed arguments. It suffers from lack
of elaboration of ideas and a rather simplistic exposition. It also
seems to overlook the complex social relations which had already
come into existence. Obviously his scheme is utopian, even if the idea
is laudable. Yet, it was the manifestation of a quest for a social and
political order different from the hegemonic ideals represented by
colonial rule. In that quest the past was the most important source of
inspiration.

A variety of traditional sources—Vedic *samhitas*, Brahmanas,
Dharmasutras, epics and Bhakti literature—appear to have moulded
the philosophical and socio-political views of Vishnubawa. The
adoption and synthesis of ideas from these sources are evident in his
writings. An eclectic influence of tradition is apparent in the content
as well as in the mode of articulation. A major source of inspiration
was the Vedic *samhitas* from which the central idea of the treatise,
namely, the king as the head of the family, was derived.[36] So too the
method of recruitment and training of people for discharging different
functions in society.[37] The spiritual and religious duties of the king
were conceived on the basis of a combination of the philosophies of

---

[34] Ibid., p. 12.
[35] Ibid.
[36] U.N. Ghoshal, *A History of Indian Political Ideas*, Madras, 1966, p. 149.
[37] Ibid., p. 55.

Vedanta and Bhakti.[38] In *Vedokta Dharma Prakasha*, Vishnubawa has suggested that if speaking truth endangered one's religion, true morality, and the world's and one's own existence, it would be better not to speak at all.[39] This is clearly a paraphrase of Bhishma's statement on truth in the Mahabharata.[40] What is as important in these examples—many more could be cited—is that the idiom of articulation was derived from the indigenous cultural tradition.

Like many others in the nineteenth century who looked inward for charting a path of development, Vishnubawa has also been stamped a revivalist, 'making a plea for a return to the past'.[41] That the past was an important influence on his scheme, and that he looked upon the Vedas as the source of all knowledge, is beyond doubt.[42] Yet, he did not seek to resurrect the past. 'The past', he said, 'has gone, and the future is to come.'[43] He was not looking to replicate the past but to selectively appropriate it. Consequently, he was opposed to several traditional institutions and practices. He was a critic of the caste system, idolatry, untouchability and seclusion of women.[44] He was also severe on the brahmin 'priestly clique' who, he held, were responsible for the worst frauds, namely, the hypocrisies of religion.[45]

Despite Vishnubawa's familiarity with traditional sources of knowledge, he was not reluctant to respond to contemporary developments. He was not opposed to mechanization, even if he advocated a rather primitive mode of social and economic organization. It is paradoxical, but significant, that the railways and telegraph had a

---

[38] 'The King should cause all *Jiwatmas* who are duped by the senses, exist but in mere *Abhawa,* and are however ignorant of themselves, to offer a daily prayer in the following manner to "Parmeshwar", who though omniscient and formless, appears to be the very universe of which their bodies form a part, and is moreover, the image of knowledge itself.' *Essay on Beneficient Government,* p. 5.

[39] N.R. Inamdar, 'Political Thought of Vishnubawa Brahmachari', *Journal of the University of Poona: Humanities Section,* No. 21, 1965, p. 169.

[40] Ghoshal, *A History of Indian Political Ideas,* p. 226.

[41] Inamdar, 'Political Thought of Vishnubawa Brahmachari', p. 169.

[42] 'When you make a study of Vedic religion you find more knowledge because Vedas are knowledge—nothing exists which is not contained in the Vedas'. Quoted in Conlon, 'The Polemic Process', p. 20.

[43] *Essay on Beneficient Government,* p. 16.

[44] Ibid. See Inamdar, 'Political Thought of Vishnubawa Brahmachari', p. 171.

[45] Ibid.

place in his scheme.[46] What he envisioned was culturally specific development of society, not alienated from the past, but not trapped in it either. His concern was not with the past, but with the present.

> That which intervenes between the past and future is the stirlessness which is the Present Time; and until you possess yourselves of the knowledge of said stirless true Present and until you do away with the belief in the passage of the future into the past, by means of that knowledge your beliefs are hollow shadows.[47]

Vishnubawa wrote at a time when a capitalist order was emerging in India under colonial dependency. The capitalist mode was slowly but surely entering different areas of production. Vishnubawa's scheme was an alternative to this new order. So also in the realm of political institutions, as it envisaged a polity totally different from the western liberal model which the Indian intelligentsia was then yearning for. That Vishnubawa's ideas, at that juncture of liberal hegemony, did not enthuse the intelligentsia, is not surprising. But it did indicate, with all its limitations, the intellectual quest for an indigenously rooted path of development. It particularly becomes meaningful in the context of the desperate but unsuccessful effort by post-colonial societies to catch up with the west.

[46] Ibid., p. 4.
[47] Ibid., p. 16.

6 Creating a New Cultural Taste: Reading a Nineteenth-Century Malayalam Novel

Cultural Hegemonization

All over the world, transforming indigenous cultures had been an agenda central to colonial domination. Attempted with a view to ensure the consent of the colonised and distinct from the physical control exercised by military success and territorial conquest, the colonial state and its agencies, both through direct intervention and indirect influence, communicated and reproduced a cultural ideal attractive and powerful enough for the colonial intelligentsia to internalize and in turn disseminate in society. The new cultural situation ushered in by the Spanish in Latin America, the Dutch and the Portuguese in south and south-east Asia and the French and the British in Africa and Asia, was as much a result of the intervention of the ideological apparatuses of the state as of the participation and collaboration of the intelligentsia in the process of colonial hegemonization. Culture and politics were thus integrated, even if the conjunction between the two was not perceived or realized by the colonised.

The cultural engineering, possible only with the effective organization of state institutions, was not undertaken in a hurry. On the contrary, it was a deliberately cautious venture. The officials of the East India Company in India, during the early period of colonial consolidation, were conscious that they had entered an unknown territory, the topography of which they could not ascertain easily.[1]

---

[1] Alexander Dow articulated one dimension of this difficulty. 'Excuses . . . may be found for our ignorance concerning the learning, religion and philosophy of the Brahmins. Literary inquiries are no means a capital object to many of our adventurers in Asia. The few who have a turn for researches

Any attempt at disturbing the existing cultural sensibilities, they feared, might engender violent reaction. Many among them viewed the Revolt of 1857 as a confirmation of this apprehension; the popular uprising, in their perception, was essentially a conservative reaction to colonial cultural intervention.

While engaged in conquest and initial administrative organization, the Company's officials had hardly any time or the opportunity to gain knowledge about the civilization they encountered. The customs, habits, traditions and social institutions of the newly-subjected people remained an enigma to them. Their bewilderment was not only because of the discernible cultural plurality, but also because of the lack of access to knowledge about the subjected. Even to conduct day-to-day administration the officials, not being conversant with the local languages, had to depend upon the 'natives'.[2]

An easy and cautious option exercised by the early colonial administration was to draw upon the pre-colonial institutional structures.[3] Warren Hastings, who was involved in setting up the administrative infrastructure in Bengal, preferred to depend upon the pre-colonial system rather than to revamp it immediately. For instance, in the case of the judiciary he laid down that

> in all suits regarding inheritance, marriage, caste and other usages and institutions, the laws of the *Koran* with respect to Mahomedans and those of the *Shastras* with respect to Gentoos shall be invariably adhered to; on all such occasions the *moulavis* or Brahmins shall respectively attend to expound the law, and they shall sign the report and assist in passing the decree.[4]

Preliminary to the setting up of the administrative structure and formulating the methods of appropriating the surplus, the East

---

of the kind, are discouraged by the very great difficulty in acquiring that language in which the learning of the Hindus contained, or by that impenetrable veil of mystery with which the Brahmins industriously cover their religious tenets and philosophy.' Quoted in O.P. Kejariwal, *The Asiatic Society of Bengal and the Discovery of India's Past*, Delhi, 1988, p. 20.

[2] R.E. Frykenberg, *Guntur, 1788–1848*, Oxford, 1965.

[3] B.B. Misra, *Central Administration of the English East India Company*, Manchester, 1959.

[4] Kejariwal, *The Asiatic Society of Bengal*, p. 23.

India Company ascertained the resources of the conquered territories through enquiries into their historical, moral and material conditions. These enquiries were not just an exercise in assessing resources for revenue purposes. In fact, they marked the beginning of the collection of cultural and ethnographic data which later became the knowledge base for the formulation of colonial policy. In doing so, the colonial state and its agencies both promoted and appropriated indigenous knowledge which substantially contributed to the political task of manufacturing consent.

> Every accumulation of knowledge [wrote Warren Hastings] and especially such as is obtained by social communication with people over whom we exercise a dominion founded on the right of conquest, is useful to the state . . . it attracts and conciliates distant affections; it lessens the weight of the chain by which the natives are held in subjection; and it imprints on the heart of our own countrymen the sense and obligation of benevolence.[5]

What was suggested by Warren Hastings was actively pursued during the course of the late eighteenth and early nineteenth centuries by the Company's administration, by bringing to life a network of cultural institutions and practices which would ensure easy accessibility to knowledge about the colonised.

Attention, to begin with, was focused on textual knowledge and how it could be made available to the officials who were engaged in bringing the natives under the colonial cultural and ideological umbrella. The codification of Hindu laws and the translation of Indian epics into English undertaken by Nathaniel Halhed were early expressions of this. Francis Gladwin and William Davy followed the example of Halhed. Gladwin compiled an English–Persian vocabulary and translated the *Ain-i-Akbari*; Davy composed a history of *The Civil and Military Institutes of Timour.*[6]

The most important contribution in this regard came from the British orientalists who, in the words of William Jones, founder of the Asiatic Society of Bengal in 1784, enquired into 'whatever is performed by the one [man] and produced by the other [nature] in

[5] Ibid., p. 24.
[6] Ibid., p. 23.

Asia'.[7] The researches the Society promoted brought to light knowledge about the Indian civilization which fulfilled two needs of the
empire. First, the achievements of the past helped to highlight the
decadent present which explained and legitimized the colonial intervention. Second, they armed the imperial rule with valuable insights
into the world of the subjected. Both thus formed an integral part of
colonial control. It was, as Edward Said has aptly remarked, 'the
great collective appropriation of one country by another'.[8]

The permanence of the empire, however, was not to base
itself on cultural appropriation. Once the foundations of the empire
were laid, focus shifted from appropriation to expropriation of the
indigenous cultural heritage. Unlike in the African and Latin American
countries, colonialism did not attempt to destroy indigenous culture
in India; it only sought to hegemonize through a controlled and
guided process of acculturation. The ideological apparatuses of the
state played a crucial role in this process by actively intervening to
reorder the intellectual and cultural domain of the 'natives'. Through
this effort of the state the English-educated intelligentsia became the
receivers and carriers of a new cultural taste and sensibility. But not
they alone. Even if the expectations of cultural filtration entertained
by colonial administrators did not materialize, and the popular and
traditional elite cultures did transgress the limits of the English-
educated middle class, to many outside this social stratum the new
cultural possibilities, though difficult to realize, were alluring. The
significance of the accultured middle class lies in the fact that it
became the ideal and legitimizer of this vision.

The New Literacy

The make-up of the cultural world of the middle class, to a
great extent, drew upon the possibilities inherent in the new literacy
that colonialism introduced in India. The colonial system initiated by
Macaulay and Bentinck and elaborated during the course of the
nineteenth century had many facets and functions, among which its
contribution to the creation of a new cultural 'common sense' figures
as one of the most enduring and critical. Both in content and in

[7] Ibid., p. 35. Also see S.N. Mukherjee, *Sir William Jones*, Cambridge, 1968,
pp. 73–90.
[8] Edward Said, *Orientalism*, London, 1978, p. 84.

organization it was qualitatively different from the pre-colonial system. So too in intent, assumptions and epistemological foundations. The limitations in knowledge notwithstanding, the pre-colonial system had the distinct advantage of being indigenous; it had grown out of the intellectual experience of the Indian people. In contrast, the body of knowledge the colonial system sought to inculcate had not evolved from within and therefore its epistemological assumptions were alien to the Indian mind. What it replaced was the 'beautiful tree', verdant because it was rooted in the cultural tradition which shaped the collective consciousness of society.

The new literacy was important in another way. It opened up large areas for cultural intervention by the state and its agencies. The debate about the nature of education to be imparted to Indians, as embodied in the anglicist–orientalist controversy, in fact, reflected the cultural space the colonial state was seeking for establishing its hegemony.[9] By then the East India Company was moving away from the orientalist task of acquiring knowledge about the subjected, to the anglicist task of imparting knowledge to them. The concern of the state now was the construction of a colonial subject, a cultural symbol for Indians in quest of modernity. The importance of the educational policy initiated and evolved by the anglicists, particularly Macaulay and Bentinck, lay precisely in this cultural dimension. The oft-quoted statement of Macaulay deserves reiteration in this context:

> I feel that it is impossible for us, with our limited means, to attempt to educate the body of the people. We must at present do our best to form a class who may be interpreters between us and the millions whom we govern—a class of persons Indians in blood and colour, but English in tastes, in opinions, in morals and in intellect. To that class we may leave it to refine the vernacular dialects of the country, enrich those dialects with terms of science borrowed from the western nomenclature and to render them by degrees fit vehicles for conveying knowledge to the great mass of the population.[10]

---

[9] B.K. Boman-Behram, *Educational Controversies in India: The Cultural Conquest of India under British Imperialism*, Bombay, 1943.

[10] H. Sharp, *Selections from Educational Records, Part I: 1781–1839*, Calcutta, 1920, p. 116.

The elaboration of this policy by the colonial rule through cultural engineering and institutional practices, embedded in society a concept of literacy which privileged reading in the English language. The cultural universe opened up by this practice had its epicentre in the colonial metropolis which in turn created in the colonised what O. Mannoni has called a dependency complex[11] and Edward Shills a sense of provinciality.[12] The cultural ideal—in literature, theatre, painting, music, dress, food, conversation, etiquette, and so on—was drawn from the coloniser's world. The new literacy thus tried to transform India into a cultural province of the colonial metropolis, and neoliterate Indians into cultural compradors.

The development of printing during the colonial period played a central role in disseminating the cultural content of the new literacy. Its cultural possibilities were realized by the printed word by 'setting up new networks of communication, facilitating new options for the people, and also providing new means of controlling the people'.[13] By facilitating access to literary products, print contributed to the making of a new cultural taste and sensibility and thus of a new cultural personality. The cultural impact of the new literacy was not confined to English-literates alone. It had a spill-over effect on vernacular readers as well, for, its cultural essence invariably found its way into the Indian languages and through them to a larger audience. The growth of printing facilities in these languages during the course of the nineteenth century further helped this process, for the new cultural taste could thus enter the arena of 'popular' reading. The catalogues of the Registrar of Books of the Bengal, Bombay and Madras Presidencies which listed the publications for each year, reflect the new concerns in vernacular literatures. Two trends were clearly evident by the beginning of the twentieth century. First, a groundswell in the publication of pamphlets, tracts and other 'popular' genres in the vernacular languages; second, their receptivity to the colonial cultural discourse.

---

[11] O. Mannoni, *Prospero and Caliban: The Psychology of Colonisation*, Ann Arbor, 1990, pp. 39–48.

[12] Edward Shills, *The Intellectual between Tradition and Modernity: The Indian Situation*, The Hague, 1961.

[13] Natalie Zemon Davis, *Society and Culture in Early Modern France*, London, 1965, p. 190.

Incorporation of colonial cultural elements was marked in textbooks in the Indian languages produced by the government, Christian missionaries, voluntary organizations and private individuals. These books, both through diction and content, guided the impressionable minds of young children to a cultural universe alien to their life experience. It appears, colonialism, like fascism, believed in 'catching them young'. This was not always achieved through a dismissal or denigration of indigenous culture, but by locating the cultural ideal in the achievements of western society. The west, therefore, loomed large in the cultural productions promoted by colonial rule. For instance, in textbooks and other reading materials for children a shift to the 'western' was pronounced, both in text and illustrations. A good example of this is some of the Hindi books prescribed in the schools of the North-Western Provinces. In one of them a popular Indian tale is illustrated with the sketch of a boy wearing a coat, trousers and a top-hat. This was not an aberration, but an expression of the larger colonial project, which sough to make India meaningful only when related to the west.

The written word as a cultural factor became increasingly important and influential during the course of the nineteenth century. The context in which it occurred was the access to print technology and the consequent commodification of 'vernacular' literature. The importance of this development was not limited to the physical presence of the 'book' in the marketplace and thus its easy accessibility, but was also seen in the new relationship it forged between the reader and the book. Printed matter now penetrated the readers' private world, 'mobilizing their sentiments, fixing their memories and guiding their habits'.[14] The colonial cultural conquest through a remodelling of beliefs and behaviour was facilitated by print. A transition from group reading to individual reading was an immediate and important consequence. Since books could now be possessed by individuals, the need for group reading and public recitals sharply declined. Increasingly, reading became a private activity, enabling the reader to go back to the book again and again at leisure and to internalize the contents of literary products. The availability of

---

[14] Roger Chatier, *The Cultural Uses of Print in Early Modern France*, Princeton, 1987, p. 233.

printed literature contributed to a change in the attitude towards leisure itself. Leisure in the past was defined mainly in terms of participation in group activities, be it gossip within the family or with friends, or sports and games in the locality. The educated middle class found in reading an entirely different way of spending the leisure time. Leisure activity, therefore, became increasingly individual, a means by which the cultural world of the west came within their grasp and in turn facilitated its internalization.

New literary genres like the novel were a product of this process; they emerged in concurrence with the educated middle class being drawn into the colonial cultural world. Although prose was not unknown in Indian literatures, 'its potentiality and possibilities as an effective instrument of communication, both literary and non-literary, was realized only during the course of the nineteenth century.'[15] The emergence of the novel as a popular literary form was part of this process. The first novel in Bengali, *Alaler Gharer Dulal,* by Pearey Chand Mitra appeared in 1858, followed by Bankim Chandra Chatterji's *Durgeshnandini* and *Kapalakundala* in 1865 and 1866 respectively. In Marathi, Baba Padmanji's *Yamuna Paryattan* appeared in 1857, and in Gujarati, *Karan Ghelo* by Nanda Shankar Tiliya Shankar Mehta in 1866. In the South Indian languages novels were written much later. The first novel in Malayalam, *Kundalata* by Appu Nedungadi, was published in 1887; in Tamil, *Piratapa Mutaliyar Carittiram* by Samuel Vedanayakam Pillai in 1879; and in Telugu, *Rajasekhara Caritra* by Kandukuri Veeresalingam Pantulu in 1880.[16]

Why did the novel as a popular genre come into being during the second half of the nineteenth century? This is a question many have attempted to answer. Its imitative or derivative character has often found uncritical acceptance.[17] Modern literature in the Indian languages itself is seen within the rubric of the western impact and the Indian response, as the title of the Sahitya Akademi-sponsored history of nineteenth-century literature suggests.[18] The influence of

---

[15] Sisir Kumar Das, *A History of Indian Literature, 1800–1910,* New Delhi, 1991, p. 70.

[16] Ibid., pp. 197–216.

[17] See, for instance, K.M. George, *Western Influence on Malayalam Language and Literature,* New Delhi, 1972.

[18] Das, *A History of Indian Literature, 1800–1910.* The sub-title is 'Western Impact: Indian Response'.

English on early novels in India is indeed unmistakable, but the novel as a literary form was not generated exclusively by an external stimulus; it was rooted in the intellectual needs and aesthetic sensibility of the burgeoning middle class. Naturally, the contradictions, ambiguities and uncertainties of the members of the middle class in their social and cultural life, arising out of the hegemonizing colonial culture and the contending traditional cultures, set the context in which literary sensibility found expression in the nineteenth century. Their cultural perspective was neither entirely hegemonized by the colonial nor confined within the traditional, but was posited in a dialogue between the two. They looked beyond the colonial and the traditional; neither received their unqualified approval. The dialogical possibilities of the novel as a literary genre created the space for incorporating this cultural ambience.

Reading 'Indulekha'
Contending Sensibilities

What follows is an attempt to read one of the early Malayalam novels, *Indulekha*, published in 1889, in the context of the cultural situation engendered by colonialism and to explore the ways in which it contributed to the making of cultural taste in Keralam. By the time *Indulekha* was published print technology was well entrenched in literary production, but *Indulekha* was the first expression of its immense potential in Keralam. Highly acclaimed by discerning readers and informed critics, its popularity was so overwhelming that the first edition sold out within three months and several imitations vainly tried to emulate its success.

To the author this came as a pleasant surprise, because 'Malayalis who had not till then read any book like an English novel so suddenly liked and enjoyed' reading his book.[19] By 1971 the novel had gone through sixty editions with the print order for each edition ranging from 1,000 to 6,000.

The author of the novel, Oyyarath Chandu Menon, was born in 1847 in a Nair family of north Malabar. Like many of his contemporaries he received both a traditional and a colonial

---

[19] O. Chandu Menon, *Indulekha*, Preface to the second edition, Kottayam, 1971, p. 23.

education. Beginning in a vernacular school where he learnt Sanskrit, he moved to the Basel Mission school at Tellichery and acquired proficiency in English. Subsequently, he passed the uncovenanted civil services examination and began his official career as the sixth clerk in a small cause court in 1864. After three years he was promoted as the first clerk of the sub-collector's office where he had the good fortune to receive the patronage of William Logan, the celebrated author of *Malabar Manual*. Eventually Menon rose in the official hierarchy to retire as the sub-judge of Calicut in 1897.[20]

Robert Darnton is of the opinion that 'despite the proliferation of biographies of great writers, the basic conditions of authorship remain obscure'.[21] In Chandu Menon's case, there is no good biography, in fact, we know nothing more than a bare outline of his life. This makes it all the more difficult to ascertain the conditions in which *Indulekha* was written. However, Chandu Menon has recounted the circumstances in which he took to writing a novel, while he was a munsif at Parappanangadi. Among other things, Chandu Menon's account reflects how a new literary taste and through that a new cultural taste was developing among the vernacular intelligentsia. Parappanangadi being a small moffussil town where the demands of official duties were relatively light, Menon had considerable leisure to read a large number of English novels. This new-found love of literature in him supplanted the normal leisure-time activity of *vedi parayal* (gossip) among friends and members of the family. Consequently, Menon's 'circle of intimates' felt somewhat neglected. To offset this he 'attempted to convey to them in Malayalam the gist of the stories of novels' he had been reading. Initially they were not particularly interested in these stories of English romantic encounters, but they soon developed a 'taste' for them. One of them, Menon says, 'was greatly taken with Lord Beaconsfield's *Henrietta Temple* and the *taste then acquired for listening to novels* translated orally, gradually *developed into a passion*'.[22] Inspired by this interest in

---

[20] P.K. Gopalakrishnan, *O. Chandu Menon*, Thiruvananthapuram, 1982.

[21] Robert Darnton, *The Kiss of Lamourette: Reflections in Cultural History*, London, 1990, p. 125.

[22] *Indulekha*, translated into English by W. Dumurgue, Preface to the first edition, Calicut, 1965, p. x. Emphasis added. All quotations in this chapter are from this translation, and are included in the text in brackets.

Beaconsfield's novel, Menon decided to translate it, but soon gave it up as an impossible task. Instead, he undertook to write a new novel 'after the English fashion'.[23] His reasons for doing so were:

> Firstly, my wife's oft-expressed desire to read in her own language a novel written after the English fashion, and secondly, a desire on my part to try whether I should be able *to create a taste among my Malayalam readers* not conversant with English, for that class of literature represented in the English language by novels, of which at present they have no idea, and to see whether they could appreciate a story that contains only such facts and incidents as may happen in their own households under a given state of circumstances. (p. xvi; emphasis added)

The story of *Indulekha* is set amidst the social and ideological changes in Malabar in the nineteenth century as a consequence of the administrative, economic and social policies of the colonial government. A social phenomenon of far-reaching significance, arising out of the agrarian policy of the Company, was the emergence of an affluent class of intermediary tenants, almost exclusively drawn from the community.[24] The bulk of the English-educated middle class came from this social stratum who had the necessary financial resources as well as social vision to send their wards to educational institutions which imparted English education.[25] The opportunities thus opened up in government employment and professions and a new world view informed by the individualism and liberalism they imbibed from western thought, led to critical introspection about prevalent social institutions and practices. The reform and change initiated by them sought to transform existing relationships, both in the social and domestic spheres, which curbed individual liberty and upward mobility. What attracted most attention was the matrilineal family and marriage system which the Nairs had followed, probably

---

[23] The author of the first novel in Malayalam, *Kundalatha*, was also influenced by a similar urge. He regretted that those who are ignorant of English are not acquainted with novels in English. His attempt was to write a story on the lines of English novels. Appu Nedungadi, *Kundalatha*, Preface to the first edition, Calicut, 1887.

[24] K.N. Panikkar, *Against Lord and State*, New Delhi, 1989, p. 28.

[25] *Report of the Malabar Tenancy Committee, 1927–28*, Madras, 1928.

from the ninth century onwards. *Indulekha* reflects these concerns as well as the tensions they gave rise to.

The universe of the novel is a Nair *taravad* in which forces of change and continuity struggle for supremacy. The *karanavan,* Panchu Menon, exercises control over the resources of the family, and by virtue of that over the lives of its members, represents the force of continuity. He is affectionate and sincere, but being strongly anchored in traditional ideology, is indifferent to the aspirations of the younger generation in the family and insensitive to the changes occurring around him. The novel opens with an allusion to a dispute between Panchu Menon and Madhavan, the hero of the novel, over the education of the children in the family. Madhavan wanted one of the boys to be sent to Madras for an English education, which the *karanavan* was not prepared to agree to. The dispute was not just over distribution of the resources of the family; it symbolized a struggle between the status quo and change. It is curtain-raiser to the central concern of the novel: an exploration of the different ways in which Malabar society was trying to grapple with the cultural situation in the nineteenth century.

The plot of the novel, conceived by Chandu Menon on the lines of English storybooks, is rather simple. It revolves around the love between two cousins in a Nair *taravad,* Madhavan and Indulekha, whose marriage is traditionally sanctioned in the matrilineal system. The intervention of a Nambudiri brahmin who, enamoured of the reported beauty of Indulekha, seeks her hand in marriage, gives rise to misunderstanding and temporary separation of the lovers. The story predictably ends in the happy marriage of the lovers.

If *Indulekha* had only narrated this love story, as many of its puerile imitations did later, it would not have been a literary event of any consequence demanding continued attention thereafter.[26] The novel went through so many editions and has been at the centre of literary discussions not only because of its narrative excellence, but also because of its significance as a social and cultural statement of the times. The love story is only the necessary skeleton, the flesh is

---

[26] *Indulekha's* success led to several aspirants for fame trying their hand at writing novels. None of them made an impact on the reader. George Irumbayam (ed.), *Nalu Novalukal* (Malayalam), Trichur, 1985.

provided by the contending cultural sensibilities which inhered in the colonial society of Malabar. *Indulekha* thus transcended the limits of a storybook on the lines of English novels and reflected the struggle for cultural hegemony in civil society.

Chandu Menon conceived the three main characters in the novel—Madhavan, Indulekha and Suri Nambudiripad—to reflect the main cultural traits which were in contention in Malabar society in the nineteenth century. Madhavan is English-educated, socially progressive, politically alive, and at home with European customs, manners and knowledge. He is adept at lawn tennis, cricket and other athletic games. At the same time he is not an anglophile or contemptuous of Indian tradition; rather, he is well-grounded in it. He has 'profound critical knowledge' of Sanskrit literature, he can appreciate the nuances of traditional art forms, and can recite Malayalam poems from memory with ease. The evolution of his character represents the intellectual process which reflects the contradiction within colonial hegemonization which not only generated consent but also contestation. Located in this milieu, Madhavan is not a static character, symbolizing the accultured Indian of Macaulayian vintage. That part of his make-up is indeed quite evident, but he goes beyond it to embody the elements of the newly emerging national consciousness (pp. 2–4).

A combination of the indigenous and colonial cultures is more sharply and elaborately etched in the character of Indulekha. She has been brought up by her uncle, a Dewan Peishkar, who was 'well versed in English, Sanskrit, Music and other accomplishments'. Under his tutelage, Indulekha's cultural attainments were of a high order. She was

> thoroughly grounded in English; her Sanskrit studies included the works of the dramatic authors; and in Music she not only learned the theory of harmony, but also became an efficient performer on the piano, violin and the Indian lute. At the same time her uncle did not neglect to have his charming niece instructed in needle work, drawing and other arts in which European girls are trained. In fact his darling wish was that Indulekha *should possess the acquirements and culture of an English lady*, and it can be truly said that his efforts wee crowned with the success due to a man of his liberal

mind and sound judgement, so far as this could be compassed within the sixteenth year of her age. (p. 10; emphasis added)

Chandu Menon was conscious that this picture of Indulekha was too idealized to be true in Malabar of the nineteenth century. He expected that 'some readers may object that it would be impossible to find a young Nair lady of Indulekha's intellectual attainments in Malabar'. He, however, believed that there are 'hundreds of young ladies in respectable Nair *taravads* who would undoubtedly come up to the standard' of 'Indulekha in beauty, personal charms, refined manners, simplicity of taste, conversational powers, wit and humour' (p. xx). The only quality not possessed by them which distinguishes Indulekha is her knowledge of English. The justification for this was as follows:

> One of my objects in writing this book is to illustrate how a young Malayali woman, possessing, in addition to her natural charms and intellectual culture, a knowledge of the English language would conduct herself in matters of supreme interest to her, such as choosing of a partner in life. I have thought it necessary that my Indulekha should be conversant with the richest language of the world. (p. xx)

The English accomplishments notwithstanding, Indulekha, unlike Madhavan, does not consider the Nair system of marriage to be devoid of merit. The conversation between Indulekha and Madhavan on the man—woman relationship prevalent among Nairs encapsulates the discussion then raging in society about marriage reform. Madhavan feels that men suffer untold misery due to the freedom and opportunities which the women of Malabar enjoy. Disapproving of the freedom enjoyed by women in marital affairs, Madhavan observes:

> . . . in Malabar, the women don't practise the virtue of fidelity so strictly as do the women of other countries. Why, in Malabar a woman may take a husband and cast him off as she pleases, and on many other points she is completely at liberty to do as she likes. (p. 40)

Madhavan's allusion to the impermanence of Nair marriage

is obviously nuanced against women. He overlooks the fact that the impermanence is more due to the libertine male than the freedom-loving woman. Yet, Madhavan's argument echoes the patriarchal demand for establishing what is 'natural' and ideal in man–woman relations. Indulekha's defence of Nair women strives to reconcile patriarchal rights and female freedom:

> What, did you say that Malayali women are not chaste? To say that woman makes light of the marriage tie is tantamount to saying that she is immoral. Did you then mean that all or most of women in the land of palms are immoral? If you did, then I for one certainly cannot believe him. If you intended to signify that we Nairs encourage immorality, because, unlike the Brahmins, we do not force our womenfolk to live lives worthy only of the brute creation by prohibiting all intercourse with others, and by closing against them the gates of knowledge, then never was there formed any opinion so false. Look at Europe and America, where women share equally with men the advantages of education and enlightenment and liberty! Are these women all immoral? If, in those countries, a woman who adds refinement of education to beauty of person, enjoys the society and conversation of men, is it to be straightaway supposed that the men whom she admits into the circle of her friends are more to her than mere friends? (p. 41)

Indulekha's spirited defence, however, reflects the gender equality that Nair women had enjoyed for centuries, which the reforms contemplated by the government and supported by the educated middle class was likely to upset. Whether the practice which had evolved as a part of the cultural tradition needed to be changed was itself a matter of doubt for many. In the evidences and discussions of the Malabar Marriage Commission and the public response to its recommendations, this uncertainty found varied expression. Chandu Menon, who was a member of the Marriage Commission, in a note of dissent argued that Nair marriages had validity both in law and religion and that no legislative interference was needed in this matter.[27] The Madhavan–Indulekha conversation was in many ways

[27] *Malabar Marriage Commission Report*, Memorandum by O. Chandu Menon, Enclosure C, Madras, 1891.

a precursor to the debate among the educated middle class generated by the marriage reform proposal. Indulekha's arguments can perhaps be identified with the largely unstated opinion of women which did not altogether match the patriarchal urge to control women's sexuality and independence.

The character of the 'fickle-minded and libertine' Suri Nambudiripad has multiple functions and meanings in the plot. His escapades are not intended as purely comic interludes in an otherwise serious novel, but as the expression of a cultural ethos which the middle class in Malabar was contending with. In almost every aspect—in looks, in knowledge, in character—he is contrasted, implicitly if not explicitly, with Madhavan. While Madhavan is 'remarkably good looking', Nambudiripad is 'neither good looking nor elegant'. 'When he laughed his mouth stretched from ear to ear, his nose, though not deformed, was far too small for his face, and, instead of walking, he hopped like a crow.' Madhavan is courteous and respectful towards women, whereas Nambudiripad is arrogant and condescending. He looks upon women only as objects of sexual pleasure, regardless of age or marital status. He is enamoured of every women he meets, whether she is a young girl like Indulekha or an elderly lady like her mother or an unattractive girl like her servant. Reflecting the traditional Nambudiri attitude, he believes that it is his right to marry any woman in a Nair family who takes his fancy (pp. 95–96).

Even in traditional knowledge, in which Nambudiris are generally well-grounded, Suri Nambudiri cannot match the accomplishments of Madhavan or Indulekha. Despite his 'madness' for Kathakali and pretensions to scholarship in Sanskrit literature, he can hardly remember or recite a few lines of poetry. His efforts to do so provide comic relief. Indulekha, however, recites with great ease the poems which he struggles to remember. Another dimension of Suri Nambudiri's character is his contempt for the new cultural situation, arising more out of ignorance than reflection or understanding. Consequently, he is trapped in sexual obsession. He believes that English 'destroys romance and hinders all love making'. Even Panchu Menon, whose fealty to traditional ideologies led him to welcome the Nambudiripad, finds him an 'unmitigated fool, destitute of intellect and intelligence' (p. 191).

Chandu Menon's reservations about the proposed legisla-tive intervention notwithstanding, *Indulekha* underlines the growing awareness about the iniquity of the Nair–Nambudiri marriage alliance. The new generation resented sexual exploitation by the Nambudiris and questioned the ideological dominance which sanctioned it. Indulekha's rejection of Suri Nambudiripad is a powerful statement of this cultural consciousness. Yet, ideologies hardly fade so quickly. That is why Nambudiripad is able to marry one of Indulekha's cousins, despite his clumsy and offensive mannerisms.

From 'Region' to 'Nation'

Apart from being a means to contrast the feudal and the modern, the Nambudiripad episode has yet another function in the plot. It is used as a device to take the story outside the 'region' to the wider arena of the nation. Madhavan, under the false impression that Suri Nambudiripad has married Indulekha and taken her with him, seeks solace in travel which takes him to Calcutta, the centre of nationalist activity at that time. At Calcutta he befriends those who are active in the Indian National Congress and participates in their meetings. This sojourn and experience provides the context for an extended discussion on religion, the colonial state and the Congress movement, which takes up about one-sixth of the novel.

The participants in the discussion, apart from Madhavan, are his father Govinda Panikkar and his cousin Govindankutty Menon. They represent three different strands of thought. Govindankutty Menon is an atheist and a liberal reformist, Govinda Panikkar is a theist who values belief in and reverence for spiritual preceptors, and Madhavan is a critical rationalist and a supporter of the Congress. Their discussion broadly covers two main issues. First, the place of religion in human life, and second, the nature of the Congress movement in the context of colonial rule.

The discussion on religion reflects the intellectual ferment which stirred Indian society during the religious and cultural regeneration of the nineteenth century. All three strands of 'renaissance' thought are articulated during the discussion: a defence of religious tradition, a rational critique of religious practices and an atheistic attitude towards religious faith.

The conversation opens with a critique of the nonconformist

attitude of young men which Govinda Panikkar attributes 'solely to the ideas and mode of thinking adopted in consequence of English education'. The influence of education is such that reverence, faith and love for spiritual preceptors and family elders, and belief in god and piety have ceased to exist. The educated youth, according to him, have scant regard for the good old practices of the Hindus and think that the Hindu religion is altogether contemptible. He has no doubt that the acquisition of knowledge and culture are 'utterly worthless if they came into conflict with faith in things divine' (pp. 299–300).

This opening statement leads to an animated discussion on god, religion and ideology, from which three distinct positions emerge. Holding that 'the origin, preservation, growth and decay of the whole world are due to natural forces', Govindankutty refuses to believe that there is any supreme power which can be called God. As for religion, he thinks that it is 'simply a fabric of each man's brain' and that as human knowledge increases, faith in religion must decrease. Madhavan, on the other hand, is 'firmly convinced that there is a God', but fails to see any connection between temples and God (pp. 301–02).

The views of these young men who are 'wonderful examples of the times' are shocking to Govinda Panikkar who believes that any departure from the faith of his forefathers is undesirable. Realizing that any attempt to convince the young radicals on God and religion would be a difficult task, he confines his defence to the need for temples. Temples, he argues, were meant as a reminder of 'the admiration and homage due to the Almighty' since people are likely to ignore His presence 'in every place, even the most secret'. Madhavan interprets his father's argument to mean that there is no 'essential connection between temples and God' and that 'temples are nothing but symbolical institutions founded by pious individuals for the benefit of those who have no natural inclination to piety'. He not only questions the connection between temples and God, but also the relevance of temples for true believers. Acknowledging that God is present throughout the world and that the powers of creation, preservation and destruction are vested in Him, Madhavan feels that it would be 'a gross mockery to go to a temple and pretend that the image set up therein was my God and worship it and prostrate myself before it' (pp. 303–04).

Anti-idolatry was a major idea around which religious reform in the nineteenth century was organized and propagated. Since there is no authorial intervention in this, Chandu Menon's views on the subject are not clear. But Govinda Panikkar's defence of idolatry appears weak when compared with the forceful articulation of the anti-idolatry argument by Madhavan. It is reinforced by the discussion on the role of religious leaders in perpetuating superstition. Govinda Panikkar's experience of an ascetic living for ten days on seven pepper berries and seven neem leaves is dismissed by Madhavan as the trick of an impostor, for it was not done under verifiable conditions and hence was not acceptable (pp. 305–07).

The critique of religion and religious practices, though undertaken in the context of tradition, does not involve its rejection. Instead, it leads inevitably to an exploration of the relative relevance of tradition and modernity. Steeped in western thought and influenced by the ideas of Charles Bradlaugh and Darwin, Govindankutty Menon is contemptuous of the knowledge contained in traditional texts which he dismisses as 'crammed with incongruities and impossibilities'. Citing from the works of Darwin and Bradlaugh, he seeks to establish that the scientific and rational ideas which European thought contain are totally absent in the Indian tradition, represented by the Puranas and other ancient texts. An altogether different view, sensitive to the importance and strength of tradition, is articulated by Madhavan, who argues that Govindankutty Menon's contempt for traditional knowledge is more due to ignorance than a proper understanding of the contents of ancient texts which have contributed to the advance of European thought and ideas. He reminds Govindankutty Menon that the atheism the latter has adopted from Bradlaugh was very much in existence in the Sankhya system of Kapila (p. 322). That there were atheists in India comes as a surprise to both Govindankutty Menon and Govinda Panikkar, suggesting how both the 'modernists' and the 'traditionalists' are equally ill-informed about their own past. The entire discussion is so conceived as to underline a cultural–intellectual perspective, advocated by Madhavan, which is in favour of the new, without renouncing the old.

Reminiscent of what happened to the intellectual concerns of the nineteenth century, the engagement with religion and tradition shifts to the realm of politics. The discussion covers two inter-related dimensions of political reality: the nature of colonial rule and the character of the Congress movement. All three discussants share the colonial view about the benevolence of British rule, but their assessment of the possible benefits from the Congress movement are sharply different. They believe that the British government is far superior to earlier regimes—'[un]like our old rulers, [who were] guilty of injustice, irregularity and oppression' (p. 342)—and would eventually lead India to progress. Madhavan expresses this common conviction in unambiguous terms:

> The fact is that the establishment of the British Empire has been productive of indescribable benefits to this country. In no other nation do we find intellectual capacity so fully developed as it is in the English, and the statesmanship they display is one proof of this fact. Another proof lies in their impartiality, a third in their benevolence, a fourth in their valour, a fifth in their energy and a sixth in their endurance. It is through the preponderance of these six qualities that the English have succeeded in bringing so many countries of the world under their domination and protection, and the subjection of India by a people endowed with such vast natural ability is the greatest good fortune that could have befallen us. (p. 346)

This assessment of British rule provides the necessary context to envision the possible ways in which the Indian polity could develop. One of them, the liberal—reformist view articulated by Govindankutty Menon, is through gradual change and reform introduced by the British government. To facilitate this process Indians could prove themselves socially worthy of political advancement by changing their 'imperfect and disgraceful customs and institutions' and raising India to a state of equality with England. Popular assemblies, self-government and enfranchisement could only follow, not precede it. In the absence of this necessary improvement, the Congress is 'worthless' and nothing but 'pompous bombast', 'vain agitation and waste of money'. It is hence 'altogether contemptible' (p. 337).

Articulating the moderate view and emphasizing the positive role of the Congress, Madhavan attributes to it an instrumentalist function, which is to bring to 'maturity and perfection' the indescribable benefits afforded by the British by striving 'to instil into the English greater faith in us, greater affection and greater regard for us, and thus to persuade the English government to make no difference between us and Englishmen' (pp. 339–40). Such an objective could be achieved neither by resorting to violence nor by lapsing into inactivity but by making every legitimate effort to raise our position higher and higher. Such efforts, he believes, would be rewarded by the establishment in India, as in England, of a free government (p. 343). With Govindankutty Menon almost agreeing with Madhavan's contention, a resolution of the conflict between social and political reform is posited.

This long and laboured discussion, as argued by many literary critics, would appear to be unconnected with the plot, but is in fact integral to the theme of the novel. Baffled by this supposedly unnecessary detour, some have criticized it as 'a stone blocking the unhampered progress of the plot'.[28] If the discussion on atheism and the Congress were left out, as some later editions actually did, perhaps it would not do any harm to the story. Chandu Menon's stated intention of writing a 'story book' would also have been fulfilled. But, then, Chandu Menon was attempting more than narrating a story. He was making a powerful cultural and political statement, integrating into the plot the vital issues Indian society faced at that time.

Indulekha is not merely a story set in the context of colonial history. It collapses and encapsulates the historical process of nineteenth-century Malabar into a literary genre consciously borrowed from the English. The novelty of the genre and the possible attraction of a love story do not fully account either for its popularity or for its importance. Its significance and success are to great extent rooted in its ability to capture the cultural and political experience of the intelligentsia, nuanced by the contradictions, ambiguities and uncertainties inherent in it.

By internalizing the colonial cultural values and political ideas the intelligentsia objectively fulfilled a legitimizing role for

---

[28] M.P. Paul, *Novel Sahithyam*. Also see P.K. Balakrishnan, *Chandu Menon, Oru Patanam*, Kottayam, 1971, pp. 112–17. (Both in Malayalam.)

colonialism. This dimension is effectively projected in *Indulekha* through an emphasis on the modernizing potential of English education and the benevolent, liberal character of British rule. The characters, conversations and authorial interventions unmistakably articulate this early consciousness. Madhavan and Indulekha are forceful representations of this colonial ideal. At the same time, a disjunction between the cultural consequences of English education and the liberalism of British rule is also posited. Govinda Panikkar, for instance, is a cultural critic of English education but a political supporter of British rule. He holds that English education subverted tradition and encouraged atheism, but at the same time initiated the beginnings of a liberal polity in India.

Despite the influence of English education Madhavan and Indulekha are not colonial cultural stereotypes. Their personalities are a complex admixture of the colonial and the indigenous, reflecting the cultural introspection embodying the intelligentsia's alienation from the struggle against colonial culture. They are neither completely hegemonized by the colonial nor fully distanced from the traditional. Thus their identity is rooted in a new cultural taste, anchored in both the western and the indigenous without fully identifying with or rejecting either of them. In the field of politics as well this duality is evident: the acceptance of British rule on the one hand and the transition to national consciousness on the other. Capturing this historical process is what makes *Indulekha* a classic.

7 Indigenous Medicine and Cultural Hegemony

During the initial phase of colonial rule in India the indigenous system of knowledge and cultural practices came under severe strain. Exposed to western intellectual and cultural forces, Indian intellectuals developed a world view that was critical of traditional cultural and social practices.[1] Their agenda for change, however, was not based on westernization, but on a selective rejection and reform of the present. The progress achieved by the west pointed to possible directions for the future, but how the past should figure in the new order was quite uncertain. The increasing influence of colonial culture heightened this uncertainty and underlined the possible loss of the cultural heritage. As a result, the intellectuals were caught in a paradox: to discard the old and create a new cultural milieu, or, to preserve or retrieve the traditional cultural space so that the past is not swept off the ground. The efforts to reconcile this paradox led to a critical inquiry into both the past as well as the present. The movement for the revitalization of indigenous medicine was a part of this quest in Indian society during the late nineteenth and early twentieth centuries. This essay examines the movement in Keralam initiated and led by P.S. Variar of Kottakkal and reflects on its implications for cultural hegemony in colonial India.

Introducing Western Medicine

At the time of the British conquest the medical needs of the Indian population were being met by a variety of indigenous practi-

---

[1] All intellectuals in colonial India, however, were not the products of western influence, as held by scholars like Edward Shills. For an elaboration, see the chapter titled 'Historiographical and Conceptual Question's.in the

ces—Ayurveda, Unani, Siddha and folk medicine. Fruitful interaction between these systems, particularly between Ayurveda and Unani, led to the enrichment of their pharmacopoeia and the improvement of diagnostic skills. Reviewing the practice of medicine in ancient and medieval India, A.L. Basham has underlined the collaboration that existed between the practitioners of the two systems: 'whatever the ulama and the Brahman might say, we have no record of animosity between Hindus and Muslims in the field of medicine.'[2] The efforts of Bahwa Khan, a minister of Sikander Lodhi, and Hakim Yoosufi, a physician in the court of Babar and Humayun, to develop a composite and integrated medical system through a synthesis of Arabian, Persian and Ayurvedic thought was an expression of this collaboration.[3] During the medieval period several others had tried to bring the two systems together; the notable examples are Abdul Shirazi, the personal physician of Shahjahan and Muhammad Akbar Arsani, the court physician of Aurangzeb. The Unani and Ayurvedic systems also adopted drugs from each other. Muhammad Ali lists 210 plant drugs of Indian origin added by Unani physicians to their *materia medica*,[4] just as Ayurveda incorporated in their pharmacopoeia several medicines from the Unani system.[5] This interaction, cooperation and collaboration, Charles Leslie argues, made the traditional beliefs and practices of Ayurvedic physicians 'radically different from the classic texts'.[6] Even if the change was not as pronounced as claimed by Leslie, it is evident that indigenous practitioners did not lack the will and ability to incorporate knowledge from other systems with which they came in contact.

Western medicine initially introduced for the benefit of

    volume.

[2] A.L. Basham, 'Practice of Medicine in Ancient and Medieval India', in Charles Leslie (ed.), *Asian Medical System: A Comparative Study*, Berkeley, 1976, p. 40.

[3] A. Abdul Hameed, *Physician-Authors of Greco-Arab Medicine in India*, New Delhi, n.d., p. 17. Bahwa Khan's Persian Text, *Madan-us-Shifa-i-Sikander Shahi* (fifteenth century), has been recently translated into English under a project sponsored by the National Institute of Science and Technology and Development Studies, New Delhi.

[4] M. Ali, 'Ayurvedic Drugs in Unani Materia Medica', *Ancient Science Life*, April 1990, pp.191–200.

[5] P.V. Krishna Variar, *Arya Vaidya Charitram*, Trichur, 1904–05, pp. 52, 89.

[6] Charles Leslie, 'The Ambiguities of Medical Revivalism in Modern India',

Europeans in India and later made accessible to the Indian population, was a 'tool' of the empire.[7] It was, as suggested by Roy Macleod, a cultural force, 'acting both as a cultural agency in itself, and as an agency of western expansion'.[8] The attitude of Indian intellectuals clearly bears out Macleod's contention. To the intellectuals modern science, viewed as integral to western culture, was an important modernizing force. What 'raised the natives of Europe above the inhabitants of other parts of the world', Rammohun Roy had argued eloquently, was scientific knowlwdge.[9] In contrast, science was underdeveloped in the indigenous tradition and it was received from the west with unqualified admiration:

> While we looked forward with pleasing hope to the dawn of knowledge, thus promised to the rising generation, our hearts were filled with mingled feelings of delight and gratitude, we offered up thanks to providence for inspiring the most generous and enlightened nations of the West with the glorious ambition of planting in Asia the arts and sciences of Modern Europe.[10]

Rammohun's famous letter on education addressed to Lord Amherst from which the foregoing statement is quoted is laden with a running comparison between western and indigenous knowledge. In contrast to 'the real knowledge' developed in post-Baconian Europe, what India had was nothing more than 'valuable information'.[11] If Indian minds continued to be enclosed within the indigenous system, Rammohun argued, the country would remain in darkness. The only way out, according to him, was to internalize western knowledge and thus embark on a path of progress.

It was in this cultural and ideological context that western medicine was implanted in India. That the intelligentsia welcomed its

in Leslie (ed.), *Asian Medical System,* p. 356.

[7] The phrase is used by Daniel Headrick in *The Tools of Empire: Technology and European Imperialism in the Nineteenth Century,* New York, 1981.

[8] Roy Macleod, 'Introduction', in Roy Macleod and Milton Lewis (eds.), *Disease, Medicine and Empire: Perspectives on Western Medicine and the Experience of European Expansion,* London, 1988, p. 1. Also see David Arnold (ed.), *Imperial Medicine and Indigenous Societies,* Delhi, 1989.

[9] Rammohun Roy, 'A Letter to Lord Amherst on English Education', in *The English Works of Raja Rammohun Roy,* Allahabad, 1906, p. 472.

[10] Ibid.

introduction was but natural, even though there was some hesitation and scepticism initially. Religious prejudices prevented some from taking to the new system, while others were influenced by rumours, not altogether unjustified, about the methods and consequences of practices like vaccination. The reaction of K.T. Telang, reformer and nationalist leader, to a suggestion to undergo surgery, reflects some of the prejudices of the times. He refused the simple operation, which would have probably saved his life, in deference to the feelings of his father and mother who had 'the most inveterate objection to the slightest use of the knife, to the shedding of a drop of blood'.[12] Despite such initial reservations, however, the treatment proffered by western medicine was attractive to the intelligentsia: it was looked upon as a means of embracing the modern and defying the old and thus be a part of the new cultural world.

During the course of the nineteenth century the administrative and institutional infrastructure necessary for the practice of western medicine was set up by the state. Although a limited enterprise, the hospitals, dispensaries and colleges established by the state formed the nucleus from which colonial medicine sought to establish its hegemony and thus to marginalize and delegitimize the indigenous system. In the process, the role of the colonial state went beyond its administrative functions. It not only promoted western medicine, but also sought to assert and establish its superiority over all other systems. Western medicine thus became the officially preferred system; it was accorded the status of official medicine and the attitude of the state towards other systems became discriminatory, even hostile.

Although the colonial state's preference for western knowledge was expressed at the time of the orientalist–anglicist controversy and institutional arrangements were made thereafter, administrative and legislative interventions in its favour took time to mature. In the case of medicine, it occurred in the last quarter of the century when the demand for colonial medicine could not be met by the existing infrastructure. The void was filled by irregularly qualified doctors who had either received training in unrecognized medical institutions or had no training at all. This endangered the hegemonic

---

[11] Ibid., pp. 472–74

potential of western medicine, as its acceptance was based on a perception of its effectiveness, and that perception was likely to be affected if its practice were to be left to quacks. The Principal of Grant Medical College, Bombay, suggested a solution in 1881: the exercise of state control through a system of registration of medical practitioners. The proposal found favour with the Bombay government, but the Government of India considered it inexpedient at that juncture and refused sanction for legislation on this matter.[13] The Bombay government, however, persisted with the idea and moved another proposal in 1887, confining the operation of the proposed legislation to the town and island of Bombay. The Government of India still did not consider the situation alarming enough to justify intervention by the state. It took about thirty years for the government to revise this stand. The change was influenced by the rapid increase in the number of unrecognized medical institutions and persons holding degrees and diplomas from such institutions passing themselves off as qualified medical practitioners. Consequently, when the Government of Bombay revived its proposal in 1909, it had a smooth passage, culminating in the Bombay Medical Registration Act of 1912.[14] The other Presidencies soon followed the Bombay initiative.

Apart from constituting a medical council, the Act provided for the registration of medical practitioners. Only those who were registered under the Act were now to be considered competent to issue medical certificates or eligible for appointment to public offices.[15] The registration was open only to 'Doctor, Bachelor and Licentiate of Medicine, and Master, Bachelor and Licentiate of Surgery of the Universities of Bombay, Calcutta, Madras, Allahabad and Lahore and holders of a diploma or certificate from a government medical college or school'.[16] The Act thus constituted a body of 'legally qualified medical practitioners' exclusively trained in western medicine.

The Act, by implication, excluded the indigenous system from its operation and thus from the patronage of the state. More important, the practitioners of indigenous medicine were relegated to an inferior status, as they were unrecognized by the state and

[12] Vasant N. Naik, *Kashinath Trimbak Telang,* Madras, n.d., p. 41.
[13] Government of Bombay, Legal Dept., Vol. 3, 1912, p. 17.
[14] Ibid., p. 18
[15] *Bombay Medical Act 1912,* paras 10 and 11.

therefore deemed unqualified. The idea of disallowing them to practise itself was mooted at that time, but the government turned it down as 'impracticable at present'. It was, however, hoped that 'when the time becomes ripe', a law would be introduced for 'excluding unqualified practitioners'.[17] The Act did not debar the practice of indigenous medicine, but it did not have the approval of the state. The partisan attitude of the state was thus unambiguously articulated through the Act.

The discussions that followed the passing of the Act made it clear that the government's intention was not limited to protecting the medical profession from 'the irregularly qualified doctor'. When the time was opportune, it meant to fully supplant the indigenous system with western medicine. The rationale put forward for doing so was that the former was unscientific, antiquated and inadequate. In its place the government was trying to impart to Indians the benefit of a modern system. The Governor of Madras, Lord Pentland, expressed this view, ironically, while inaugurating and Ayurvedic dispensary at Cheruthuruthy in Keralam. The indigenous system, he asserted, had hardly any knowledge of anatomy, its medicines were deplorably poor in quality and its practitioners had no ability to establish cause–effect relationships. Such a system, the Governor argued, had no claim on public money.[18] Similar sentiments were voiced by Lord Hardinge, the Governor-General, in his speech at the foundation-laying ceremony of the Ayurvedic-Unani Tibbia College at Delhi. What was implicit in the Governor's speech was made explicit by the Governor-General: government support would be made available only to western medicine.[19]

The policy of the colonial state that followed from the triumph of the anglicists, culminating in the Medical Act, was not only geared to the implementation of a practice embodying western knowledge, but also directed at delegitimizing indigenous knowledge. In 1822 the government started a school for native doctors in Calcutta with a course of study combining indigenous and European medicine. Similar schools were also proposed in Bombay and Madras. Anatomy and modern medicine were introduced in the cur-

[16] Ibid., 'The Schedule'.
[17] Government of Bombay, Legal Dept., Vol. 3, 1912, p. 19.
[18] *Dhanwantari*, 16 November 1917.

ricula of Calcutta Madrasa and Sanskrit College.[20] The idea of a possible synthesis inherent in these experiments was given up after 1835 in favour of confining the cultural and intellectual horizon of the subject people to western knowledge. Consequently, the schools for native doctors were abolished, medical science was dropped at Sanskrit College and the Madrasa, and medical institutions with curricula exclusively devoted to western science were set up.[21] To the protagonists of indigenous medicine the government policy of denying them unhampered space was an act of cultural oppression and deprivation, as knowledge and practice of medicine were viewed as a part of their culture.

The Indigenous Systems

Despite the expressed intention of promoting western medicine, the 'benefits' of colonial medicine were limited to a small section of the population. Doctors were few in number and hospitals and dispensaries could hardly cater to the needs even of a small section of the population. For instance, in Madras Presidency there were only 2,272 registered western medical practitioners and 578 medical centres in 1921. On an average each medical institution catered to 40,000 people.[22] Since most of the medical centres were located in urban areas, colonial medical facilities were almost unavailable to the rural population. A comparison of Madras and Cuddappah districts would indicate the disparity between the urban and rural areas. In Madras district there was one medical centre per 1.4 square miles, covering a population of 27,298, whereas the corresponding figures for Cuddappah district were 589.2 and 89,399.[23]

In contrast, available statistics for different regions indicate that every village had more than one practitioner of indigenous medicine. During his survey of education in Bengal in 1835–38 William Adam found 646 medical practitioners in Nattore district,

---

[19] Ibid., 6 November 1917.

[20] Charles Leslie, 'The Professionalizing Ideology of Medical Revivalism', in Milton Singer (ed.), *Entrepreneurship and Modernization of Occupational Cultures in South Asia,* 1973, p. 220 and O.P. Jaggi, *Western Medicine in India: Social Impact,* Delhi, 1980, p. 10.

[21] Poonam Bala, *Imperialism and Medicine in Bengal,* New Delhi, 1991, p. 47.

[22] *Report of the Usman Committee on the Indigenous System of Medicine,* Vol. I, Madras, 1923, p. 9.

with a population of 195,296 distributed across 485 villages.[24] According to the Census of 1921 there were 21,000 practitioners of indigenous system in Madras Presidency.[25] More important, indigenous medical knowledge was not the preserve of any particular caste and hence had a popular character and easy accessibility. In Keralam, for instance, the practice of Ayurveda was not limited to the *ashtavaidyans,* the eight upper-caste families, and their disciples. A large number of Ayurvedic practitioners belonged to the lower, untouchable castes who have formulated several medicines mentioned in popularly used Malayalam texts.[26] The early popularity of Narayana Guru, the social reformer of Ezhavas, was built around his knowledge of medicine and ability to cure diseases.[27] Knowledge of Ayurveda, at least in Keralam, was not a monopoly of the upper castes—it transcended caste and religious barriers.

The facilities afforded by colonial medicine were at no point of time sufficient to supplant the indigenous systems. The Committee on the Indigenous System of Medicine noticed that these systems 'minister to the medical needs of nearly nine-tenths of our vast population who are quite unprovided for by any official medical aid'.[28] Even in areas where western medical centres existed, indigenous medicine continued to be in demand. A comparison between Ayurvedic and western medical dispensaries situated in the same locality of Madras city indicates a clear preference for the former. While the Ayurvedic dispensary treated 122,238 patients in 1921–22, the western medical dispensary attracted only 37,626. There are two other factors worth recording. First, among the patients in the Ayurvedic dispensary, there were a good number of Muslims, Christians and Eurasians. Second, the average cost per patient per day in the western medical dispensary was about 400 per cent more than in the Ayurvedic dispensary.[29]

---

[23] Ibid.

[24] William Adam, *Reports on the State of Education in Bengal, 1835 and 1838,* Calcutta, 1941, p. 515.

[25] *Report on the Indigenous System,* p. 19.

[26] N.V. Krishnan Kutty Variar, *Ayurveda Charitram,* Kottakkal, 1980, p. 344.

[27] P. Chandra Mohan, 'Social Consciousness in Kerala', unpublished M. Phil. dissertation, Jawaharlal Nehru University, Delhi.

[28] *Report on the Indigenous System,* p. 13.

An important implication of the limited reach of colonial medical facilities was that indigenous medicine had enough space to operate, particularly in rural areas. Yet, a sense of insecurity gripped the minds of indigenous practitioners, as they envisioned an unequal confrontation with western medicine. Conscious of a possible marginalization due to the challenge caused by western medicine, the protagonists of indigenous medicine were forced to take a critical look at the state of their art. Their assessment of the situation was a complex amalgam of pride in the past, dissatisfaction with the present and apprehension about the future. The efforts to revitalize indigenous systems during the late nineteenth and early twentieth centuries stemmed from this assessment.

Tarashankar Bandhopadhyaya's Bengali novel, *Arogya Niketan,* is an admirable representation of the crisis faced by indigenous medicine at a time when colonial medicine was making its presence felt in rural Bengal. The crisis is embodied in the life of Jeevan Moshai, the central character of the novel, who despite his uncanny skill for diagnosis and unmatched ability for prognosis, is increasingly marginalized by the presence of western medical practitioners in the village. As a result, his practice dwindles and the family dispensary, Arogya Niketan, which had for three generations successfully looked after the medical needs of the village, becomes deserted and dilapidated. The novel opens with the following description of the dispensary:

> It [Arogya Niketan] was established about 80 years ago. Now it is in a state of ruin. The mud walls are broken here and there. The roof has several holes; its central part is hanging down—like the posterior of a hunchback. Yet, the dispensary manages to exist— awaiting its end, expecting the moment when it would collapse.[30]

Tarashankar's description of the state of the dispensary is symbolic of what had happened to indigenous medicine. That its condition was deplorable and 'pitiable' was an opinion shared by almost everyone concerned about its future. There was no doubt in the mind of anyone that an all-round decline had taken place—in

---

[29] Ibid., p. 6.
[30] Tarashankar Bandhopadhyaya, *Arogya Niketanam* (Malayalam transla-

knowledge, in the quality of medicine and in the training of physicians:

> The antiquity of Ayurveda is a matter of pride for all of us, but nobody can deny that its present state is quite deplorable. Due to reasons both internal and external, our medical system has steadily declined, while in contrast, other systems have progressed in an equal degree. The people of the West examine the laws of nature and invent new dimensions of science, thereby repeatedly revising the earlier scientific knowledge. We, on the other hand, blindly believe that old sciences are perfect. As a result, we have not only failed to progress but have also been pushed down the ladder by others. If this state of affairs continues for some more time there is no doubt that Ayurveda will become totally extinct.[31]

Implicit in this view of the contemporary conditions was a notion that Ayurveda was the source of all medical knowledge. Referring to its antiquity, borne out by classical texts, it was argued that all other systems in the world derived their initial knowledge from Ayurveda. 'It is frankly admitted by every savant in the world', said Jaminibhushan Roy Kavirathna, President of the All India Ayurvedic Conference, 'that rudimentary principles of almost every science had their origin in this country. There is ample evidence to prove that the root principles of the science of medicine were first preached in Arabia by Indian professors and physicians. From Arabia Ayurveda travelled through Egypt to Greece, thence to Rome, and from there, again spread all over Europe and gradually throughout the world.'[32] Ayurveda was the *janani* (mother) of all medical knowledge, a point repeatedly made by all advocates of the indigenous system.[33]

Antiquity, however, was not the sole criterion in assessing the past: the emphasis was equally on the state of knowledge in ancient texts and practice. In both knowledge and its application Ayurveda had attained a high level of perfection, as was evident from the texts of Charaka, Susruta and Vagabata. The commentaries on

tion), Kottayam, 1961, p. 1.

[31] *Dhanwantari,* 16 August 1913.

[32] Presidential Address, All India Ayurvedic Conference, 7th Session (Madras, 1915), Calcutta, 1916, p. 6.

these texts and later independent compositions elaborated a system of treatment which could meet all possible contingencies. Their proficiency was not limited to medicine; surgical skills were also not wanting. A number of surgical instruments along with actual opera-tions are listed and published in the ancient texts. Some of surgi-cal areas in which Indians excelled were rhenoplasty, skin grafting, eye surgery, trepanning, bone setting and amputation.[34] Moreover, Indians neither lacked a knowledge of anatomy nor refrained from conducting dissections.[35]

This reading of the past by the advocates of indigenous medicine was not entirely drawn from the European orientalists' Asiatic researches. They, unlike the western-educated intelligentsia, had access to and the ability to read and interpret classical texts. The orientalist discovery of India's past was however handy to them. In fact, they often referred to the authority of European scholars in support of their views. The opinions of H.H. Wilson, T.A. Wise and Royle, which highlighted the achievements of the indigenous systems, because they came from Europeans, were particularly useful for countering the colonial bias.[36] But then, the views of Indian prota-gonists and the orientalists were not similar, or when similar their motivation and purpose were not identical. The orientalist quest was either antiquarian or was an arm of the empire to construct a knowledge of the subjected, and was thus a part of the colonial hegemonic project. That the latter dimension is true of almost every field is often overlooked. For instance, in the case of education a scholar has recently tried to underplay the distinction between Indian and colonial ideas on the ground that the views of the Indian

---

[33] *Sudha Nidhi,* Vol. 2, No. 2.

[34] S.M. Mitra, *Hindu Medicine,* London, 1914.

[35] *Sudha Nidhi,* Vol. 2, No. 4.

[36] 'It was most probably at this early period (three centuries before the Christian era) that they studied the healing art with such success as to enable them to produce systematic works on medicine, derived from that source of knowledge which the prejudice of mankind is so much opposed to. Susruta informs us that a learned physician must combine a knowledge on books, or theoretical knowledge with dissection of the human body and practice. This explains why the ancient system of Hindu medicine was so complete in all its parts, and so permanent in its influence and warrants the inference that several centuries were required to form it.' T.A. Wise, *The Hindu Sys-*

intellectuals and colonial officials were similar in several respects.[37] Such a view overlooks the fact that their projects were totally different; while the former had a long-term view of social regeneration, the latter had a limited aim of management. This difference in perspective was applicable in the case of indigenous medicine as well.

Given the above perception of the past, a major point of inquiry revolved around the circumstances which led to the making of the present. Such an inquiry was not an attempt to invent a theory to justify revival, as Leslie argues, but was conceived as a necessary prelude to reform.[38] Hence the focus on the causes of decline which were identified as both internal to the systems and as created by external forces.

The internal causes rested on three factors: stagnation of knowledge, ignorance of the practitioners, and non-availability of quality medicine. The main drawback of the systems was that their knowledge had become dated. However good the classical texts were, the knowledge contained in them had remained stagnant, as there were no substantial efforts to improve upon them through experimentation and by relating knowledge to new experience. Ayurveda, by and large, had remained indifferent to the ecological and social changes which occurred after the composition of these texts and hence its method of treatment had lost touch with reality.[39] Thus, Ayurveda failed to keep pace with times and laboured within the parameters of knowledge developed centuries before.

Even this knowledge contemporary practitioners did not imbibe sufficiently. The classical texts were either not easily available or if available, most practitioners did not have the necessary language skills to assimilate their contents. The more easily accessible texts and commentaries in the vernacular languages were also not adequately made use of. In preference to the arduous task of mastering these texts and thus the fundamentals of the discipline, most practitioners adopted the easier method of oral instruction during short spells of

tem of Medicine, New Delhi, 1986 (reprint), p. xviii.

[37] Krishna Kumar, *Political Agenda of Education: A Study of Colonialist and Nationalist Ideas,* New Delhi, 1991.

[38] Leslie, 'The Ambiguities of Medical Revivalism in Modern India', in Leslie (ed.), *Asian Medical System,* p. 362.

[39] Poonamchand Tansukh Vyas, 'The Present Abject State', *Sudha Nidihi,* Vol. 1, No. 2. Also see P.S. Variar's evidence, *Report on the Indigenous*

apprenticeship under senior physicians. As a result, by the end of the nineteenth century an overwhelming majority of indigenous practitioners were ignorant of their art, purveying borrowed prescriptions to unsuspecting patients. Their only aim and interest was to earn a livelihood.[40] It is not a matter of surprise that in their hands indigenous medicine lost its effectiveness and credibility.

The methods adopted for preparing medicines, it was realized, were another major weakness of the indigenous systems. Medicines in prepared form were few and hence the patients had to prepare them on the basis of the ingredients prescribed by physicians. What was prepared by the patients often did not measure up to the prescription, either in content or method. Consequently, there was a wide gap between what the physician intended and what was actually administered to the patient. In the absence of any effective method to ensure the quality of medicine, treatment by even a competent physician was often ineffective.[41] These internal weaknesses were not unrelated to the decline in patronage, both political and social. Commenting on the contemporary neglect, the Committee on the Indigenous System observed that indigenous systems were subjected to, 'on the one hand, a cold and even chilling neglect of the State and of others who should have been their natural and grateful patrons, while, on the other, there is the severe handicap from unequal competition with a "rival" favoured with the monopoly of State recognition and State support. Under these circumstances, the wonder is not that the Indian systems have decayed, but that they are living at all.'[42]

In all discussions of the decline of the indigenous systems, the impact of the hostile attitude of the colonial state figured prominently. Under the new political conditions they were not only deprived of patronage but were also denied a chance to compete with western medicine on an equal footing. The crucial factor for the decline was, therefore, seen as loss of political power. 'Give us political power', said a militant supporter, 'then we will show which system is effective, scientific and superior. The reason for the success

---

System, Vol. II, Evidence, pp. 215–19.
[40] *Dhanwantari*, 15 December 1916.
[41] Ibid., 13 February 1916.

of western medicine in India is undoubtedly the support of the government.'[43]

The implications of alien political domination were not limited to loss of patronage and of opportunities for employment. They were equally pronounced in the sphere of social support to the system. The erstwhile Indian ruling classes had been a major source of sustenance for the indigenous systems.[44] Their displacement from the structure of power as a consequence of the establishment of colonial rule deprived the indigenous system of crucial support. So too the preference shown by the educated classes for the more systematic and professionally organized western medicine. The indigenous systems were thus marginalized, both in terms of political patronage and social support.

Although the discriminatory policy of the colonial state was the immediate problem, the stagnation and decline of the indigenous system has been traced to the ancient period itself. It was realized that over a period of time the connection between theory and practice which Susruta had emphasized had been lost sight of. One of the causes for this disjunction, it was argued, was the influence of Buddhism which discouraged dissection of animals.[45] The impact of this on the art of surgery was particularly pronounced; by the nineteenth century it was almost irretrievably lost. The decline continued during the medieval period when the preference accorded to Unani medicine by Muslim rulers and nobles proved to be disadvantageous to Ayurveda.[46] What happened during these phases was, however, qualitatively different from the developments during the colonial period when indigenous systems faced the possibility of imminent extinction. The movement for the revitalization of indigenous medicine emerged in the context of this possibility.

The revitalization movement was part of the general cultural–intellectual regeneration taking place during the late nineteenth and

---

[42] *Report on the Indigenous System,* p. 10.

[43] V. Narayanan Nair, 'Our Present State and Future Prospects (An Appeal for the Spread of Ayurveda)' (Malayalam), Kottakkal, 1921, pp. 12–13.

[44] The Ashtavaidyans in Kerala received rent-free lands from the state. *Dhanwantari,* 14 June 1917.

[45] Ibid.

[46] Variar, *Arya Vaidya Charitram,* pp. 88–89. It may, however, be noted that

early twentieth centuries; it was not an isolated phenomenon. Consciousness about the decline was manifest in almost all regions of India, particularly in Bengal, Maharashtra, Rajasthan, Tamil Nadu and Keralam. These two characteristics were intrinsic to the movement—it was cultural in its ambience and regional and national in its manifestation. The exploration of possibilities within the system by individuals and institutions at a regional level eventually merged into a common endeavour, organizationally represented by the Ayurveda Maha Sammelan in 1907.[47] The cultural connections and linkages beyond regional limits imparted to the movement a social and political meaning. Yet, different streams of indigenous systems did not evolve a common platform, despite a perception of the identity of interests and similarity of principles governing their practice. The earlier interaction between different systems also seems to have ceased; each one of them was now more concerned with western medicine. Despite this, the revitalization movement underlined the cultural concerns and also reflected the struggle for hegemony in colonial society. The movement in Keralam under the leadership of P.S. Variar throws some light on these dimensions.

The Kottakkal Initiative
Sankunni Variar

Panniyinpalli Sankunni Variar was born on 16 March 1869 into an orthodox but talented family of the temple service caste in Kottakkal, a small township near Kozhikode. Members of the family were trained in painting, music and Sanskrit literature.[48] Sankunni's mother, Kunhikutty Varasyar, had considerable knowledge in Sanskrit and was also well-versed in classical music. The reputation of the family was, however, based on the achievements of its members as Ayurvedic physicians. The artistic, religious and medical atmosphere in which young Sankunni grew up appears to have had an abiding impact on his precocious mind. Even as a small child he knew the

---

the Unani system was considered an indigenous system.
[47] Poonam Bala, 'The State and Indigenous Medicine: Some Explorations on the Interaction between Ayurveda and the Indian State', unpublished M. Phil. dissertation, Jawaharlal Nehru University, New Delhi, 1982, p. 94.
[48] The mural paintings of Ambalapuzha temple were executed by Achutha

names of medicines well enough to prescribe them to those who feigned illness as a practical joke to tease him.[49]

After exposure to such a family environment, Sankunni's education proceeded on traditional lines. He learnt Sanskrit under some of the reputed scholars of his time, Chunakkara Kochukrishna Variar and Kaikulangara Rama Variar. He was introduced to the rudiments of Ayurveda by Konath Achutha Variar, after which he studied for four years under Ashta Vaidyan Kuttancheri Vasudevan Mooss, who was a highly accomplished Ayurvedic physician.

By the time Sankunni completed his education at the age of twenty and started practice at Kottakkal, western medicine was becoming popular in the region. Curious by nature, he was eager to acquaint himself with the new system. His ignorance of the English language was the first stumbling block, which he overcame by learning it privately. An opportunity to acquire the skills of western medicine soon presented itself, although fortuitously, when he was afflicted by an eye disease, granular ophthalmia, for which he consulted Dr V. Verghese, an assistant surgeon of the government hospital at Manjeri near Kottakkal. On completion of the treatment, Dr Verghese offered to teach him western medical methods, if he so desired. He gratefully accepted the offer and received training in the hospital for three years.[50] He learnt methods of diagnosis, dispensing medicines, administering anaesthesia and performing minor operations. His knowledge of medicine thus embraced both the indigenous and the western systems. Although firmly rooted in Ayurveda, which he conceived as integral to his religion and culture, he developed a respect and admiration for western medical knowledge, particularly surgery, anatomy and physiology, which considerably influenced his perspective of reform.

Variar was a man of liberal and catholic outlook. Although deeply religious and orthodox in belief and practice, his attitude towards other faiths was influenced by universalist principles. The entrance to his house was adorned with Christian, Islamic and Hindu symbols. When Dr Verghese came to visit him, Variar presented to his teacher, as a token of his respect, a bejewelled gold cross.[51] His non-

---

Variar and Madhava Variar, two grand-uncles of P.S. Variar, Kizhedath Vasudevan Nair, *Vaidyarathnam P.S. Variar,* Kottakkal, 1983, p. 2.
[49] P.S. Variar, *Shashti Varshika Charitram,* Kottakkal, 1929, p. 26.

sectarian attitude was best expressed during the revolt of 1921 in which Mappila rebels killed Hindu landlords and fought against British troops. Variar's house was a place of refuge for both Hindus and Muslims. He did not hesitate to extend help and hospitality to them even when the police was present in his house. Despite the opposition of government officials, he advocated that the families of Mappilas involved in the revolt deserved as much relief as the Hindus. Variar's name was so respected that it became a password to safety during the troubled times of the revolt. The Mappilas not only refrained from attacking his house, but even stood guard to protect it from roaming bands of rebels, as a demonstration of their respect and gratitude.[52] Free from many of the prejudices of his times, Variar had an open and critical mind. He was imaginative but practical, enthusiastic but patient, and energetic but systematic. These qualities contributed to the success of his institution-building efforts, be they in the field of medicine, literature, or art.

Cultural Roots

The movement for the revitalization of indigenous medicine revolved around three issues. (i) The retrieval, systematization and dissemination of knowledge. (ii) The creation of institutional facilities for training physicians. (iii) The preparation and distribution of medicine. In none of these fields can P.S. Variar be called a pioneer in the national context. Gangadhar Ray and Ganga Prasad Sen in Bengal, Shankar Shastri Pade in Maharashtra and Gopalachari in Madras had in some ways anticipated his efforts.[53] There were also several contemporaries of Variar, like Gananath Sen and Lakshmipati, who charted a similar course. Variar's efforts, apart from being the first in Keralam, laid great emphasis on institution-building; more importantly, they were closely linked to the cultural awakening in colonial Keralam.

Immediately after he started practice at Kottakkal he became conscious of the weaknesses of his art and began exploring steps to

[50] Kizhedath Vasudevan Nair, *Vaidyarathnam,* pp. 23–25.

[51] Ibid., p. 25.

[52] Ibid., pp. 60–65. Also see K.N. Panikkar, *Against Lord and State: Religion and Peasant Uprisings in Malabar,* New Delhi, 1990.

[53] P.M. Mehta, *Luminaries of Indian Medicine,* Bombay, 1968, and

remedy at least some of them. The formation of an association of physicians, the Arya Vaidya Samajam, in 1902, was the first step in this direction.

The inaugural session of the Samajam was held at Kottakkal with delegates drawn from all over Keralam. Subsequently annual conferences were held at different places. The Maharajas of Travoncore and Cochin and the Samuthiri of Calicut were its patrons; P.S. Variar was nominated its permanent secretary.[54] The annual conferences were conducted with great fanfare: they became cultural events, with music, exhibitions and public processions.[55] The organizational structure and activities of the Samajam covering all the three political divisions—Travancore, Cochin and Malabar—emphasized the unity of Keralam. It was perhaps the first public body to do so, much before the Indian National Congress organized its first Kerala conference in 1920.

The Samajam was essentially a voluntary public platform to exchange views and share experiences. In the process it became the ideational ground of the revitalization movement. Most of the programmes and activities of the movement either originated from or were discussed in its meetings. A good example is the *pathasala*, an institution for training physicians, the need for which was repeatedly stressed in the deliberations of every annual conference.[56] The main contribution of the Samajam was that it occasioned a 'creative introspection'—to borrow a term from D.D. Kosambi—into the past and present of Ayurveda, both its knowledge and practice. The proceedings of the conferences had two parts. The first, general speeches—eulogistic, uncritical and nostalgic about the past—intended to instill self-confidence in the system. Although repetitive and superficial, they created a sense of urgency to bring about changes in the existing conditions. The second, the reading of papers, led to more professional discussions on illness, treatment and medicine. This was perhaps the most significant aspect, as it brought together uncodified experience and innovations and thus underlined both the problems and the potential of the discipline.

The deliberations in the conferences had an unmistakable

Brahmananda Gupta, 'Indigenous Medicine in Nineteenth and Twentieth Century Bengal', in Leslie (ed.), *Asian Medical System*, pp. 368–77.

[54] *Shashti Varshika Charitram*, pp. 81–82.

tendency to underplay the effectiveness and suitability of western medicine and to highlight the superiority of the indigenous system for the treatment of Indians. The argument was not so much based on which system was currently better equipped and developed, but more on the links of a medical system with nature and society. Each system, it was argued, developed in specific natural and social conditions which influenced its pharmacopoeia and the methods of treatment. The fundamental question of relations between body, ecology and medicine was underlined:

> In Europe warmth is considered an indicator of happiness, as evident from the use of the words 'warm reception'. The climate being cold Europeans feel happy with a little warmth. We, on the other hand, living in a tropical region are fond of cold. If any medicine to generate heat in the body is to be administered to Europeans, it has to be quite strong. Their medicines prepared to suit the body of Europeans are too hot for us. For those living in tropical countries, an important quality of medicine is the ability of cooling the system. The medicinal herbs from the Himalayan region are therefore considered by many as more effective than those from the Vindhyas. There is a general impression in India that English medicines give only temporary relief. But the Europeans do not impute the same weakness to their system. It is so because their medicines are effective for their diseases but no suitable for the conditions of our body.[57]

One may pick several holes in the above argument, but it forcefully draws attention to the fact that the western and indigenous systems orginated and developed in different environmental and cultural conditions. Given these differences, whether western medicine was suited to the body and the mind of Indians was the basic question. In this context, its indigenous character was perceived to be the strength of the indigenous system; it was 'in harmony with the nature of the inhabitants of the country.'[58] It was a part of their culture, integrated with their pattern of life and hence attuned to a culturally specific concept of health-care.

[55] *Dhanwantari,* 14 January 1917.
[56] Ibid.

Disseminating Knowledge

Although the speeches and writings of the advocates of indigenous medicine were often self-adulatory, the deliberations in the Arya Vaidya Samajam were self-critical and directed to the formulation of a plan of action. A major concern was the contemporary state of knowledge, two dimensions of which called for immediate attention. The first was stagnation and loss of knowledge, and the second, lack of knowledge among practitioners.

Loss of knowledge had occurred both due to the non-availability of texts as well as their lack of use in actual practice. From the time of the early texts of Charka, Susruta and Vagabata a considerable body of literature had come into existence, either as original compositions or as commentaries. Of them only a few, like those of Madhavacharya (*Madhavanidhanam*), and Moreshwar Bhatt (*Vaidyanritam*) were in actual use. The existence of large number of other texts, particularly those composed in the regional languages, was unknown even to those active in the profession. The loss of regional language texts of later provenance was all the more grievous as they alone recorded attempts at innovation in the treatment of difficult cases. Innovations based on experience were crucial, as the texts did not prescribe the actual composition of ingredients, for this was determined by a variety of considerations. Innovations were certainly not lacking: some of the unorthodox methods used by *ashtavaidyans* to cure different cases are on record.[59]

The non-availability of later texts was particularly unfortunate as they contained information about additions made by them to the pharmacopoeia. Almost every text contributed to the enrichment of the existing *materia medica*, as evident from the works of Madanapala, Narahari, Shodalan, Moreshwar Bhatt and several others.[60] These additions took place either due to external influences or because of the need to meet new challenges. Thus, the notion that the stagnation of the indigenous system was due to the inability or unwillingness of practitioners to depart from the given, requires some re-examination.

A positive feature of the revitalization movement was the retrieval of knowledge and its dissemination through systematic

[57] Ibid., 14 May 1917.
[58] Ibid.
[59] *Kottarathil Sankunni, Eithihyamala*, Kottayam, 1974, pp. 141–46 and

collection and publication of texts. Judging from the results, the assumption about the existing of texts and commentaries not easily accessible or not currently in use, was not wide of the mark. Shankar Shastri Pade, the main inspiration behind the movement in Maharashtra, prepared an index of 702 texts and commentaries and published about 70 books.[61] The Usman Committee on the indigenous system of medicine in Madras Presidency listed 288 Sanskrit, 400 Telugu, 63 Malayalam and several hundred Siddha texts and commentaries available in different repositories. It also identified 49 texts which could not be located anywhere.[62]

The dissemination of knowledge available in the classics and later texts was conceived as an urgent task of revitalization. Aided by the printing infrastructure developed during the colonial period, the protagonists of indigenous medicine tried to transform the hitherto relatively inaccessible knowledge into social knowledge as well as a shared system of knowledge among the practitioners. Publication of both texts and popular commentaries was, therefore, undertaken in fairly large numbers in different parts of the country. By the end of the nineteenth century there were as many as fifty medical journals in the Indian languages[63]—*Sanjeevini* in Bengali edited by Ganga Prasad Sen, *Raja Vaidya, Arya Bhishak* and *Sadvaidya Kostubha* in Marathi edited by Shankar Shastri Pade, and *Dhanwantari* in Malayalam edited by P.S. Variar, to mention a few.[64]

Codification and dissemination of existing knowledge was an area to which P.S. Variar devoted considerable attention. One of his early efforts was to prepare and publish a catalogue of medicine, with details of dosage and other information which would enable patients to use medicines without the prescription of a physician. He wrote a book, *Chikitsa Samgraham,* to acquaint the public with the rudiments of Ayurvedic medicines and treatment. The other important works authored by Variar were a book on cholera, a Malayalam rendering of *Ashtanga Hridayam,* and a history of Ayurveda jointly

268–77.

[60] P.S. Variar, *Arya Vaidya Charitram,* pp. 49–64.

[61] *Sudha Nidhi,* Vol. I, No. 3.

[62] *Report on Indigenous Medicine,* Appendix IX. Also see N. Kandaswamy Pillai, *History of Siddha Medicine,* Madras, 1979, pp. 372–402.

written with his cousin P.V. Krishna Variar.[65] These publications
created a corpus of literature in Malayalam easily accessible to the
practitioners and the public and thus gave rise to social consciousness
about the use and importance of Ayurveda.

    Dhanwantari, a fortnightly journal published by P.S. Variar
from Kottakkal, played a very important role in this regard. Started
in 1902, it was the mouthpiece of the revitalization movement in
Keralam and reflected most of the tendencies inherent in it. It
provided an open forum for debate and discussion, as is evident from
some articles critical of the reform efforts.[66] P.S. Variar was a regular
contributor and some of his essays focused on the nature of the choice
Indians should make to achieve proper health-care. He wrote a series
of articles entitled 'Western and Eastern Medicine', which was a
candid assessment of the strengths and weaknesses of the two
systems. While conceding the advances made by western medicine, he
argued for selective adoption of ideas and methods from it. He
underlined the past achievements as well as the divine origin of
Ayurveda, but at the same time stressed the need for introducing
changes in it. On a comparison of the two systems, what he emphasized was the relative merit and potential of Ayurveda for effective
health-care of Indians, given the climatic conditions in which the
body was located.[67] This article was an indication of the lines on
which he wanted the revitalization movement to proceed.

The 'Pathasala'

    The retrieval of knowledge would become meaningful only
when internalized by the existing body of practitioners and integrated
into their practice. A majority of them did not have the training or
intellectual equipment to do so. Like many of his contemporaries,
P.S. Variar realized the urgent need to rectify this situation by creating
the necessary infrastructure to bring into existence a group of
physicians well-versed in the discipline. Given the indifference of the
colonial state in this matter, mobilization of internal resources
became important.

---

[63] *Sudha Nidhi,* Vol. I, No. 3.

[64] Mehta, *Luminaries,* pp. 84–88.

[65] Kizhedath Vasudevan Nair, *Vaidyarathnam. Ayurveda Charitram* was
per-haps the first history of Ayurveda to be written in an Indian language.

There are very few knowledgeable and experienced Vaidyans in Kerala today. Even if there are some they have no facilities to train and teach their disciples. There is enough reason to believe that after one more generation the conditions of Ayurveda would become so critical that any effort to remedy the situation is likely to be futile. The general opinion, therefore, is that arrangements for imparting training should be made as early as possible.[68]

This was an idea repeatedly raised by Variar in almost every meeting of the Arya Vaidya Samajam. Although it received enthusiastic approval and support, he was conscious of the limitations of resources, both men and material, for undertaking such a venture. Therefore, the proposal to set up a *pathasala* remained in a state of incubation for about fifteen years. Meanwhile, he took some initiative to create a body of qualified practitioners by evolving a system of public examination for those who were already carrying on practice. Under this scheme the Samajam organized early examinations in three towns of Keralam. That only 17 out of 315 who took the examination managed to qualify was indicative of the existing state of knowledge and training of the practitioners. Interestingly, a majority of those who took the examination belonged to the lower castes; there were also a few Christians.[69]

Institutional arrangements for teaching and training materialized only in 1917 when a *pathasala* was set up at Calicut. It was an important step towards the professionalization of indigenous medical practice through systematic instruction and a well-defined curriculum. The *pathasala*, as evident from its prospectus, was conceived as the lynchpin of the revitalization movement. The objectives of the *pathasala*, the prospectus stated, were to revive the 'once prosperous and now increasingly declining Ayurveda', to bring about timely changes in it, to train physicians with sufficient knowledge and experience who can conduct the practice 'without others' assistance and to acquaint the British government about the merits of the indigenous system'.[70]

The *pathasala* adopted a five-year course, with Sanskrit as

---

[66] *Dhanwantari*, 14 May 1917.
[67] Ibid.
[68] Prospectus of 'Arya Vaidya Pathasala', *Dhanwantari*, Vol. 12, No. 11.

the medium of instruction first and later both Malayalam and Sanskrit. The curriculum of the *pathasala* was based on a combination of indigenous and western knowledge. The emphasis was indeed on mastering Ayurvedic texts and through that acquiring knowledge of medicines and their preparation. They were supplemented with instruction in physiology, anatomy, chemistry, midwifery and surgery incorporated from the western system.[71]

Knowledge of Sanskrit was a prerequisite for admission and preference was given to those who were also conversant with English. Admission was open without caste or gender discrimination. Education was free, but there was an admission fee of Rs 5. To begin with there were five scholarships, four for boys at the rate of Rs 8 per month and one for girls at the rate of Rs 10.[72] Later the number of scholarships increased considerably, so much so that an overwhelming majority of students received financial assistance to pursue their studies.[73]

The publication of the prospectus of the *pathasala* and the nature of the curriculum proposed in it stimulated some thinking about the course and character of the revitalization movement.[74] The curriculum of the *pathasala* articulated a definite view on this, a view which Variar had repeatedly expressed in several of his writings. While preferring Ayurveda as the ideal system suitable for Indian conditions, he was not in favour of isolationism. He believed that the western and Indian systems should be brought together so that the latter could benefit from this interaction. However, Variar's conception of this interaction, although programmatic, was superficial and inadequate. Like many of his contemporaries, Variar was also inclined to borrow from the west rather than create a dialogue between the indigenous and the European. Given their perception of European progress, the Indian mind during the colonial period tended to be eclectic, grafting ideas and practices into their own intellectual–cultural universe. The curriculum of the *pathasala* which incorporated some elements of western medical knowledge in the final year of the course was a good example of this weakness. What

[69] *Dhanwantari*, 16 August 1913.
[70] Prospectus of the 'Arya Vaidya Pathasala'.
[71] Ibid.
[72] Ibid.

was borrowed hardly merged with the rest of the course and remained a separate and curious entity.

In the discussions and debates that followed the establishment of the *pathasala* two distinct views came to the fore. The first was represented by the purists who strongly resented the efforts of Variar to depart from tradition. Taking a revivalist posture, they wanted the curriculum to be confined to the classical texts and their later commentaries. The other view placed greater reliance on western knowledge, particularly in anatomy and physiology.[75] Variar was not in agreement with either of these views, as he was not in favour of either blind adherence to tradition or uncritical acceptance of the west. The curriculum of the *pathasala* was one area where he tried to bring together the western and the indigenous.[76] The establishment of the *pathasala*, therefore, was an important event in the intellectual–cultural life of Keralam, as it was a pioneering institutional effort to reach out to western knowledge from a perspective strongly rooted in tradition.

Marketing Medicines

The most successful institution-building effort of P.S. Variar was in the manufacture and marketing of medicines. Variar realized that Ayurveda could be effective and popular only if its medicines were standardized and prepared in conformity with textual prescriptions. This was possible only if the practitioners took initiative and joined together to form companies for the manufacture and marketing of medicines. In this respect the practice of western medicine, he felt, was worthy of emulation. The popularity and effectiveness of western medicine was largely dependent on its easy availability, in accordance with the prescription of doctors. Indigenous medicine could contend with the increasing influence of western medicine only if it developed similar infrastructure. With this in view he established the Arya Vaidyasala in Kottakkal in 1902. The advertisement published on the occasion is an interesting document reflecting Variar's business acumen, ability for innovation, and will to change according to contemporary needs. He had no hesitation in following the western

[73] Ibid.
[74] Ibid.

example, discarding old prejudices and thus bring into operation a system of manufacture of medicine on modern and scientific lines and market them on a commercial basis.[77]

P.S. Variar was indeed not the first to undertake largescale manufacture and sale of indigenous medicine. Chandra Kishore Sen in Bengal had opened a dispensary in 1878 in Calcutta for selling medicines at a cheap rate. His firm, C.K. Sen and Company, started largescale production in 1898. So did N.N. Sen and Company in 1884 and Shakti Aushadalaya of Dacca in 1901.[78] But the bottling of *kashayam*, a medicinal brew which could not be kept for more than a few days, was an innovation others had not attempted.

The sale of medicines in Arya Vaidyasala was moderate to begin with. During the first four-year period sales amounted to only Rs 14,000 but it increased to Rs 57,000, Rs 1,23,000 and Rs 1,70,000 during the subsequent four-year periods.[79] The venture proved to be a great success. Arya Vaidyasala is a flourishing institution today with more than one sale outlet in every town in Keralam as well as in some cities outside. Following Variar's initiative, several others established Vaidyasalas and began selling medicines. The social reach and acceptance of Ayurveda in Kerala society today is mainly due to the vision and enterprise of P.S. Variar.

Cultural Renaissance and Medicine

The revitalization movement in Keralam occurred in the context of a cultural awakening of which Kottakkal was an important centre. Integral to this awakening was the quest to realize the political and cultural personality of Keralam through a construction of its political unity and cultural identity. Despite the existing political divisions, Keralam was conceived as one territorial entity— extending from Gokarnam to Kanyakumari. The writing of history, which seems to have suddenly flourished during the late nineteenth century, underlined this unity by tracing the origin of Keralam to the legend of Parasurama, according to which the area was reclaimed from the sea and donated to the brahmins. Among many such

---

[75] Ibid.
[76] Ibid.
[77] *Shashti Varshika Charitram*, pp. 70–74.

histories written during this period, the one composed in verse by Kodungallur Kunhikuttan Thampuran, renowned for his translation of the Mahabharatam, is particularly significant. Thampuran traced the origin, antiquity and historical development of the region.[80] His description of the territory anticipated the romantic invocation of the land of Keralam by Vallathol Narayana Menon during the national movement. The period between Thampuran and Vallathol witnessed the formation of a consciousness about the identity of Keralam in the realm of history, politics and culture, in fact, in all areas of social endeavour. During this time the novels of O. Chandu Menon and C.V. Raman Pillai which had social and political significance had made their appearance, Narayana Guru and V.T. Bhattathiripad had initiated reform movements, and G. Parameswara Pillai and his associates had presented the Malayali Memorial. All these events were expressions of a social resurgence, rooted in the intellectual and cultural perception of the changing situation in Keralam. So too the movement for the revitalization of indigenous medicine.

Several intellectual and cultural activities took shape around the movement at Kottakkal: a history society, a literary magazine, a Kathakali troupe and a drama company were some of them. Arya Vaidyasala was the nucleus around which these activities blossomed and P.S. Variar was the moving spirit behind them, not merely as patron but as active participant.[81] The work of Arya Vaidasala thus became part of a multi-pronged cultural endeavour—the expression of a cultural renaissance, as described by N.V. Krishnan Kutty Variar, an outstanding physician of Kottakkal and the author of *Ayurvedacharitram.*[82]

The existing literature on the state of indigenous medicine has mainly focused on three issues—revivalism, professionalization and elitism. That the movement within the indigenous systems, for that matter in all realms of cultural and intellectual life in colonial India, was essentially revivalist in character, is a very common and often uncritically accepted idea. In the case of medicine, Charles Leslie, the most articulate advocate of this view, argues that since the

[78] Gupta, 'Indigenous Medicine', in Leslie (ed.), *Asian Medical System,* p. 374.

[79] *Dhanwantari,* 14 March 1920.

[80] Kodungallur Kunhikuttan Tampuran, *Keralam,* Trissur, 1912.

protagonists of indigenous medicine 'believed literally in the author-ity of the classic texts, and at the same time were impressed by the accomplishments of modern science, they set out to demonstrate that the institutions and scientific theories of consmopolitan medicine were anticipated in the ancient texts.'[83] He implies in his analysis that the inquiry into the causes of decline was to formulate a theory which would justify revival. He dismisses 'the revivalist theory of decline', as there is no evidence to support the assumption that the general level of Ayurvedic practice in the nineteenth century was less efficacious than that of antiquity.[84]

Another view, both popular and influential, relates the revitalization movement to professionalization. Given the main concerns of the movement—systematization of knowledge, institu-tionalization of training, and standardization of medicine—professionalization was inherent to it. As a consequence the move-ment is identified with professionalization, taking place under the influence of modern (read western) medical practice. An advocate of this view, Paul Brass, describes the movement—'a major revivalist movement in modern Indian history'—'as an attempt by a tradition-alistic interest group to legitimize itself and achieve recognition and status'.[85] The movement, in his reckoning, had a limited objec-tive—to act as an instrument of political pressure in support of Ayurveda and to counteract the influence of the 'entrenched and hostile' modern medical profession. This argument seems to focus on the interests of a social group and thus underplays the significance of the quest to revitalize the system as a body of indigenous knowledge and as an aspect of the cultural identity of a subjected people.

Another view of the movement underlines its elitist character as it sought 'to replace popular practices that were seen outside the

[81] The script for plays were written by P.S. Variar which are preserved in the library of the Arya Vaidyasala.

[82] Interview with the author at Kottakkal, 15 April 1991.

[83] Leslie, 'Ambiguities of Medical Revivalism', in Leslie (ed.), *Asian Medical System*, p. 365. A similar view is held by Ralph C. Crozier; see 'Medicine, Modernization and Cultural Crisis in China and India', *Comparative Stud-ies in Society and History*, Vol. 12, pp. 275–91.

[84] Ibid.

scientific systems'.[86] Elaborating this point, Barbara Metcalfe, in a study of Hakim Ajmalkhan states:

> In some was the technique of creating intellectual equivalence was the same in all subjects, namely the return of texts of the literate culture at the expense of customary or local practice. Thus the adversaries of the reformers were practitioners of unsystematic folk medicine, often midwives and other women and poorly trained yunani practitioners. As in the case of religious education this is scripturalist reform, but here reform by the cosmopolitan, not the sharia-minded.[87]

The movement within indigenous medicine indeed had elements of all there features, yet any one of them individually or all of them collectively, did not constitute the character of the movement. All reform movements in colonial India, in the social, cultural or religious spheres, were not without an element of revival inherent in them. Yet, they were not exclusively revivalist movements, seeking to resurrect the past as an alternative to the present. The past was indeed a reference point in all these efforts, though the invocation of the past was not so much an expression of the concern for tradition, as recently argued,[88] as a device to contend with contemporary conditions.

In the case of indigenous medicine too a revivalist tendency, supported by the landed aristocracy, was quite evident. A report on the Arya Vaidya Samajam stated that its meetings were attended at one time or the other by almost all rajahs, landlords and physicians.[89] As mentioned earlier, the patrons of the Samajam were the two ruling chiefs of Travancore and Cochin and the former ruler of Calicut. Members of the erstwhile ruling families of Malabar enthusiastically participated in the activities of the Samajam. Financial support for the movement also came from the same sources.[90] Although poli-

[85] Paul R. Brass, 'The Politics of Ayurvedic Education: A Case Study of Revivalism and Modernization in India', in Susan H. Rudolph and Lloyd I. Rudolph (eds.), *Education and Politics in India*, Delhi, 1972, pp. 342–43.

[86] Barbara Metcalfe, 'Nationalist Muslims in British India: The Case Study of Hakim Ajmalkhan', *Modern Asian Studies*, 9, 1, 1985, pp, 1–28.

[87] Ibid.

[88] Lata Mani, 'Contentious Traditions: The Debate on Sati in Colonial India', in Kumkum Sangari and Sudesh Vaid (eds.), *Recasting Women*, New Delhi, 1989, pp. 88–126.

[89] *Dhanwantari*, 14 January 1917.

[90] Ibid.

tically loyal to the British, the members of this class were quite critical of the colonial cultural system—the obverse of the attitude of the
intelligentsia which disapproved and opposed colonial domination,
without, however, rejecting colonial culture. To members of the
landed aristocracy the movement appealed as an opportunity to
revive the practices of a traditional society in which they had
exercised political and social power. Hence, their attitude towards it
was nostalgic and revivalist, just as their attitude towards western
medicine was hostile and confrontationist. Such a perspective was
not wholly shared by the movement, but it did not dismiss it either.
What it attempted was to go beyond this perspective in an effort to
modernize the system, by reconciling it with the knowledge of
western medicine.

The revitalization movement essentially operated within the
literate tradition and its social universe remained within the confines
of literate groups—those who knew Sanskrit and English. A large
number of popular practitioners who were not literate and had no
textual knowledge were inevitably marginalized by the movement. In
fact, the leaders of the movement decried the ignorance and inefficiency of these practitioners and one of the stated aims of the
movement was to create in their stead a body of knowledgeable
physicians. The impact of professionalization, particular, was
quite adverse on this group, as they in comparison were deemed
untrained and unqualified. However, the movement did not look
upon them as adversaries, as suggested by Barbara Metcalfe, but as
objects of reform, even if reform turned them into victims.

Multiple Voices

The historiography of colonial India is quite often informed
by a simplistic opposition between colonialism and nationalism.
Consequently, the historical process during this period is telescoped
into a unilinear development of anti-colonial consciousness, over-
looking contradictions and differentiations within it. If located
within this perspective, the revitalization movement informed by an
unmistakable tendency of confrontation with colonial medicine
would appear to be an expression of cultural nationalism, contesting
colonial cultural hegemony. The movement, however, had multiple
voices within it. While opposing the cultural ambience created by

colonial medicine, the movement was not averse to incorporating elements of western knowledge perceived as superior and yet undeveloped in the indigenous system. A change which the movement tried to refute was the unscientific character of indigenous medicine, yet it levelled the same charge against popular medical practices and tried to make them comply with textual prescriptions.

The quest to revitalize indigenous medicine reflected a multi-pronged struggled for cultural hegemony, not only between the coloniser and the colonised, but also between different classes within the colonised society.

8 Marriage Reform: Ideology and Social Base

It is important for an enquiry into the changes in family organization and marriage system of the Nairs in Keralam during the second half of the nineteenth century to investigate the nature and basis of their self-perception of their own social position and relations. Since self-perception, to a great extent, is influenced by the dominant ideology in a society, it would also be necessary to examine the role of the ideological system that came into being in the wake of the social dominance of the Nambudiri brahmins. Some of the relevant questions in this context are: How did the Nairs come to accept an unequal marital relationship with the Nambudiris? Were the Nair family organization and marriage system linked with Nambudiri privileges? More importantly for our present discussion, how did the ideological struggle of the Nairs against Nambudiri dominance, which resulted in a revaluation and reform of their social institutions and social practices, develop during the course of the nineteenth century?

Ideologies being material and not ideal in their origin and existence, changes in the influence of the dominant ideology are related to changes in the material conditions of existence. The nature, direction and momentum of these changes as well as the ideological forms in which men become conscious of these changes, constitute the basis for the creation or adoption of an alternate system of beliefs, as also for the struggle against the dominant ideology. The factors which helped the development of this struggle and the consequent efforts to restructure social institutions during colonial rule—a period in which India not only underwent rapid socio-economic transformation, but was also beleaguered by western ideas—were several: the employment of Indian intermediaries by European traders, the new pattern of appropriation and distribution of peasant surplus and changes in the nature and requirements of state patronage, and, above all, the integration of the Indian economy with the world capitalist market. This chapter seeks to examine the impact of some of these factors on the family organization and marriage system of Nairs in Malabar.[1]

Nambudiri Privileges: Historical Roots

By the beginning of the twelfth century almost the entire land of Keralam had come under the control of the Nambudiris. The process by which they came to occupy this dominant position is linked to the nature of temple administration and control of temple property. In Keralam, as in other parts of south India, temples were the centres of social life. They fulfilled 'the role of today's schools, reading rooms, religious centres, cinema houses, theatres, parks and even brothels'.[2] Almost every town in ancient Keralam had developed around a temple. The temples had extensive landed property as well as gold and other valuables in abundance, contributed by rulers and devotees.[3] The land grant of Karunandadakkan to Parthivapuram temple and the gold offered to the temples at Suchindram, Tirunanthikarai, Tiruvalla and Trikkakara by several other rulers may be cited as examples in this context.[4] The expenses incurred by temples also indicated their prosperity. The Tiruvalla temple, for instance, had earmarked land requiring one lakh *paras*[5] of seed for *tiruvagram* (a feast for the brahmins). The temple also incurred expenditure on daily service, payment of salaries to employees and

[1] During British rule Malabar was a district of Madras Presidency. It continued to be a district of the state of Madras till 1956, when, according to the recommendations of the States' Reorganization Commission, it was made a part of Keralam. Later, it was divided into four districts—Kannur, Kozhikode, Palakkad and Malappuram.

[2] Elamkulam Kunjan Pillai, *Studies in Kerala History*, Kottayam, 1970, p. 332.

[3] Rajan Gurukkal, 'Socio-Economic Role of the Kerala Temple, 800–1200', M. Phil. dissertation, Jawaharlal Nehru University, New Delhi, 1978.

[4] *Travancore Archaeological Survey (TAS)*, I, Madras, 1910, p. 115; and II, Madras, 1921, p. 42.

[5] A local measure equal to approximately five kilograms.

maintenance of a school and a dispensary.[6] The expenses of Parthivapuram temple were equally heavy.[7]

The temple properties were administered by *sabhas* or committees consisting, in all probability, of brahmins and representatives
of *karalar* (tenants of temple lands).[8] They enacted certain rules and
regulations—*mulikkalakkaccam, kadamkattu kaccam, Sankaramangalath kaccam, kottivayira veli kaccam* and *tavanur kaccam*—
for preventing possible embezzlement of temple property and for
protecting the interests of the tenants.[9] Between the tenth and twelfth
centuries changes occurred in the constitution of these committees
and their membership devolved almost exclusively upon the Nambudiri
brahmins, which enabled them to establish ownership over temple
properties and in course of time emerge as *janmis* or absolute proprietors of land.[10] Our present knowledge of the history of ancient
Keralam is not adequate to explain the process of this transformation
in detail. Elamkulam Kunjan Pillai has suggested that it was integral
to the socio-political changes taking place during this time: the
disintegration of the Chera kingdom as a result of the invasion of
Rajendra Chola in 1028, the introduction of the *kalari* (gymnasium)
system, compulsory military service and the emergence of the Nairs
as a separate caste of warriors.[11] This explanation, however, raises a
series of questions: was there any secular control over the administration of temples before the Chola invasion; what was the relationship
between the Nambudiri brahmins and the ruling chieftains; and if the
karalar were inducted into military service, who replaced them and
what relationship was established with their successors by the
brahmin trustees? However, it is enough for our present purpose to
observe that a major part of the land came under the control of the

---

[6] *TAS*, II, pp. 175–97.

[7] Kunjan Pillai, *Studies*, pp. 327–28.

[8] Kunjan Pillai, *Keralacharitrathile Iruladanja Edukal* (Malayalam),
Kottayam, 1963, p. 37.

[9] Kunjan Pillai, *Studies*, pp. 336–37.

[10] In the case of Suchindram temple, by the middle of the thirteenth century
control over the temple administration was exercised by a group of
Malayali brahmins. Southern Travancore, where Suchindram temple is
situated, was conquered by the ruler of Travancore only in the twelfth
century. K.K. Pillai, *The Suchindram Temple*, Madras, 1953, p. 148.

[11] Kunjan Pillai, *Studies*, p. 432.

Nambudiris by the twelfth century and that exemption from taxation helped them to further consolidate their position during the subsequent period.

An ideological system rationalizing and perpetuating this dominance soon came into being—legend, religion and literature contributing to its making. Keralam, according to a legend which is still an inseparable part of the historical consciousness of the Malayalis, was reclaimed from the sea by Parasurama, and bestowed upon the brahmins for their exclusive enjoyment. Early 'histories' of Keralam like *Kerala Mahatmyam* and *Keralolpatti,* composed in all probability by Nambudiri landlords, authenticated this legend. *Keralolpatti* describes the position of brahmins as follows:

> Parasurama created Malayalam, the *Keralabhumi* and gave it as a gift to the Brahmans of the 64 *gramams* together for their enjoyment is called *janmam.* . . . . Afterwards he gave the right called *rajamsam* to 3600 Brahmans of 10 *gramams* by pouring water on the sword. They can put their finger in water and say 'this is my *janmam*'; but the others may not put their finger in water and say 'this is my *janmam*'.[12]

Thus, Nambudiri land-ownership was represented as divine dispensation and, therefore, inviolable.

The rules of social conduct and caste relations ensured a superior and privileged position for the Nambudiris and the subjection and acquiescence of the lower orders to a value system which helped to perpetuate their privileges. Ranked the highest in the caste hierarchy and in ritual status, and regarded as the repository of Vedic knowledge and as scholars of Sanskrit, the authority of the Nambudiris was supreme in all religious matters. Probably initially they also had some technical expertise like knowledge of the calendar and the ability to forecast weather cycles.[13] They were 'the holiest of human beings, representatives of God on earth', whose person and property were sacred. They also wielded considerable political influence and acted as neutral channels of communication between various

[12] Quoted in C.A. Innes and F.B. Evans, *Malabar,* second edition, Ernakulam, 1951, p. 305.

[13] D.D. Kosambi, 'The Basis of Ancient Indian History', *Journal of American Oriental Society,* 1955, p. 36.

chieftains.[14] They enjoyed immunity from the normal processes of
law, being subject only to the authority of the head of their own
community.[15]

The duty of the lower castes was to serve the brahmins by
protecting and maintaining their properties. Their salvation lay in
submitting themselves to the will and pleasure of the Nambudiris.
The virtues of serving the brahmins were set forth in literature,
religious discourses and temple arts like *chakyarkuttu*. The subservience of lower castes was manifest in all realms of social intercourse.
A Nair could not touch a Nambudiri, a Tiyya had to keep at least
thirty-two feet away from him, and a Cheruma sixty-four feet.[16] Even
the style of conversation indicated the superior/inferior status.[17] The
violation of these rules led to excommunication—the denial of village
services like those of a barber or washerman and the facilities of
village temples and wells.

The influence of the Nambudiri value system and of their
material position is best reflected in the marriage system and the law
of inheritance. The Nambudiris followed patriliny and primogeniture,
with only the eldest son allowed to marry within the caste, which was
obviously intended to keep the family property intact.[18] The younger
sons established liaisons, known as *sambandham*, with matrilineal
Nair women—these were not regarded as marriage by the Nambudiris,

---

[14] L.A. Krishna Iyer, *A Short History of Kerala*, Ernakulam, 1966, p. 129, and
K.K. Pillai, 'Aryan Influence in Kerala History', in *History on the March,
Proceedings of the Kerala History Convention*, Ernakulam, 1965, p. 143.

[15] Francis Buchanan, *A Journey from Madras through the Countries of
Mysore, Canara and Malabar*, II, London, 1807, p. 425.

[16] Adrian C. Mayer, *Land and Society in Malabar*, Bombay, 1952, p. 26. Also
see V.P.S. Raghuvanshi, *Indian Society in the Eighteenth Century*, New
Delhi, 1969, p. 64.

[17] A Nair, while conversing with a Nambudiri, described his house as a
'rubbish heap', food as 'old *kanji*', whereas a Nambudiri's food is 'nectar'
and all his actions are described in honorific forms. Gopala Panikkar,
Malabar and its Folk, Madras, 1900, p. 202, and A. Chandra Shekhar,
'Degrees of Politeness in Malayalam', *International Journal of Dravidian
Languages*, January 1977, pp. 85–96.

[18] For details regarding Nambudiri marriages, see Joan P. Mencher and Helen
Goldberg, 'Kinship and Marriage Regulations among the Nambudiri
Brahmans of Kerala', *Man*, II, No. 1, March 1967. Also David M. Schneider
and Kathleen Gough, *Matrilineal Kinship*, Berkeley, 1962, pp. 319–23,
357–63.

though the Nairs viewed them as such. Even the eldest son, who was permitted poliginy within his own caste, often entered into temporary liaisons with Nair women. These relationships were loose and, at best, semi-permanent arrangements—an arrangement for 'a night's sleep' as the Nambudiris called them—which could be terminated without notice by either party. Nair matriliny and Nambudiri primogeniture denied to the offsprings of these alliances any share in their father's property; reinforcing this was the popular belief that accepting *brahmaswam* (brahmin property) was a great sin. Thus, the *sambandham* system met the sexual needs of the Nambudiris without any obligation on their part.

It is generally accepted that the *sambandham* system came into vogue only after the arrival of the brahmins,[19] prior to which the Nairs followed communal or group marriages. Did its origin represent the stage of transition from group marriages to separate marriages, and did ecological and agrarian factors necessitate this change? Was it that the brahmins, who had migrated to Keralam in the period when this transition was taking place, became a part of this system in the absence of an adequate number of women in their own community, as well as due to the immediate need of preserving their family property from disintegration? Whatever its origin, in the post-twelfth century period, the Nambudiris, aided by their control of land and a value system based on their scriptural knowledge and spiritual powers, succeeded in rationalizing it as the ideal marital arrangement for the Nairs, whereas in reality it was a system of privileges for themselves.

The Nairs lived in matrilineal joint families, known as *taravads*, which consisted of a woman, her children, her daughters

---

[19] Scholars are unanimous in their opinion that the Nambudiris were originally migrants from north India. Even E.M.S. Namboodiripad, who differs from other scholars regarding the details of the evolution of the Nambudiri community, accepts the migration hypothesis. He writes: 'It need not at all be disputed that small groups of Brahmins came from the North and settled themselves in Kerala: nor need it be disputed that it was they who brought the culture of the North Indian Brahmin to the people here.' *Kerala: Yesterday, Today and Tomorrow*, Calcutta, 1968, p. 22. The only exception is K. Damodaran who is of the opinion that all castes, including the Nambudiris, emerged out of the changes in the mode of production. *Kerala Charitram*, Trichur, 1962, p. 157.

and grand-daughters and their children, her brothers, descendants through her sisters, and her relations through her dead female ancestors. The members of a *taravad* were co-partners of all family property, whether inherited or acquired by the efforts of individual members. The *karanavan*, the seniormost male of the family, was the manager and guardian of family property. Though he had no right of alienation, he possessed enough powers to act as a patriarch, subjecting the other members of the family to his authority. The junior members had practically no say in the management of the property; yet the rule of impartibility held together the various *tavazhis* (lineages) within the *taravad*. The members were entitled to daily needs such as food, clothes and oil from the common pool. The males also drew upon the family income to make customary gifts of plantains, clothes and betel-leaves to their wives during the three festivals—Vishu, Onam and Thiruvatira.[20] Both males and females were totally dependent on the *taravad* for their economic needs. The money received by junior members for serving as retainers of local chieftains was just sufficient for their food and other necessities while on the march or in service in towns.[21] The organization of the *taravad* was ideal and viable so long as the income of the family was sufficient to meet the needs of its members.

According to Louis Dumont, the Nambudiri 'lived in close symbiosis with the Nair in marriage and sexual relationships'.[22] But except for the status accorded by a hypergamous marriage, the advantages of 'symbiosis' lay exclusively with the Nambudiris and, therefore, the real question is not, as Dumont has suggested, how the higher-caste Nambudiris complied with it,[23] but how the Nairs came to accept a system of unequal partnership. Since the Nambudiris did not permit hypogamy, the Nambudiri–Nair liaison was qualitatively different from the reciprocal alliances among the Nairs, even within the framework of the *sambandham* system.

The Nair acceptance of Nambudiri privileges as a social ideal

---

[20] For further details of family structure, see Schneider and Gough, *Matrilineal Kinship*, pp. 334–36.
[21] Ibid., p. 337.
[22] Louis Dumont, 'Marriage in India: The Present State of the Question', *Contributions to Indian Sociology*, No. VII, March 1964.
[23] Ibid.

was the result of the latter's ideological hegemony and control of land. The sexual morality of the Nairs, as laid down by the Nambudiris, did not emphasize chastity as a virtue. According to *Keralolpatti*, for instance, the duty of Nair women was to satisfy the desires of the brahmins. Quoting the *Smritis*, Ashtamurthi Nambudiri told the Marriage Commission that 'if a Brahmin wished to have sexual intercourse with a Sudra's wife, the Sudra would be bound to gratify the wish.'[24] Apart from this religious rationale, brahmanic traditions propounded the idea that the Nambudiris, living in accordance with Vedic rites, were the ideal sexual partners from whom alone brave and intelligent progeny could be conceived. Buchanan observed in 1800 that 'they were the most favoured lovers, the young women of rank and beauty seldom admitting any person to bed, but a Brahmin, and more especially a Nambudiri.'[25]

The ideological influence was so strong that the privileges of the Nambudiris arising out of their social dominance were perceived by the Nairs as a matter of prestige and privilege for themselves. Where ideology failed, the Nambudiris had their material position to fall back upon. Being landlords with absolute proprietory rights, they could assign land to the families of women whose favours they sought or, in the event of refusal, cancel the assignment if one already existed.[26] Mencher and Goldberg have noticed cases 'where a Nambudiri took a fancy for a pretty Nair girl whose family held land on some form of subsidiary tenure from his *illom*, and was able to force her to become his mistress, even if she was already married and devoted to her Nair husband'.[27]

Thus, the traditional pattern of family organization, the system of marriage, and the law of inheritance of the Nairs were

---

[24] *Malabar Marriage Commission Report (MMCR)*, 1891, p. 11.

[25] Buchanan, *A Journey*, p. 426.

[26] 'If a Nambudiri takes a fancy', wrote a correspondent in *Kerala Sanchari*, 'for a girl in the family of any of his unhappy tenants and is not allowed to have her as his concubine, the consequences to the tenant are disastrous. He will either be ejected from his holdings or his lands put on *melchart* (overlease).' *Madras Native Newspaper Reports (MNNR)*, *Kerala Sanchari*, 27 May 1876.

[27] Mencher and Goldberg, 'Kinship and Marriage Regulations': 'Nambudiri landlords successfully use their influence that their wealth and position in Malabar give them to seduce Nair women'; Memorandum of O. Chandu Menon, *MMCR*, p. 10.

closely linked with the nature of land relations and the over-riding influence of the values and ideology of the Nambudiris.

The Colonial Impact

The trading activities of the Europeans and the subsequent colonial rule considerably altered the pattern of traditional property relations and the related ideological system. The advent of Europeans led to the expansion of trade and the emergence of new urban centres. The agents and intermediaries of Arab trade, mostly Mappilas, were replaced by new groups for procurement of pepper and other spices from the interior, enabling at least a few of them to occupy positions of importance in the new politico-economic system.[28] More important factors of social significance were the extension of commercial agriculture, the expansion of a money economy, and the increasing use of cash transactions, especially by the aristocratic elements in villages.[29] These paved the way for major changes in the traditional agrarian structure and relations, the full impact of which, however, was felt only after the British conquest of Malabar in 1792.

The traditional agrarian structure was based on a three-tier relationship between *janmis* (landlords), *kanakkar* (tenants) and *verumpattakkar* (sub-tenants). As explained earlier, most of the land was controlled by the Nambudiris as *janmam* or as *devaswam* (temple lands) and by a few Nair chieftains, mainly in north Malabar. The Nambudiris did not undertake cultivation; further, unlike brahmins in other parts of the country, they did not enter into secular vocations like administration, account-keeping, etc. They lived on the rent received from their tenants, mostly Nairs, to whom they leased out or mortgaged their lands. Most of the Nairs, who were military retainers of feudal chieftains, too did not cultivate their own lands. They sub-leased the land to Nairs of inferior economic position, to untouchable castes like Tiyyas, or to Mappilas, extracting, obviously, a higher rent from them. It is not clear whether a well-defined hierarchical relationship of these categories based on legal or

---

[28] K.M. Panikkar, *Malabar and the Portuguese*, Bombay, 1929, pp. 181–82, and *Malabar and the Dutch*, Bombay, 1937, pp. 162–63; Ashim Das Gupta, *Malabar in Asian Trade*, Cambridge, 1966, p. 4.
[29] Panikkar, *Malabar and the Portuguese*, pp. 58, 206–08.

customary sanction existed during the early period. William Logan was of the opinion that Nair *kanakkar* were initially nothing but a protector guild and that they claimed a part of the produce in their capacity as protectors or supervisors.[30] The customarily enforceable three-tier hierarchical relationship crystallized only in the post-fifteenth century period, under the immediate impact of the money economy and greater occupational mobility. In the traditional system, the net produce of land was shared equally by *janmis, kanakkar* and actual cultivators. If Logan's opinion about the role of *kanakkar* is true, the distribution of surplus was based on a principle of mutual dependence within the framework of feudal exploitation.

The above description points to the caste/class correlation, especially at the upper level, during the early period, a fact testified to by several European travellers and contemporary observers.[31] But a certain erosion of this monopoly, both of *janmam* and of *kanam*, was taking place after 1500. Thomas Warden noted in 1801:

> The Nambudiris are the principal landholders of the country.
> . . . The lands which belong not to Nambudiris are either
> the property of the *pagodas,* rajahs or *naduwaries.* There are ryots
> who have become by purchase the rightful owners of landed
> property, but they are few in proportion to the number of the
> others.[32]

Warden was referring to a slow process over a period of three hundred years by which at least a few Nair *kanakkar* graduated to the position of landlords. The table on the following page shows the caste composition of a section of *janmis* in the nineteenth century.[33]

---

[30] William Logan, *Report of the Malabar Special Commission (RMSC)*, Madras, 1881, para 59.

[31] Buchanan, *A Journey*, pp. 366–67; Thomas Warden, *Report on the Condition of the Palghat, Congad, Monoor, Eddatenah, Kowilparah, and Narnattum Divisions of the District of Malabar*, Madras, 1801, para 36.

[32] Warden, *Report*, para 36.

[33] For data for 1803, see India Office Records, F/287/36, pp. 7960–66. The data for 1887 are compiled from a petition of the landlords of Malabar to the Governor of Madras, 3 December 1887, Legislative Department G.O. No. 81, 10 December 1887, Tamilnadu Archives.

Caste	1803		1887	
	Number	Percentage	Number	Percentage
Nambudiris	37	35.60	217	24.00
Upper intermediary castes	11	10.60	69	7.66
Nairs	46	44.20	41	45.60
Mappilas	8	7.70	92	10.22
Tiyyas	1	0.96	112	12.50
Total	103		901	

The table indicates a decline of Nambudiri monopoly of land to the advantage of the Nairs and other lower castes.[34]

During the post-1500 period changes also occurred in the nature of *kanam* tenure, control of *kanam* land, and appropriation of rent by various sections of society. In the traditional system, the *kanam* was a simple lease, stipulating an annual rent payment mainly in kind. With the expansion of the money economy, the landlords, hard-pressed for cash, resorted to the device of leasing land against an initial payment of a lump sum, which, along with its interest, was adjustable against rent during the lease period. The tendency of landlords was to realize the full rent without adjusting the *kanam* amount and, therefore, the renewal of lease at the end of the period became automatic, till, due to the increasing pressure of land, there were enough competitors to invest in land. The British policy of recognizing the *janmis* as absolute proprietors and the *kanam* as a terminable tenure at the end of the lease period facilitated the alienation of *kanam* lands from their original occupants through evictions and *melcharts* (overlease), and their concentration in the hands of a class of rent-paying, rent-receiving intermediary *kanakkar*.[35] This class, mostly Nairs, sub-leased land to *verumpattakkar* at a

---

[34] The data from which this conclusion is drawn are not entirely satisfactory. They do not account for all *janmis* of the district, nor for the extent of their landholdings. It is also likely that the land held by lower castes was less in extent compared to that of brahmins. However, it does indicate a changing trend.

[35] For details of British land revenue policy and its social consequences, see K.N. Panikkar, 'Peasant Revolts in Malabar in the Nineteenth and Twentieth Centuries', in A.R. Desai (ed.), *Agrarian Unrest in India*, Bombay, 1978.

highly enhanced rate of rent. By the beginning of the twentieth century they were appropriating as much as 35 to 40 per cent of the net produce, whereas the landlords' and cultivators' share ranged between 2 and 12, and 15 and 25 per cent, respectively.[36] The rent thus appropriated was used for acquiring more *kanam* land, resulting in its concentration in the hands of this class. The pattern of land control and, more importantly, the share of the surplus appropriated, shifted in their favour. The section of *kanakkar* who benefited thus was not the old Nair aristocracy but a new group which readily grabbed the opportunities offered by the administration of the East India Company.[37] Most of the important Nair families whose members became prominent in political and administrative spheres built up their fortunes through this process during the nineteenth century. While the old aristocracy continued to cherish feudal values, the new group gave their children English education and sought and obtained employment in the administration of the British.

Among the Indians employed by the British immediately after the annexation of Malabar, Nairs constituted a fairly large proportion. In 1799 the Indian complement of the Company's administration consisted of 107 from outside Malabar, mainly Maratha brahmins, and 89 from Malabar, of which 44 were Nairs.[38] The reluctance of the Madras government to appoint village *mukhyasthans,* 'men of respectability and wealth', as *parbattis* due to their alleged participation in rebel activities, opened up opportunities for Nairs of inferior economic status.[39] Most of the village officials, Adhikaris and Menons, appointed after the reorganization of the village administration in 1822, were also Nairs. They were in charge of revenue assessment, settlement and collection, and they used these positions to great advantage. Instances of Nair families amassing wealth and rising in social prestige and position by means of their official status are many. Quick to realize the importance of English

---

[36] C.A. Innes and F.B. Evans, *Note on Tenancy Legislation in Malabar,* Madras, 1915, Appendix.

[37] *RMSC,* para 329.

[38] Malabar District Records, Gl. No. 20998, Tamilnadu Archives.

[39] Madras Board of Revenue Proceedings, 18 July 1803. P287/36 (IOR), Board of Law, 26 May 1803; Cons. No. 31, 13 July 1801; Nos. 31–33, 9 March 1801; Cons. No. 32, 2 April 1801; and Cons. No. 23, Tamilnadu Archives.

education in the new political set-up, they sent their children to schools and colleges, and they were in turn absorbed in the judicial and revenue administration, whereas the Nambudiri and Nair landlords lived within the security of feudal privileges, and the Mappilas and Tiyyas did not have the necessary resources to meet the expenses of education. At the end of the nineteenth century, the number of graduates, undergraduates and matriculates in the district was about 1,000, and the number of officials drawing a salary of more than Rs 10, 20 and 50 a month was 1,063, 245 and 90 respectively, the majority of whom were Nairs.[40] In many Nair fami-lies the first generation at the beginning of the nineteenth century began as petty village officials, but the second generation rose to the higher posts of munsiffs, magistrates and judges.[41] The Malabar Tenancy Commission noted that the '*kanomdar* form a large section of the middle class of Malabar, chiefly drawn from the professional classes, government servants and people of like status'.[42] In fact, the sequence was in reverse order: the middle class had its social origins in the rent-receiving, rent-paying class of intermediary *kanakkar*. The families of Chettur to which Sir C. Sankaran Nair belonged, or of Mannath into which M. Krishnan Nair was born, and a large number of other Nair families whose members rose to high positions in the civil and subordinate services of the British government, belonged to this category. It was the members of this class who had, on the one hand a certain degree of economic independence, and on the other, a new cultural and ideological perspective, that initiated a critical evaluation of their own social customs and institutions.

Marriage and Family: Reordering Institutions

The first expression of social awakening among the Nairs was a struggle against the existing value system as reflected in the institutions of the *taravad* and marriage. During the second half of the

---

[40] *MMCR*, The President's Memorandum, p. 9.
[41] Sir C. Sankaran Nair once told Lord Hardinge that his family had the honour of holding the highest as well as the lowest post under the government. His ancestor was a village official and he was a member of the Viceroy's Executive Council. His father was a *tahsildar* and his father's brother was a *sheristadar*. K.S. Menon, *C. Sankaran Nair*, New Delhi, 1967, pp. 10–11.
[42] *Malabar Tenancy Commission Report*, Madras, 1929, p. 6.

nineteenth century, these two institutions were increasingly subjected to critical evaluation. The educated sections of Nairs had by then begun to perceive the connection between land control and their 'symbiotic life' with the Nambudiri landlords, and their own family organization and marriage customs.[43] Therefore, their reform efforts were directed at the *taravad,* marriage customs and tenurial relations.[44]

The emergence of a money economy and socio-economic changes during British rule considerably undermined the cohesion and utility of Nair *taravads.* The following table represents the structure of four Nair *taravads* at the end of the nineteenth century.[45]

1	2	3	4	5	6	7	8	9	10	11	12
A	2,800	18	87	41	46	12	13	4	1	2	33
B	1,200	7	58	266	32	13	13	2	1	2	11
C	2,500	82	256	126	130	35	52	2	1	6	36
D	680	21	104	52	52	17	32	–	–	2	49

Note: 1: *Taravad*; 2: Assessment paid to the government in rupees; 3: Number of *tavazhis* in each *taravad*; 4: Total number of members; 5: Males; 6: Females; 7: Boys above 5 and under 20; 8: Men from 20 to 40; 9: Boys in school; 10: Men who knew English; 11: Government servants; 12: No occupation.

The above data confirm our earlier observation regarding the income

[43] *MNNR, Kerala Patrika,* 23 May 1891. Almost everyone who was involved with the question of marriage reform viewed the Nair law of inheritance, family organization and marriage custom as linked with Nambudiri dominance either in their origin or in their perpetuation. K. Kannan Nair, 'The Matrimonial Custom of the Nayars', *Malabar Quarterly Review,* 1903; Gopala Panikkar, *Malabar and its Folk,* p. 36; and *Kerala Patrika,* 31 May 1890. A correspondent wrote in *Kerala Patrika* of 23 May 1891: 'Several tenants in Malabar are afraid to give evidence before the Marriage Com-mission for their landlords threaten them with evictions and *melcharts,* if they were to do so. Any reformation in the Malayali marriage customs is impossible unless it is made compulsory that all Nambudiri Brahmins should marry girls of their own caste.'

[44] The tenancy movement was a struggle for a larger share of rent between the landlords and intermediary *kanakkar.* See K.N. Panikkar, *Against Lord and State,* New Delhi, 1989, pp. 120–21.

[45] M. Othena Menon, *Remarks on C. Karunakara Menon's Observation on the Malabar Marriage Bill,* Madras, 1890, p. 22.

of the family—a substantial income from land and an additional independent income through government service. It is also clear that the resources of the first three families were much more than what was required to meet the subsistence needs of their members. The government assessment being 30 per cent, the net produce of family 'A' was worth Rs 9,337 per annum. If the family was that of an intermediary *kanakkar*, it would get Rs 3,755 after deducting   the shares of the cultivator, landlord and the government, at 10, 20 and 30 per cent respectively. At the prevailing price of Rs 60 per 1,000 Macleod seers of paddy,[46] the family would have 62,000 Macleod seers of paddy at its disposal, or 713 seers per individual including children. If one seer of paddy per day is considered sufficient for one individual's consumption, the family would have 30,276 seers, or Rs 1,817, per annum as excess income. If it was a *janmi* family or part of its holdings was *janmam*, the income would go up proportionately.[47] But this excess income was not generally distributed among the junior members of the family, their share remaining at the same level when the family was comparatively poor, just enough to meet their daily needs. The *karanavan*, being the manager of the property, controlled this income and most often spent it on himself, his wife and children.[48] The junior members, whose needs had considerably increased due to changes in the social climate and in the nature of the internal market, soon perceived the disparity between what was due to them and what was actually received by them. The existence of the *taravad* and the joint management of property were no longer to their advantage. Therefore, their loyalty and sense of belonging to the family and faith in the principle of impartibility were rudely shaken.

The opportunities provided by colonial rule for independent incomes for junior members, particularly through government service, was another important factor which affected the solidarity of

---

[46] K.N. Krishna Swami Aiyyar, *Statistical Appendix for Malabar District*, Madras, 1933, p. ccli.

[47] Not only cash crops like coconut and pepper, but even paddy had a ready market during this period.

[48] One of the witnesses reported to the Marriage Commission: '*Karanavans* misappropriate the *taravad* property, and alienate it in favour of their wives and children. The *anantaravans* misbehave, are disobedient and will not work.' *MMCR*, p. 30.

the *taravad*. The data regarding four *taravads* cited earlier show that there were several *tavazhis* in each *taravad*, each of them forming a separate unit. At least some of these units had independent sources of income, a husband or a son employed in government service. Eager to provide better facilities to the members of their immediate kin group, they were reluctant to pool their income in the common fund. The organization of the *taravad* also militated against the newly acquired ideas of individual freedom and equality. These 'marginal men' viewed the *taravad* as an impediment to their progress rather than as a source of security and strength. The comparatively more affluent and 'modern' *tavazhis* became catalysts for the dissolution of *taravads*, not simply because of their desire for independence, but equally, if not more, due to the sense of deprivation they created in other units of the family. Given an example for emulation which promised social prestige and economic rewards, the less fortunate *tavazhis* were quick to demand English education for their children also. This became a matter of major dissension in the family. The *karanavans* were in most cases reluctant to part with money, and even if they were prepared to educate one or two children, it was difficult to reconcile rival claims. In the four *taravads* mentioned earlier there were 77 boys of school-going age, but only 8 were attending schools. The *karanavans* were pressurized by various means, including civil suits, to provide for education. The *Kerala Patrika* of December 1885 published a letter praising a junior member of a Nair family for instituting a civil suit against a *karanavan* for the expenses of English education.[49] In the absence of support from the *taravad*, some of them depended upon the income of their fathers, which in turn, affected their loyalty to and sense of solidarity with the *taravad*.[50]

While affluence acted as a catalyst for change, inadequacy of resources was an equally important factor in the dissolution of the *taravad*. The socio-economic changes resulting in the concentration of *kanam* land in the hands of a few intermediary *kanakkar*, and the

---

[49] MNNR, *Kerala Patrika*, December 1885.

[50] Mr Rozerio, one of the witnesses who deposed before the Marriage Commission, observed: 'I know hardly any instance of a *karanavan* educating a junior member. It is almost invariably the father who educates.' *MMCR*, p. 30.

increase of population[51] during this period led to severe economic distress for a majority of Nair families which, in turn, adversely affected *taravad* solidarity. For instance, family 'D' had 15,000 Macleod seers of paddy at its disposal, or each member had 144.5 seers per annum, which was short by 110.5 seers at the notional rate of 1 seer per person per day. Evidently, the family income was not even sufficient to meet the subsistence needs of all its members. To smaller *tavazhis* and those with independent incomes, the *taravad* was more a burden than an advantage, and their emancipation lay in its break-up. In other words, by the second half of the nineteenth century, the economic and ideological props of the *taravad* system had come under severe strain. Strife and litigation between *karanavans* and junior members of the family became the order of the day. 'A house divided against itself cannot stand', reported the Marriage Commission, 'and most *taravads* in Malabar are in this condition.'[52]

The movement for reformation of the social customs, practices and institutions of the Nairs was a direct outcome of the collapse of the economic basis of the *taravad* and the new ideological and cultural perspective acquired by the educated middle class. What came under attack first was the impartibility of family property, the customary law of inheritance, and the traditional system of marriage.

The Legislation

A memorandum submitted to the government in 1869 was the initial effort in this direction.[53] Newspapers carried several letters and articles advocating changes in the *marumakkathayam* law of inheritance and impartibility of property.[54] One paper observed:

> Formerly, wealth acquired from any source by either the males or the females of a *taravad* was considered as the joint property and was enjoyed by all the members of the family, but in these days this

---

[51] In 1822 H.S. Graeme, the Special Commissioner, had estimated the population of Malabar at 7,07,556 out of which 1,64,626 were Nairs. *Report on the Revenue Administration*, p. 6. By 1881, the Nair population had risen to 3,21,674—an increase of almost 100 per cent.

[52] *MMCR*, p. 31.

[53] *MNNR, Kerala Sanchari*, 9 September 1891.

[54] *MNNR, Kerala Mitram*, 11 March 1882; *Kerala Patrika*, October 1886 and 12 April 1890.

rule is entirely ignored. The property derived from a father or from *anantaravans* or *karanavans* or even property obtained by women from their husbands is found to be considered private property. Not only so, but endeavour is made to have, if possible, a separate house. And when this endeavour succeeds, instead of addition being made to the *taravad* property, opportunity is taken to get all that can be got from it. This causes splits, litigation and quarrels in the *taravads*, which are thereby ruined. It is doubtful whether there is a *taravad* in Malabar *where there is no enmity between the karanavans and anantaravans*. It is quite inevitable that a man will not love any one more than his wife and children. He may probably have some affection for his brothers and sisters but not for his nephews and nieces. Similarly between the nephews and *karanavans*. We do not say that a customary affection will never be shown by the nephews, but if shown at all, it is in our opinion, a mere pretence and cannot last. The real object of this affection is the ancestral property. If the custom of *marumakkathayam*, the basis of so many evils, be still continued, it will soon be difficult to find rich families among the Malayali people.[55]

Contemporary newspapers circulated stories, often exaggerated, about the temporary nature of Nair marriages and around the common jibe that a Nair does not know who his father is.[56] At Trichur a married woman was 'married' and taken away by a Thampuran;[57] a district munsiff's wife was forcibly taken away by her people to be given in marriage to someone else; and a sub-registrar at the time of a secret interview with a married woman asked if she 'would accompany him to his house' to which she consented and thus became

[55] *MNNR, Kerala Patrika,* 20 April 1893. Emphasis added.
[56] M. Othena Menon has recorded an interesting anecdote: 'N. Sankara Marar, the late subdivisional *sherishtadar,* Tellichery, was once invited to a *kalyanam* [marriage] by a high official. . . . All being seated, the host, on the entrance of an old man, an invited guest, got up and with much reverence introduced him to the *sherishtadar* as his father. The visitor passed into the interior apartments and in few minutes more another old guest made his appearance. The same ceremony was gone through by the host who again introduced the newcomer as his father. Sankara Marar tried to control his tongue, but could not, and on resuming his seat said: "Please Mr . . . excuse if I do not get up when another of your father comes".' *Remarks,* p. 19.
[57] *MNNR, Kerala Patrika,* 16 May 1891.

his wife.[58] 'Repudiations of wives by their husbands and husbands by their wives are so reprehensively practised with impunity among the Sudras, who are not bound by any ties of matrimony, that the necessity of some legislation on the subject in the present improved state of society is undoubted.'[59]

These incidents were highlighted because they were exceptional and not universal and they differed from the life-style of at least one section of society. Many contemporary observers have noted the change that had occurred in the traditional norms of marriage. Participating in a debate in the Viceroy's Legislative Council in 1872, Sir James Stephen said:

> Among the Nairs, there is, legally speaking, no such thing as marriage at all. In spite of this custom, marriage is practically as common and as binding among the Nairs as in many other races. The connections which they form usually last for life and are marked by a great degree of mutual fidelity.[60]

But these marriages were not recognized by law. The Madras High Court had decreed in 1869 that 'the relation (*sambandham*) is in truth not marriage, but a state of concubinage into which the woman enters of her own choice and is at liberty to change when and as often as she pleases.' The lack of legal sanction was seen as a great impediment to progress. Sir C. Sankaran Nair felt that 'but for English law and English courts new customs would have been adopted and followed, that the law of marriage and inheritance would have been different from what they are now and that the Malabar *taravads* would long since have broken up into families each headed by a male, if our courts had allowed them to do.'[61]

The Malabar Marriage Association founded in 1879 drafted and presented a bill to the government seeking legal sanction for Nair marriages.[62] The government did not take any action on this. How-

---

[58] Othena Menon, *Remarks*, p. 9.

[59] *MNNR, Kerala Patrika*, 11 March 1882.

[60] NAI Legislative Department, December 1890, Nos. 138–42. In 1881 Logan also made a similar observation: 'a Nayar usually marries only one wife, lives apart with her in their own home, and rears her children as his own also.' *RMSC*, para 483.

[61] Ibid.

[62] Othena Menon, *Remarks*, p. 2.

ever, Logan pressed the question of both marriage and inheritance in drawing the attention of the government to his report on the tenancy problem. He recommended that 'all adults should have the power of disposing of their self-acquired property by will and if he died intestate, a man's children should get one-third of his property.'[63] Logan's recommendations implied legal recognition of Nair marriages. These recommendations were examined by a committee consisting of Sir Madhava Rao, William Logan, H. Wigram, C. Karunakara Menon and C. Sankaran Nair. The committee unanimously recommended the enactment of a marriage and succession law on the lines suggested by Logan and drafted a bill which was approved by the Madras High Court. The bill introduced by Sir C. Sankaran Nair in the Madras Legislative Council on 24 March 1890 to provide a form of marriage for Hindus following the *marumakkathayam* law, was in pursuance of the recommendations of this committee.[64] Moving the bill, Sir Sankaran Nair said, '... our wives are concubines and our children bastards in a court of law, and the necessity therefore for a bill to legalize marriage and to provide for the issue of such marriage seems apparent.'[65] His bill sought to give legal validity to Nair marriages, to make bigamy a punishable offence, and to provide for dissolution of marriages, divorce and restitution of conjugal rights.[66] The Government of India did not sanction the bill but instead directed the Madras government to gather more information on the subject before the bill was taken up for consideration.[67] Accordingly, the Malabar Marriage Commission was appointed in 1891 with T. Muthuswami Aiyar as its president.[68]

The Commission concluded its work rather hurriedly. Its first meeting was held at Kozhikode on 18 May and its last on 27 June 1891. During the course of its investigations, 121 witnesses were examined orally, of whom 79 were in favour of legislation, and

---

[63] *RMSC*, paras 481–88.

[64] Ibid.

[65] Ibid.

[66] Ibid.

[67] *Judical Proceedings*, 22 December 1890, No. 1863.

[68] The other members of the Commission were H.M. Winterbothan, C. Sankaran Nair, Kerala Varma Valiya Kovil Tampuran, Rama Varma Tampuran, O. Chandu Menon and M. Mundappa Bangera. *Legislative Department Proceedings*, February 1894, P.B. Nos. 47–58.

interrogatories were sent to 474 of whom 322 responded. Out of these 322, 178 were in favour of legislation.[69] The Commission also received petitions and resolutions which had been passed in meetings held in various parts of Malabar. Thirteen petitions signed by 2,733 persons were in favour of legislation and 25 signed by 2,131 were opposed to it; 632 Nair women submitted separate petitions of whom 245 supported legislation and 378 opposed it.[70] The above statistics collected by the Commission seem to indicate that there was considerable resistance to the proposed measure. Statistics are often deceptive, and in this case particularly so, since they did not correctly reflect the various shades of opinion within each category, and also the nature of the groups which mobilized opposition or support to the bill. The opposition came mainly from the Nambudiris and big landlords like Ashtamurthi Nambudiri, the Zamurin of Calicut, Ettan Tampuran of Padinjare Kovilakam and Kolathur Varrier,[71] who were the beneficiaries of the traditional system and defenders of feudal values. Even a section of educated Nairs opposed it, not because they did not favour the socially recognized institution of marriage, but because they believed that such an institution already existed among the Nairs. O. Chandu Menon, the celebrated author of *Indulekha*[72] and a member of the Marriage Commission, and C. Karunakara Menon, sub-editor of *The Hindu*, belonged to this category. Opposition also came from a good number of *karanavans* who were apprehensive that 'seven-eighths of the *anantaravans* will give their earnings to their wives and children and *taravads* will be ruined if the proposed Act is passed.'[73] With Sankaran Nair's bill as the model, what was foreseen as a consequence of the enquiry was not merely a legal validation of marriages but total ruination, not reform, of the entire fabric of social life.[74] The opposition of a large number of people, including a section of the educated still under the influence of feudal

---

[69] *MMCR*, p. 35.

[70] *Legislative Department Proceedings*, February 1894, Nos. 47–58, NAI.

[71] *MMCR*, p. 11.

[72] When Madhavan remarks that Malayali women do not observe chastity, Indulekha makes a strong defence of Nair women and argues about their high sense of sexual morality. O. Chandu Menon, *Indulekha*, pp. 57–58.

[73] *MMCR*, p. 34.

[74] C. Karunakara Menon, *Observations on the Malabar Marriage Bill*, 1890, p. 19.

ideology, was a result of this fear. The Commission rightly rejected this opinion as inconsequential and hoped that 'the uninstructed majority will rapidly follow the lead of the enlightened classes'.[75] The latter being seen as the catalyst of changes in society, the Commission concluded that 'the great majority [of the enlightened section] desire a modification of the succession law in favour of wife and children or a marriage law or both'.[76] Though the members had differences of opinion on the details of the proposed measure, five of them considered legislation desirable in one form or the other.[77] The Madras government generally concurred with this view and decided to introduce a marriage law which 'would graft upon the *marumakkathayam* custom a method whereby the ordinary legal incidence of marriage could be attached to existing form of the people'.[78] Accordingly, the Malabar Marriage Act of 1896 was passed, which provided that when a *sambandham* was registered it would have the status of a legal marriage: the wife and children would be entitled to maintenance by the husband and father respectively, and would succeed to half his self-acquired property, if he died intestate.[79]

The Act of 1896 was the result of a long struggle by the enlightened sections of Nairs, but it did not, as feared by the conservatives, destroy the *taravad* system. It indeed made the first breach, but the most crucial demand, namely the partition of property, was not incorporated in the Act. Even the provision for marriage registration, the Act being a permissive law, was not very effective.[80] However, the pressure of legislation was kept up[81] and consequently

---

[75] *MMCR*, p. 34.

[76] Ibid., p. 35.

[77] Only four out of six members signed the main report and of these Rama Varma Tampuran dissented from the conclusions in several important particulars. The president and O. Chandu Menon disagreed entirely from the conclusions arrived at by the signatories to the report and with each other and recorded their views in separate memoranda.

[78] *Legislative Department Proceedings*, February 1894, Nos. 47–58.

[79] *Legislative Department Proceedings*, June 1896, Nos. 1–27.

[80] In the first fourteen months of the Act's operation, only 51 *sambandhams* were registered and after that interest rapidly declined. During the first ten years, fewer than 100 people registered their marriages. Robin Jeffrey, *The Decline of Nayar Dominance*, New Delhi, 1976, pp. 186, 313.

[81] *MNNR, West Coast Reformer*, 7 April 1910; *Manorama*, 1 November 1912; and *Kerala Sanchari*, 25 March 1914.

the Marumakkathayam Act was passed in 1933, which provided for
partition of the family and inheritance of the father's self-acquired
property. Soon after, the courts in Malabar were flooded with
partition suits and the disintegration of Nair *taravads* into smaller
units began at a brisk pace. This change, however, did not emanate
from the Act as such: on the contrary, the Act was the inevitable
culmination of a slow process which had begun as early as the
sixteenth century, destroying the economic basis of the *taravad*
system. Though the *taravad* ideology had not become totally ex-
tinct—it lingers on among certain sections even today—by the time
the Act was passed Nair families had a fair share of Madhavans and
Indulekhas,[82] and Suri Nambudiris rarely ventured into Nair families
for 'arrangements for a night's sleep'. The reform movement among
the Nambudiris, emphasizing the need for English education and
demanding the right for junior members to marry from within the
community, soon followed.

By the beginning of the twentieth century, the value system
to which the Nairs were subjected in their social and family life had
become anomalous to their material position in society. Their self-
perception of social status in relation to the upper-caste Nambudiris
was also of a different order, characterized by a sense of importance
and independence and not by subjection and subservience. The
influence of Nambudiri values was no longer decisive; an alternate
ideal based on individual freedom had come into being. What made
this rejection of the dominant ideology and related institutions
possible were the socio-economic changes which had begun with the
expansion of the money economy in the post-fifteenth century period
and intensified under British rule, and the policy of the colonial rulers
of creating an English-educated middle class for administrative
purposes. The realities of material existence being a crucial determinant
of self-perception, the ideological struggle and the efforts to restructure
social institutions would not have been possible without the economic
status the Nairs had achieved due to changes in land control, increase
in their share of the surplus, and income from government employment. By the end of the nineteenth century their world had changed—

---

[82] Characters in O. Chandu Menon's novel, *Indulekha*, published in 1889.
See the chapter titled 'Creating a New Cultural Taste' in this volume.

from a life confined to the *taravad,* the village temple and the Nambudiri *illom,* to one of competition in the government offices and judicial courts; a change from the dark recesses of the *nalukettu* to the exiciting atmosphere of urban centres like Kozhikode and Madras, besieged with modern ideas and modern ways of life. It was only logical that they tried to demolish the *nalukettu* and build it anew.

Glossary

anantaravan	junior member of a Nair family
ashtavaidyan	one of the eight traditional Ayurvedic physicians
brahmaswam	belonging to brahmins
chakyarkuthu	a form of art performed in temples
devaswam	belonging to temples
din	faith
gramam	village
illom	Nambudiri house
jahannam	hell
janmam	birthright
janmi	landlord
jati	caste
kalari	gymnasium (where martial arts are practised)
kanakkar	tenants
kanam	a form of tenancy
kanamdar	holder of *kanam* (a tenant)
karalar	cultivator
karanavan	head of a Nair family
kashayam	medicinal brew
kriti	composition
madrasa	a Muslim school
marumakkathayam	matriliny
melchart	overlease
moksha	salvation
mukhyasthan	chief
nalukettu	quadrangular matrilineal Nair house
narakam	hell
parbati	a village official
pathasala	school
sambandham	marriage alliance
taravad	Nair household
tavazhi	lineage
vedi parayel	gossip
venumpattakkar	tenants at will

Index

Abdul Hamid (Maulavi), 88*n*
Abdul Shirazi, 146
Abdul Wahid (Maulavi), 88*n*
Abdus Samad, 39
Academic Association, 88
acculturation, 2, 101, 126
Adam, William, 48, 50, 51, 52, 151;
    Report for Bengal Presidency (1835–
    38), 47
Addhya, Uday Chandra, 16, 81
Adhikaris, 187
age of consent, 112; Bill on, 87
Ahmad, Salahuddin, 58
Aiyar, T. Muthuswami, 195
Akbar, 19, 39
Alatas, Syed Hussein, 71*n*
Alavi, Syed, 84
Alivardi Khan, 36
All India Ayurvedic Conference, 154
Ambalapuzha temple, 159*n*
Amherst (Lord), 147
Amir Khan, 20, 35
anantaravan(s), 190*n*, 193, 196
Andhra, 70
anglicist–orientalist controversy, 127
anti-colonial consciousness, 79; evolu-
    tion of, 56; growth of, 57, 58; unilinear
    development of, 174; *see also* con-
    sciousness
Anti-Conversion Petition, 88
anti-idolatry, 141; Vedic authority for, 5;
    see also idolatry
Anti-Idolatory Memorial, 88
Appapanthis, 5
appropriation of rent, 177, 186, 187
Arabic, 49
aristocracy, 70; *see also* landed aristo-
    cracy
Aristotle, 66*n*

artisans, 77, 78
Arya Samaj, 112
Arya Samajists, 11, 29
Arya Vaidya Samajam, 162, 167; deli-
    berations in, 164; report on, 173
Arya Vaidyasala, 171; in Kottakkal, 169;
    sale of medicine in, 170; *see also* Ayur-
    veda; medicine; P.S. Variar
ashtavaidyans, 164
Asiatic Society of Bengal, 125
Aurangzeb, 35, 38
Ayurveda, 146, 158, 160, 167, 168, 169;
    antiquity of, 154; divine origin of,
    166; past and present of, 162; politi-
    cal pressure in support of, 172; reach
    and acceptance of, 170; use and im-
    portance of, 166; *see also* medicine
Ayurveda Maha Sammelan, 159
Ayurvedic-Unani Tibbia College, 150
Bacon, Francis, 72
Bagal, J.C., 89*n*
Bahawa Khan, 146
Balramis, 5
Bandhopadhyaya, Tarashankar, 153
Bannerji, Krishna Mohan, 17
Basham, A.L., 146
Bavaria, 45*n*
Beaconsfield (Lord), 132, 133
Benaras, 45*n*
Bengal, 70, 124
Bengal renaissance, 59, 61
Bengal Spectator, 105*n*, 106*n*
Bengali (language), 17, 18
Bentinck (Lord), 126, 127
Beveridge, Henry, 19*n*, 34, 110
Bhakti movement, 114
Bhatt, Moreshwar, 164
Bhattacharya, A.K., 61
Bhattacharya, Rameswar, 42

Bhattathiripad, V.T., 171
'Bible Minute', 83*n*, 84
Bigyan Sar Sangraha, 13
Blanc, Louis, 98
Bodajena, Brajanatha, 7*n*, 42
Bombay, 1
Bombay Darpun, 90, 91
Bombay Gazette, 74, 77, 102, 104
Bombay Guardian, 117
Bombay Medical Registration Act, 149
Bonaparte, Louis, 33
Borthwick, Meredith, 64
Bose, Rajnarayan, 8*n*, 82, 84
bourgeois–democratic ideology, 100, 101, 107
bourgeois–democratic order, 8, 33, 94, 95, 96, 97, 101
bourgeois liberalism, 25, 26, 94, 100
bourgeois–patriarchal framework, 92
bourgeoisie, 24, 29; *see also* capitalism
Bradlaugh, Charles, 141
brahmaswam, 181
Brahmo Samaj, 31, 112; non-conformism of, 28
Brass, Paul R., 172
British Association for the Advancement of Sciences, 13*n*
British rule, civilizing role of, 3; as 'chosen instrument', 73, 74; as divine dispensation, 22, 24, 69, 72, 94, 110, 115, 116–17, 119–22, 179; ideological justification of, 4; nature and consequences of, 75
Buchanan, Francis, 51, 183
Buddhism, 97, 158
Bundi paintings, 39–40
C.K. Sen and Company, 170
Cabral, Amilcar, 57*n*, 67*n*, 80, 86
Calcutta, 82, 83
Calcutta School Book Society, 88
Calcutta Society, 29*n*
Calicut, ruler of, 173; Samuthiri of, 162
Capenter, Lant, 66*n*
capital, accumulation of, 96; lack of, 73
capitalism, 37; development of, 24, 32, 96; stultified form of, 33; *see also* bourgeoisie; production
Carnatic, 48; before the French intervention, 36; music, 43–44

caste, 78; attitude towards, 69; changes in structure and organization of, 4, 6; distinctions, 5; hierarchy, 179; system, 121; *see also* untouchable castes
casteism, 8; Vedic authority for opposition of, 5
Chakrabarty, Tarachand, 13
chakyarkuthu, 180
Chandra, Moti, 39
Charaka, 154, 164
Charan Das, 5
Charandasis, 5
Chatterji, Bankim Chandra, 21*n*, 31, 79*n*, 81, 84, 97, 100, 110; *Durgeshnandini*, 130; (his) interpretation of Krishna, 97; *Kapalakundala*, 130; *Samya*, 76, 98, 100
Chatterji, Gangadhar, 13*n*
Chera kingdom, 178
Cheruma, 180
Cheruthuruthy, 150
Chetti, Gazula Lakshmi Narasu, 1
Chettur, 188
China, 10*n*, 19, 58
Chintamani (*raga*), 44
Chittu, 20, 35
Chola, Rajendra, 178
Christian missionaries, 82, 83, 102
Civil Marriage Act, 88
Cochin, 173; Maharaja of, 162
Collet, Sophia Dobson, 64, 66
colonial construction of history, 108–12, 113
colonial culture, and domination, 67*n*; and ideology, 58, 84, 88; increasing influence of, 145; intervention of, 124; intrusion of, 84, 105, 184; and hegemony, 101, 131, 174; mediation of, 107; practices of, 105; system of, 174; values of, 143; *see also* indigenous culture; traditional culture
colonial domination, 3, 24, 53, 80, 123, 174; capitalism under, 33; context of, 56; reality of, 71
colonial education, consequences of, 81; implications of, 10, 105; *see also* education
colonial hegemonization, 86, 115, 123, 135

colonial ideologues, 19, 34, 46, 113
colonial ideology, 71; dissemination of, 9, 89; role of, 60
colonial India, bourgeois ideological hegemony in, 100; cultural and intellectual life in, 33, 86, 88, 108, 171; cultural–ideological struggles in, 58; conditions in, 93; emerging consciousness in, 78, 84; historiography of, 94; humanist ideas in, 97; intellectual history of, 56; intellectual transformation in, 107; political perspectives and activities in, 94, 115; quest for modernization in, 108; reform in, 97, 173; socio-cultural regeneration in, 80
colonial intervention, 36, 53, 108, 126
colonial rule, cultural identity under, 80; economic implication of, 76; ideologues of, 19; nature of, 142 social base of, 109; *see also* colonial state; colonialism
colonial social engineering, 109
colonial state, 72, 82, 109, 123, 125, 139, 150; character of, 71, 94; cultural space of, 127; discriminatory policy of, 158; hostile attitude of, 157; indifference of, 166; role of, 148; *see also* colonialism; colonial rule
colonial stereotypes, 72*n*
colonialism, 53, 58, 61, 84, 95, 109, 126, 129, 144, 174; a critique of, 96; the cultural–ideological implications of, 79; the ideologues of, 60; the impact of, 71; the logic of, 19; *see also* colonial state; colonial rule
Committee on the Indigenous System of Medicine, 152, 165
communal differences/ideology, 32, 84
communal or group marriages, 181
communal ownership, 199
communication, 128, 130
comprador–collaborator paradigm, 56
compradors, 63, 70, 71; cultural, 128
Congress government, 139, 142
Conlon, Frank, 116, 121*n*
consciousness (social), 56, 57, 70, 74, 81; about the identity of Keralam, 171; collective, 127; cultural, 84, 139; development of, 57–58; emergence of, 79; evolution of, 70; false, 71; growth of, 64; ideology and, 56; in the nineteenth century, 77; production of, 55; social and political, 67; *see also* anticolonial consciousness
conservatism, 57
conservatives, 2, 56, 69, 89, 92, 100
cultivators, 187, 190
culture, *see* indigenous culture; traditional culture; colonial culture
cultural appropriation, 126
cultural backwardness, 34
cultural defence, 84, 107; concept of, 57
cultural engineering, 128
cultural hegemony, 71, 135, 175
cultural identity, in Keralam, 170, 171; of a subjected people, 172
cultural–ideological struggle, 56, 57, 58, 78, 79, 85, 86, 87, 94, 107
Damodaran, K., 181*n*
Dandekar, Morobhat, 117
Dard, 43
Darnton, Robert, 132
Darwin, 141
Das, Kalimohan, 13*n*
Davy, William, 125
Dawn Society, 81
Dayanand Anglo-Vedic institutions, 11
Deb, Ashutosh, 84
Deb, Radhakanta, 65, 67, 69, 84, 88*n*, 89, 93, 100
Deccan, 41
Delhi, 45*n*
Deshmukh, Gopal Hari, 78
despotism, 21, 111
Devamrita Varshini (*raga*), 44
devaswam, 184
Digby, William, 67*n*
Dikshitar, Muthuswami, 43, 44
divine dispensation, 22, 24, 69, 72, 94, 110, 115, 116–17, 119–22, 179
Dnyanprasarak Sabha, 88
Dow, Alexander, 37, 123*n*
drain of wealth, 76, 77, 96
Dubois, Abu, 37
Duff, Alexander, 103
Duff, Grant, 19*n*
Dumont, Louis, 182

Dumurgue, W., 132n
Dutt, Akshay Kumar, 10, 11, 14, 17, 26,
    27, 28, 31, 69, 74, 76, 81, 98, 103;
    Dharamniti, 100
Dutt, Kylash Chunder, 74
Dutt, Shama Charan, 74
East India Company, 20, 116, 124, 125,
    127; administration of, 187; agrarian
    policy of, 133; early policy of, 9n;
    judicial and revenue administration
    of, 23; officials of, 123
education, 10, 47, 81, 127; colonial sys-
    tem of, 47, 102; content of, 52–53,
    83; importance of, 92; medium of
    instruction in, 81; in science, 11–13;
    of women, 69, 89, 90, 93; see also
    English education; colonial education;
    mass education
Educated Natives of Bengal, 82
Elkin, Boris, 64
Elphinstone, Mountstuart, 47, 48
emancipation of women, 93; Bankim on,
    99; Rammohun and Vidyasagar on,
    97; see also women
English education, 58, 83, 140, 144;
    'baneful influences' of, 106; in India,
    67; see also education; colonial educa-
    tion
enlightenment, 67, 99; and progress, 46;
    efficacy of, 8–9; provided by British,
    52
Euclid, 66n
evangelization, 83, 102, 116, 117
Ezhava(s), 152
family, organization, 176, 189; property,
    impartibility of, 190, 192
Farquhar, J.N., 46, 58, 59
'Fatherhood of God', 30, 97
Forbes, J., 37, 49
Fort William College, 59
Framjee, Dosabhoy, 94
France, 45n
Gandhi-led temple entry movement, 114
Gangaputras, 6n
Garhmukteshwar, 68n
Geiger, Theodor, 64
geyanatakam (opera), 44
ghana raga pancharatnam, 44
Ghose, Kashi Prasad, 74

Ghose, Ram Gopal, 88
Ghose, Sharada Prasad, 74
Gita, 67; Tilak's reading of, 97
Gladwin, Francis, 125
Goetz, Hermann, 37
Gokhale, Vishnu Bhikaji, see Vishnubawa
    Brahmachari
Gopalachari, 161
Graeme, H.S., 192n
Gramsci, Antonio, 63, 87n
Grant Medical College, 149
Gujarat, 64; painters from, 39
Guru Dutt, 82, 84, 107
Gwalior, 39
Hakim Ajmal Khan, 173
Hakim Yoosufi, 146
Halhed, Nathaniel, 125
Hardinge (Lord), 150, 188n
Hariharananda, Tirthaswami, 66
Hartog, Philip, 50
Hastings, Warren, 124, 125
Headrick, Daniel, 147n
hegemony, see colonial culture; colonial
    hegemonization; colonial India
Heimsath, Charles, 58, 59, 64
heterodox sects, 5, 47, 97
Hindoo Patriot, 92
Hindu College, 16n
Hindu Intelligencer, 59, 83, 92, 106n
Hindu laws, 125
Hindu scriptures, 66, 112
Hindu Theistic Association, 31
Hinduism, 4, 104, 116, 160; defence of,
    117; followers of, 113; great prin-
    ciples of, 31; tree of, 83
Holkars, 20
Horticultural Society, 88
humanism, 2
humanist ideas, 97
Hussain, Gulam, 35
Hussain, Kareem (Maulavi), 88n
Hyderabad, 36, 38
hypergamous marriage, 182
hypogamy, 182
identity, crisis of, 1, 2, 33; redefinition of,
    84
ideological apparatuses, 123, 126
ideological system, 184; created by colo-
    nial rule, 94; role of, 176

ideology and culture, 57; *see also* colonial culture
idol worship, 28*n*; *see also* idolatry
idolatry, 4, 5, 6*n*, 8, 29, 46, 69, 121; *see also* anti-idolatry
impact–response framework, 3, 7, 60
imperialism, 61, 62
India, discussions on educational progress in, 47; dumping of British goods in, 24; European ideas and institutions in, 3; intellectual history of, 117; liberation struggle in, 25; paramount power in, 20; political and administrative reality in, 22; social and religious beliefs in, 8; social transformation envisaged in, 101
Indian civilization, 38, 126; cultural specificity of, 101; orientalist admiration of, 109
Indian historiography, 46, 54, 110
Indian literature, 42–43
Indian music, 107; *see also* Carnatic
Indian National Congress, 139, 142, 143, 162
Indian intellectual tradition, 67, 68, 116
Indian intellectuals, 115, 145; attitudes of, 58, 147; formation of, 69; organicity of, 70; two broad categories of, 65; views of, 155; *see also* intellectuals
indigenous culture, 101, 103, 106, 123, 126; denigration of, 79, 129; and institutions, 84; *see also* traditional culture
indigenous elementary schools, 50; primary object of, 48–49; *see also* education
indigenous system(s) of medicine, 149, 150, 152, 153, 155, 156, 157, 159, 160, 169, 171, 173, 175; achievements of, 155; committee on, 157; marginalization of, 148; practitioners of, 149, 152, 153, 177; professionalization in, 171 172, 174; protagonists of, 151, 165, 172; revitalization of, 145, 158, 161–66, 171; sale of, 170; source of sustenance for, 158; superiority of, 163; unscientific character of, 175; weakness of, 157;

see also Ayurveda; medicine; unani medicine
indigenous tradition, 67; a search for identity, 84
individualism, 133; development of, 98
Indulekha, 131–44
industrialization, 73, 77, 96
inequality, 76, 98–99
inheritance, law of, 180, 183, 192, 194, 195; system of, 96
instrumentality of British rule, 72, 73
intellectual activity, 54, 64
intellectual community, formation of, 87–94; ideological premises of, 94–101
intellectual history, 65; autonomy of, 32; concern of, 62–63; external approach of, 55; functional view of, 55; idealist view of, 54–55; of India, 76; internal approach of, 54; as an integrative tool, 54; major themes of, 57
intellectuals, character and role of, 33; formation of, 64; Morin's definition of, 64; *see also* Indian intellectuals; intelligentsia
intelligentsia, 64, 87, 148; attitude of, 174; of Calcutta, 89; colonial, 123; cultural and political experience of, 143; English-educated, 126; Indian, 110, 111, 122; liberal, 101; political vision of, 115; vernacular, 132; western-educated, 155; *see also* intellectuals
Islamic learning, 50
Jahangir, 39
Jai Singh, 45, 51
Jaipur, 45*n*
Jambekar, Bal Shastri, 1, 90; *Bombay Darpun*, 16; *Dig Darshan*, 16
janmam, 179, 184, 185, 190
janmi(s), 178, 184, 185–86
Japan, 58
Jones, William, 109, 125
Jordens, J.T.F., 65, 68
Jotephandas, 6*n*
kadamkattu kaccam, 178
Kaibrathas, 6*n*
kalari system, 178
kanakkar, 184, 186, 187, 188, 189*n*, 190, 191

kanam, 185
kanam land, 186, 187, 191
kanam tenure, 180
Kangra paintings, 40, 41
Kangri Gurukula, 11
kanomdar, 188
karalar, 178
karanavan, 182, 190, 191, 192, 193, 196
Karthabajas, 5
Kashmir, 39
Kayasthas, 6n
Kerala Mahatmyam, 179
Kerala Patrika, 191, 192
Keralam, Ayurveda in, 152, 170; cultural
    awakening in, 161; cultural taste in,
    131; Nairs in, 176; revitalization
    movement in 145, 159, 170
Keralolpatti, 179, 183
Kesavayya of Bobbili, 44
Khan, Hakim Ajmal, *see* Hakim Ajmal
    Khan
Khan, Karim, 20, 35
Khan, Sayyid Ahmad, 10, 11, 13, 14,
    15n, 18n, 19n, 27, 30, 81, 95
Kishan Chandra, 48
Kishangarh schools, 39, 40
knowledge, acquisition of, 100; dissemi-
    nation of, 9, 92; retrieval of, 161, 164,
    166; stagnation of, 156, 164; sys-
    tematization of, 172
Kopf, David, 58, 59, 64
Kosambi, D.D., 162
kottivayira veli kaccam, 178
Lakshmipati, 161
land control, 187, 189, 198
landed aristocracy, 173, 174; *see also*
    aristocracy
landlords, 186, 187, 189n, 190;
    Nambudiri, 188, 189
Leslie, Charles, 146, 156, 171
Levinson, Joseph, 64
Lex Loci Act, 82, 83, 88, 93
liberalism, 95, 133; and British rule, 144;
    hegemonic influence of, 115
liberation movement, 57n; role of culture
    in, 80
liberty, enemies of, 21; European ideas
    of, 3
Lingayats, 6n

Literary Society, 88
Locke, John, 60
Logan, William, 185, 194n, 195; *Malabar
    Manual*, 132
Lokhitawadi, 21, 24, 27; *Satpatre*, 16
London, 13n
Lucknow, 38
Macaulay, 126, 127
Macaulayian system, 17
MacCulley, David, 64
Macleod, Roy, 147
Madanapala, 164
Madhavacharya, 164
Madras, 1, 195
madrasa, 49; in Patna, 66
Mahajan, Bhau, 16
Maharaja of Mysore, 44
Maharashtra, intellectuals in, 77; peri-
    odicals of, 74
Majumdar, R.C., 46, 56, 64
Makti Tangal, 84, 103, 105
Malabar, 196; annexation of, 187; Brit-
    ish conquest of, 184; middle class of,
    188; rulers of, 173, 198; social and
    ideological changes in, 133; *taravads*
    in, 192, 193; tenants in, 189n
Malabar Marriage Act, 197
Malabar Marriage Association, 194
Malabar Marriage Commission, 195,
    196, 197
Malabar Tenancy Commission, 188
Malayali Memorial, 171
Malaysia, 71n
Malcolm, John, 19n, 51
Manak, 39, 40
Mandalik, Vishnu Narayan, 107
Manji Kalagada (*raga*), 44
Mannath, 188
Mannoni, O., 128
manodharma sangita, 45
Mappilas, 161, 184, 188
Marathas, 35
marriage, institution of, 196; law of, 194,
    195; and the matrilineal family, 133,
    134, 135; Nairs and, 176; system of,
    180, 188; traditional norms of, 194
Marriage Commission, 189n, 190n, 191n,
    192; *see also* Malabar Marriage Com-
    mission

Marshman, J.C., 19*n*, 34, 110
Marumakkathayam, Act, 198; custom, 193, 197; law, 192, 195
Marx, Karl, 33, 70
Marxism, 94
Marxist historiography, 62
mass education, appeal for promoting, 15; for national regeneration, 14; necessary preconditions for, 18; science and, 10
McCulley, B.T., 34
Mechanical Institute, 13
medical practitioners, 149, 151
medicine, in ancient India, 146; colonial, 148, 151, 152, 174; Hindu, 155*n*; Indian system of, 82, 107; in medieval India, 146; science of, 154; standardization of, 172; manufacture and marketing of, 169; preparation and distribution of, 161; *see also* indigenous system(s) of medicine; revitalization movement
Mehta, Nanda Shankar Tiliya, 130
melchart(s), 183*n*, 186, 189*n*
Mencher and Goldberg, 183
Menon, C. Karunakara, 195, 196
Menon, M. Othena, 171
Menon, Oyyarath Chandu, 131, 171, 195*n*, 196, 197*n*
Menon, Vallathol Narayana, 171
Menons, 187
Metcalfe, Barbara, 173, 174
middle class, English-educated, 60, 105, 110, 126, 130, 133, 137, 138, 192, 198; growth of, 131; of Malabar, 188; subjection of, 1; values, 67
Mill, James, 19*n*, 34, 60, 95, 98; *History of India*, 110–11; periodization of Indian history, 110, 111
Miller, Perry, 54
Milnikov, 64
miniature painting, 39, 40
Mir Syed Ali, 39
Mir, 42, 43
missionary propaganda, 104, 105
Mitra, Nabha Gopal, 82
Mitra, Peary Chand, 130
Mitra, Rajindra Lal, 88, 107
Mitra, Tarni Charan, 88*n*

modern science, 147, 172
modernity, 86; tradition of, 3, 101
modernization, concept of, 2; impact of, 185; intellectuals' effort at, 61; needs of, 36
money economy, emergence of, 189; expansion of, 184, 186, 198; impact of, 185
Morin, Edgar, 64
Mola Ram, 40
monotheism, 29; K.C. Sen's application of, 97; of the Vedas, 30
Mooss, Kuttancheri Vasudevan, 160
Mughal (empire), 35, 36, 37, 53
Muhammad Hashim (Haji), 105
Muhammad Akbar Arsani, 146
Muhammad Ali, 146
Muhammad Rashid (Maulavi), 88*n*
Mukherjee, Bhudev, 82, 84, 107
Mukherjee, D.P., 161
Mukhopadhyaya, Dakshina Ranjan, 23
Mula Sankara, *see* Dayanand Saraswati
Mulick, Rasik Krishan, 23
mulikkalakkaccam, 178
Mundappa Bangera, M., 195*n*
Munro, Thomas, 47, 51
Murshid Kuli Khan, 36
Muthukutty Swami, 103
N.N. Sen and Company, 170
Naicker, Ramaswami 114
Nainsukh, 39, 40
Nair, Sir C. Sankaran, 188, 194, 195
Nair, Kizhedath Vasudevan, 159*n*
Nair, M. Krishnan, 188
Nair, aristocracy, 187; *kanakkar,* 185; law of inheritance, 188*n*; marriages, 193, 194, 195; matriliny, 181; *taravads*, 189, 198; women, 180, 181, 196
Nairs, 177, 180, 181, 184, 186, 187, 188, 192, 194, 196; alliances among, 182; as a caste of warriors, 178; economic status of, 198; educated sections of, 189, 197; family organization of, 183; marriage system of, 176, 183; practices and institutions of, 192; sexual morality of, 183; social awakening among, 188
nalukettu, 199
Namboodiripad, E.M.S., 181*n*

Nambudiri, Ashtamurthi, 183, 196
Nambudiri, brahmins, 176, 178, 179–80, 181, 182, 183, 184, 185; community, 181*n*; *illom*, 199; land ownership, 179; marriage, 180*n*; monopoly of land, 186; –Nair liaison, 182; primogeniture, 181; value system, 180, 181, 198
Nambudiris, 177, 196, 198; land under the control of, 179; sexual needs of, 181; values and ideology of, 184
Naoroji, Dadabhai, 16, 95
Narahari, 164
Narayana Guru, 65, 67, 100, 152, 171; and caste, 69; in Keralam, 113, 114; role of, 70
National Educational Council, 82
National Institution for the Cultivation of Sciences, 13
national liberation struggle, 87, 94; *see also* liberation movement
nationalism, 174; in India, 64; rise of, 59
Nedungadi, Appu, 130
Nehru, Jawaharlal, 1, 2, 65, 67
New Dispensation, 28; *see also* Keshub Chandra Sen
Northbrook (Lord), 14
novel as literary form, 130
occupational mobility, 6, 185
O'Malley, L.S.S., 34
Onam festival, 182
orientalist–anglicist controversy, 47, 148
Orme, Robert, 110
Oudh, 41
Owen, Robert, 98
Pade, Shankar Shastri, 161, 165
Padmanji (Baba), 130
Paine, Tom, 60, 95
painting, 43; *see also* miniature painting
Panchalas, 6*n*
Pancham Banjigarus, 6*n*
Pantalu, Buchaiah, 16
Pantulu, Kandukuri Veeresalingam, *see* Veeresalingam
Paramahamsa, Ramakrishna, *see* Ramakrishna Paramahamsa
Parasara, 92
Parasurama, 170, 179
parbattis, 187

Parthivapuram temple, 177, 178
Pathans, 35
pathasala, 49, 162, 167–69
Pentland (Lord), 150
Persian, 49
petty-bourgeoisie, 24, 33, 79; dual alienation of, 80
Phalaranjani (*raga*), 44
pharmacopoeia, 164
Photographic Society, 88
Phule, Jotiba, 113
Pillai, C.V. Raman, 171
Pillai, Elamkulam Kunjan, 178
Pillai, G. Parameswara, 171
Pillai, Samuel Vedanayakam, 130
Pindarees, 35
Pipes, Richard, 64
poliginy, 181
political anarchy, 37, 110; pre-colonial, 34
political power, fragmentation of, 36; loss of, 157
polytheism, 4, 5, 7, 46; attitude towards, 69; Hindu, 30
poverty, and suffering, 76, 77, 98, 100
pre-colonial society, 34; institutional structures in, 20, 94, 111, 124; political system of, 94; technology in, 107, 182
Press Regulation, 23
primogeniture, 180
printing, 128
production, capitalist mode of, 122; and distribution, 118, 119; *see also* capitalism
proletariat, 70
property, fragmentation of, 96; individualization of, 37; joint management of, 190; partition of, 197; right to, 91
proprietorship in land, 109
prosopographers, 54
Proudhon, 98
Punjab, 70
Radha–Krishna theme, 40
radicals, 2, 50, 69
Raghuvanshi, 37
Rajasthan, 39, 40, 41
Rajputana, 38
Ramakrishna Paramahamsa, 29, 67

Ranade, Mahadev Govind, 11, 14, 15*n*, 18*n*, 27, 28, 96–97, 100
Rani Bhavani, 48
Ranjit Singh, 19
Rao, Sir Madhava, 195
Rao, Raghunath, 91
rationalism, 26, 27
Ray, Bharatchandra, 41, 42
Ray, Gangadhar, 161
reform, a career of, 4; community-based, 114; and regeneration, 86; programme of, 9; socio-religious, 78, 88; *see also* religion
reform movements, 96; among the Nambudiris, 198; during the pre-colonial period, 97; in colonial India, 46, 173; in Keralam, 171
reformation, 29, 32, 79
Reformer, 74, 106*n*
reformers, 2, 56, 69, 89, 92
regeneration, 17, 81; in colonial society, 80; cultural–intellectual, 158; of Hinduism, 68; of India, 13*n*, 74; national, 14; in nineteenth century, 64; religious and cultural, 139; and restructuring, 107; social, 87, 156; social and religious, 96; socio-cultural and intellectual, 58, 59
religion, civil use of, 97; dominant role of, 97; hypocrisies of, 121; purity of, 46
religious beliefs, 78, 84, 103; and practices, 82
religious conditions, in the eighteenth century, 4
religious movements, 5, 29; *see also* reform
religious orders, 101
religious particularism, 31, 32, 84
religious protest and dissent, 3, 97
religious reform, 141; *see also* reform
religious universalism, 26, 29, 31, 32
retrieving history, 112–14
revitalization movement, 58, 158, 159, 174; course and character of, 168; ideational ground of, 162; in Keralam, 170; lynchpin of, 167; mouthpiece of, 166; positive feature of, 164–65; *see also* medicine
revivalism, cultural, 84; in indigenous medicine, 171; religious, 57

revivalist, 100; movement, 172, 173; theory of decline, 172
revolt (of 1921), 161
Revolt of 1857, 115, 124
Ricardo, 70
Rizal, Jose, 71*n*
Robinson, James Harvey, 54
Rohillas, 35
Rousseau, 95, 98
Roy, Jaminibhushan (Kavirathna), 154
Roy, Raja Rammohun, 1, 9*n*, 10, 21, 22*n*, 23, 29, 30, 31, 46, 65, 66, 68, 71*n*, 73, 76, 77, 79*n*, 89, 90, 91, 97, 100, 111, 112, 116, 147; biography of, 64, 66–67; concept of Vedic infallibility, 128, 134; crisis of identity of, 2; intellectual evolution of, 69; protest against Press Regulation, 95; role of, 70; *Sambad Kaumudi,* 16; *Tuhfat-ul-Muwahhiddin,* 26, 27, 66–67, 76
Royle, 155
Rozerio, 191*n*
Said, Edward, 126
salvation 97, 98
Sambad Prabhakar, 13
sambandham, 180, 181, 182, 194, 197
Sankaramangalath kaccam, 178
Sankhya system of Kapila, 141
Sanskrit, education, 48–50; knowledge of, 168
sankritist tradition, 42; *see also* tradition
sankritization, 6
Saramati (*raga*), 44
Saraswati, Dayanand, 14, 29, 31, 64–65, 67–68, 84, 100, 107, 116; biography of, 64; intellectual evolution of, 69; role of, 70; social experience of, 68
Sarbatatva Deepika Sabha, 16, 82
Sarkar, Jadunath, 34
Sarkar, Mahendra Lal, 32
Sarkar, Susobhan, 61
sati, 113; abolition of, 82, 87, 89, 112; agitation over, 90
Satnami, 5
Sauda, 43
Savant Singh–Bani Thani love affair, 40
scientific knowledge, dissemination of, 12, 13, 16
Scientific Society, 14

Seal, Anil, 64
Seetha, S., 45
Sen, Asok, 36, 61
Sen, Chandra Kishore, 170
Sen, Ganganath, 161
Sen, Ganga Prasad, 161, 165
Sen, Keshub Chandra, 11, 12, 14, 21n, 22, 24, 27, 28, 29, 30, 31, 98, 99; application of monotheism, 97; biography of, 64; conception of classless society, 97; New Dispensation, 31; *Sulabh Samachar*, 14, 16
Sen, Ram Kamal, 88n
Shah, Walliullah, 7n, 45
Shakti Aushadalaya, 170
Shastri, Gangadhar, 117
Shastri, Lakshman, 117
Shills, Edward, 63n, 64, 128, 145n
Shiva Narayan, 5
Siddha, 146
Simon (Saint), 98
Sindias, 20
Skinner, James, 20, 35
Smritis, 183
social protest, 3
social reform, 27, 59; literature on, 64; *see also* reform
social reformers, 63; *see also* reformers
Society for Acquisition of General Knowledge, 17, 88
Society for the Promotion of National Feeling, 82
Society for Translating European Sciences, 12
Society for a Uniform Script, 82
socio-economic developments, 18, 176, 189, 191, 198
socio-economic formations, 26
socio-political changes, 24, 89, 106
Somprakash, 105n, 106n
Spear, Percival, 34
Spencer, 60, 95
spiritual enlightenment, 100; and knowledge, 89, 91
state institutions, 79, 101
Stephen, Sir James, 194
Students' Literary and Scientific Society, 88
Subaji Bapu, 90

Suchindram temple, 177, 178n
Sudhraj Nihalchand, 40
supernaturalism, 8, 77, 97
superstition, 4, 5, 141; attack on, 26; religious, 9, 98
Susruta, 154, 155n, 158, 164
swadeshi, 78
Syama Shastri, 43–44
Tagore, Devendranath, 13, 16, 81n, 84, 91, 103, 106, 107n
Tagore, Prasanna Kumar, 74
Tamil literature, 41n
Tampuran, Ettan, 195n
Tampuran, Valiyakovil Kerala Varma, 195n
Tampuran, Kodungallur Kunhikuttan, 171
Tampuran, Rama Varma, 195n, 197n
Tarachand, 34, 64
Tarkadkar, Bhaskar Pandurang, 74, 75, 77
Tattwabodhini Patrika, 13, 16, 81n, 105, 106, 107n
Tattwabodhini Sabha, 103, 107
taravad(s), 181–82, 190, 196, 199; dissolution of, 191; economic basis of, 192, 198; institutions of, 185; in Malabar, 194; marriage customs of, 189; solidarity of, 191, 192; system, 188–93, 197, 198
tavanur kaccam, 178
tavazhi(s), 182, 191, 192
Telang, K.T., 148
temple property, 177, 178
Tennant, (Rev.) W., 34
Thiruvatira festival, 182
Thomas, George, 20, 35
Tilak, Bal Gangadhar, 65, 67, 89; reading of the *Gita*, 97
Tinnelvelli riot, 83n
Tipu Sultan, 37, 53
Tirunanthikkarai/Tiruvalla, temples at, 177
Tiyya(s), 180, 184, 188
tradition, concept of, 113; eclectic influence of, 120; elements of, 112; essence of, 108; modernity of, 3; –modernity continuum, 3; and modernity, 86, 141; and religion, 114;

search for an authentic, 113, 114
traditional cultural space, 145
traditional culture, 79, 107, 131; of elites, 126; and ideology, 58, 72; vitality of, 84; *see also* indigenous culture
traditional institutions, inadequacy of, 58; orientalist respect for, 47; qualities of, 106; revitalization of, 105
traditional knowledge, 82; and achievements, 101
traditional sources, 120
Travancore, 36; Narayana Guru in, 70; ruling chiefs of, 162, 173
Trikkakara temple, 177
Troeltsch, 54
Tweeddale (Lord), 83n
Tyagaraja, 43, 44
Ujjain, 45n
Umabharanam (*raga*), 44
unani medicine, 146, 158; *see also* medicine
universal church, 31
universal religion 31
universal theism, 30, 32
universal tolerance, 32
universalism, 32
universalist principles, 160
untouchability, 121
untouchable castes, 114, 184; *see also* caste
upper-caste domination, 113, 114
Urdu literature, 43
vaccination, 148
Vagabata, 154, 164
Vaikkom Satyagraha, 114n
Varadarajan, 41n
Varasyar, Kunhikutty, 159
Variar, Chunakkara Kochukrishna, 160
Variar, Kaikulangara Rama, 160
Variar, Kolathur, 196
Variar, Konath Achutha, 159n, 160
Variar, Madhava, 159n
Variar, N.V. Krishnan Kutty, 171
Variar, Panniyinpalli Sankunni, 145, 159–71; *Chikitsa Samgraham*, 165; *Dhanwantari*, 165, 166; institution-building effort of, 161, 169; 'Western and Eastern Medicine', 166
Varma, Marthanda, 36

Vedic *samhitas*, 120
Veeresalingam, 11, 14, 15n, 18n, 24, 69, 91; *Rajasekhara Caritra*, 130; *Viveka-vardhini*, 16
Vemana, 42
Verghese, V., 160
vernacular languages, 106, 128, 156; cultivation of, 81; the medium of, 10
vernacular literature, 129
vernacularization, 43
verumpattakkar, 184, 186
Viceroy's Legislative Council, 194
Vidyalankar, Mrityunjay, 88n
Vidyasagar, Iswarchandra, 10, 11, 14, 16n, 21n, 79n, 91, 97; educational programme of, 18, life and work of, 61; 'Marriage of Hindu Widows', 90
Vigyan Sebadi, 12
village, administration, 187; *mukhya-sthans*, 187; schools, 50; temple, 199
Virabhramas, 5
Virjananda (Swami), 68
Vishnubawa Brahmachari, 91, 103, 105; 'An Essay on Beneficent Government', 104; *Sukhadayaka Rajya-praharini*, 115, 117–20; philosophical and socio-political views of, 120–22; *Vedokta Dharma Prakasa*, 104, 117, 121
Vishnushastri Pandit, 91, 107
Vishu festival 182
Vivekananda, 9n, 15n, 29, 30, 31, 65, 67, 76, 79n, 81, 97, 100
voluntary associations, 88, 101, 129
von Grunnebaum, G.B., 58n
Warden, Thomas, 185
western education, 4, 40
western knowledge, 65, 147, 150, 151; dissemination of, 3; elements of, 175; and philosophy, 67; reliance on, 169
western medicine, 146, 147, 150, 151, 153, 157, 159, 160, 166; effectiveness of, 163; hegemony of, 149; in India, 158; knowledge of 168, 174; practice of, 169; treatment proffered by, 148; *see also* medicine
western society, 59–60
westernization, 2, 145
widow marriage, 6n, 90, 112; Act on, 88;

movement for, 90–93
Wigram, H., 195
Wilson, H.H., 155
Wilson, Hayman, 111
Wilson, John, 104
Winterbothan, H.M., 195*n*
Wise, T.A., 155

women, emancipation of, 93; seclusion of, 121; status of, 113; condition of, 107; *see also* emancipation of women
Young Bengal, 13, 16, 17, 81; *Gyananveshan*, 16; members of, 23, 26
'Young India', 95
Zamurin of Calicut, 196